FOLKLORE, NATIONALISM, AND POLITICS

EDITED BY

FELIX J. OINAS

1978
Slavica Publishers, Inc.
P.O. Box 14388
Columbus, Ohio 43214

For a complete catalog of Slavica books, with prices and ordering information, write to: Slavica Publishers, Inc.
P. O. Box 14388
Columbus, Ohio 43214

ISBN: 0-89357-043-5

Editor of Slavica Publishers: Charles E. Gribble, The Ohio State University, Columbus.

Printed in the United States of America by Inter-Collegiate Press, Shawnee Mission, Kansas 66202.

Indiana University Folklore Institute
Mongraph Series, Vol. 30

The Indiana University Folklore Series was founded in 1939 for the publication of occasional papers and monographs.

CONTENTS

PREFACE

In 1974, the Editor of the *Journal of the Folklore Institute,* Professor Richard M. Dorson, asked me to prepare a special issue of the journal, devoted to folklore, nationalism, and politics. This suggestion fit perfectly into my schedule, since during this sabbatical year I was investigating these problems concerning the Soviet Union, under a Research Grant from the National Endowment for the Humanities. With the cooperation of my colleagues at the Indiana University Folklore Institute and a couple of scholars outside, I compiled a sizeable collection of essays which was published as a double issue of the *Journal of the Folklore Institute* (vol. 12, 1975, nos. 2-3). The majority of them are reprinted here, with the addition of one (by Ilhan Başgöz) from a former issue of the same journal (vol. 9, 1972, nos. 2-3).

The scope of this volume encompasses three continents. As for Europe, the center of gravity of five of the essays is Eastern Europe, with one of them dealing with Finland and one partly with Western Europe. Asia is covered by four essays, from Siberia to the Near and Far East. And America is represented by an essay about a brief, but ideologically turbulent period.

I would like to express my gratitude to all the contributors, but especially to Dr. Richard M. Dorson, Distinguished Professor of History and of Folklore and Director of the Folklore Institute at Indiana University, for his unfaltering interest in these problems and his guidance and help. Professor Charles E. Gribble, Director of the Slavica Publishers, deserves special thanks for the publication of this volume in his series.

I am grateful to the National Endowment for the Humanities for their generous grant that enabled me to devote some time, aside from my own research, to the editing of these essays.

Bloomington,
July, 1977

F.J.O.

AMERICAN FOLKSONGS AND LEFT-WING POLITICS: 1935-56

Richard A. Reuss

On September 26, 1963, Kenneth B. Keating, then Republican senator from New York, amused his colleagues and the nation at large with a witty reply to a resolution passed a month earlier by the Fire and Police Research Association of Los Angeles, Inc., which called for a Congressional investigation of American folk music as "an unidentified tool of Communist psychological or cybernetic warfare to ensnare and capture youthful minds . . . ."[1] Keating's remarks, subsequently entitled "Mine Enemy–The Folk Singer" in the *Congressional Record*, lampooned such sweeping assertions with jibes like the following:

> I had always had the impression that if anything was thoroughly American in spirit, it was American folk music. To be sure, I was perfectly aware of certain un-American influences in it, like Elizabethan balladry, English Protestant hymns and spirituals, and, with respect to jazz and in some cases the Negro spiritual, native African rhythms. But in my naivete I had never considered these un-American influences to be of a sinister nature and simply passed them off as part and parcel of the melting-pot tradition which has contributed so much in the way of variety and interest to the American cultural heritage . . . .
>
> Of course, I realize that folk music tradition is grounded in movements of political, economic, and social unrest and I did not expect to find in music which originated among sharecroppers, miners, union organizers, factory workers, cowboys, hill folk, wanderers, and oppressed Negroes–a pattern of tribute and praise to such symbols of orthodoxy as the gold standard, the oil depletion allowance, and the standing rules of the U. S. Senate . . . .

Mixing sarcasm with burlesque throughout his oration, Keating cited "evidence" from American folk and topical song traditions in "support" of the contentions of the Fire and Police Research Association. In closing his remarks, however, he forsook comedy and concluded on a serious note:

> This resolution is but another demonstration of the absurd lengths to which the amateur ferrets of the radical right will go in their quixotic sallies against the Communist menace .... Vigilante charges such as these can breed the atmosphere of suspicion and confusion which tends not only to undermine free institutions but, of equal concern, to divert our energies from tackling the real threats posed by international communism to our liberty and security. With devotion to our freedoms, with trust in the American ideal of cultural diversity, with, above all, a sense of proportion and discernment in meeting the challenges of our times, I for one have every faith that–in the words of that inspiring song–we shall overcome.[2]

Keating's speech and plea for tolerance were applauded by the vast majority of commentators, although Georgia's Senator Richard Russell grumbled over the omission of any mention of "Dixie" in the course of the address.

The Radical Right, however, continued, as it does to this day, to hammer at the perceived Communist subversion of American folk music through its press organs and spokesmen. A spate of articles written during the past decade have repeatedly criticized such casual dismissal of the whole issue by liberals and cited dubious evidence from popular magazines and old House Un-American Activities Committee documents implicating nearly every popular folksinger of the past three decades as conspirators.[3] David Noebel, a young minister in the conservative Christian Crusade organization, in fact, has carved out a part-time career attacking alleged Communist folksingers and folksong publishers in the United States; his endeavors have included numerous magazine articles, a national speaking tour, a full-length paperback book, *Rhythm, Riots and Revolution*, and a long-play record, *The Marxist Ministrels.*[4]

It is, of course, absurd to speak of a "Communist takeover" of American folk music, as the Radical Right asserts. Yet it is also a distortion not to recognize the impact the "Old Left," or the individuals and groups who formed a part of the Communist-dominated radical milieu of the 1930s and '40s, had on the early popularization of folksongs in this country. Some of its performers, mostly without their one-time partisan political commitments, subsequently achieved considerable national fame and commercial success as urban interpreters of indigenous traditional songs and styles. A new and ideologically mixed generation of radicals, reformers, and social critics, led by Bob Dylan and Joan Baez, continued the earlier movement's coupling of protest themes with rural American folksong idioms during the 1960s and '70s in the contexts of Civil Rights marches, "Ban the Bomb" parades, anti-Vietnam War demonstrations, pollution control rallies, and other causes, rendering the once novel folk-style protest songs as common in the urban United States as the soapbox. The Old Left's enthusiasm for "folk" entertainment, aural and written, was one direct contributing influence in the assembling of several different immensely successful popular anthologies of folklore in the 1940s; its belief that folk traditions ought not to be merely collected and studied passively but consciously employed in agit-prop (from agitation-propaganda) and other social contexts to improve the lot of the masses was an early voicing of an activist philosophy later revived by various non-Communist professional folklorists and others as "applied folklore."

In view of this legacy, then, what specifically was the Communist Party's policy on folksongs and folklore, and what if any structural apparatus was formally created to implement its worldview? (I speak here of the Party itself, not the broader radical movement of the 1930s to mid-1950s influenced by and surrounding it.) Why did Communists and their sympathizers react ambivalently to the pronouncements and activities of left-wing folksingers in the movement, even while generally favoring the mass popularization of folk music? Thus far, published studies have eschewed consideration of these questions, either because of lack of information or in some cases to protect individuals potentially threatened with anti-Communist harassment. Now at least some direct answers can be given, though much data still is not available and discretion in the citation of some names (where known) remains advisable. In order to comprehend the significance of party actions (or non-actions), however, it first is necessary to review briefly the broad historical outlines of what transpired in the larger Communist movement with relation to the promulgation of folksongs as a favored cultural aesthetic form and propaganda medium.

As noted elsewhere,[5] the beginnings of the American Communist interest in traditional lore of any kind were gradual and unspectacular; indeed they were hardly evident for many years. The party itself was founded in 1919 when radical segments of the Socialist Party split from the main body to form two independent revolutionary organizations which merged in 1923. Beset during most of its first decade by government political persecution and internal factional quarreling, the party membership as a whole had no time to devote to such peripheral concerns as the singing of folksongs or to the construction of music theories espousing their favorable qualities. Little music of any kind was performed, even in agit-prop contexts, and on those occasions when songs were needed for strike or other militant situations the older standardized revolutionary classics inherited from the IWW and international socialist repertoires sufficed. A few random comments on folksongs and other folklore are to be found in the Communist press of the late 1920s, but no consistent position on the merits of rural traditions, favorable or unfavorable, is indicated.[6]

In the late 1920s and early 1930s, however, the party and its allied organizations began a more intensive and dogmatic inquiry into the nature of art and culture. Based on the supposition that the class struggle was drawing to an imminent conclusion leading to revolution and the triumph of the proletariat, the movement's theoreticians attempted to formulate a series of art expressions embodying "worker" values as preferred alternatives to those perceived as central to "decadent" capitalist society. Accordingly, for several years the Workers Music League, a Communist-sponsored organization of left-wing musicians and formally trained composers, experimented with various musical forms, mostly classically oriented, in an attempt to create militant class-conscious songs which would appeal to and be sung by major segments of the working class. These attempts largely failed, primarily because both the complex, often dissonant, music structures developed and the doctrinaire political ideology of this so-called "Third Period" of Communist history were alien to most American laboring peoples. One typical propaganda "art" song of the era had as part of its lyrics:

> We are the builders, we build the future,
> The future world is in our hands.
> We swing our hammers, we use our weapons
> Against our foes in many lands . . .
> And we, the workers, who are the builders,
> We fight, we do not fear to die.
> "All power and freedom unto the workers!"
> Is our defiant battle cry.[7]

Folksongs played little part in this milieu, for few people sympathetic to the Communist Party at this time saw any connection between traditional music on the one hand, and strike, protest, or other radical activity on the other; the few who did were principally newspaper reporters and organizers in the rural South and Midwest.[8] In urban centers, the left-wing immigrant language choruses did perform some folk material from Europe, but this was not considered theoretically significant until later. Prior to 1935, folksongs ordinarily were mentioned only with reference to specific agit-prop causes, which was rare, and then only because the lyrics were deemed to be revolutionary in content. Most of the time, party ideologists took a dim view of folk music, for as music critic Carl Sands remarked in a *Daily Worker* review, "not all folk-tunes are suitable to the revolutionary movement. Many of them are complacent, melancholy, defeatist—originally intended to make slaves endure their lot—pretty, but not the stuff for a militant proletariat to feed upon."[9] A colleague was quoted in the same newspaper as saying, "one of the great faults in the field of workers' music has been that of combining revolutionary lyrics with traditional music—music which can by no means be termed revolutionary."[10]

This attitude changed dramatically with the coming of the Popular Front, the political and ideological coalition of left-wing groups in many countries, organized to combat the rising tide of fascism and formally proclaimed in 1935. In the interests of fostering good will and anti-fascist cooperation at all levels, the international Communist movement now encouraged the downplaying of themes of class struggle and stressed greater socialist identification with individual national histories, social conditions, and life-styles. In the United States the effects of the onset of the Popular Front were dramatic. The American Party dropped its militant rhetoric and made its peace with the New Deal administration of Franklin D. Roosevelt. It successfully broadened its ranks to include a sizable proportion of its membership from the middle class as well as the "proletariat"; its total enrollment swelled to a peak of about 90,000, reached just after World War II. Earl Browder, titular head of the CPUSA during its most successful decade (1935-45), coined the slogan "Communism Is Twentieth-Century Americanism," and Marx, Lenin, and Stalin soon were joined by Jefferson, Lincoln, and Franklin D. Roosevelt in the American movement's pantheon of heroes. Indeed, some of the best mass singing of "The Star Spangled Banner" in the United States could be heard at Communist sponsored rallies at Madison Square Garden.[11]

As the party veered in this new direction, it became possible for members and sympathizers to share in the burgeoning national interest in the American cultural heritage, much of it centering on folklore. Developing in the 1920s as an outgrowth of the nation's new intellectual concern with its social and historical roots, the collection and documentation of artifacts and traditions from the national experience reached its height during the decade of the 1930s, partly because of its psychological value as a counter to the trauma of the Great Depression. In these years the Lomaxes published best-selling collections of folksongs, and presently the WPA folklore projects were started. Artists like Thomas Hart Benton decorated the walls of public buildings with scenes depicting traditional life in the United States, and the Roosevelts and other important figures in the administration paid court to the lore of the people. By the mid-1930s, folksongs and folklife were much closer to the public consciousness than at any time in previous history. Communists and fellow travelers, hence, were by no means the only people keenly interested in the popularization of folklore and its promulgation as the culture of the American people, a perspective which must be maintained when discussing the events of that era.

At this time folksongs were publicized in the Communist movement through two principal music mediums. One was the workers' chorus tradition, a staple of European immigrant life now largely nativized in repertoire and language, but still firmly rooted in the formal, western, classical music heritage insofar as performance style was concerned. Left-wing choruses, however, declined in their proportionate influence as the isolation of the Old Left from the rest of American society dissipated in the years following the establishment of the Popular Front; their chief importance for us here is that they cultivated some awareness and appreciation of folksongs among many to whom traditional music in anything less than an art arrangement was too crude to be appealing.

The other medium was what might be termed a loose urban folksinger aggregate of soloists and small groups that developed toward the end of the 1930s. Packing the now familiar guitars, banjoes, and like instruments, they proved comparatively diversified in their individual approaches to the performance of folksongs, yet were much more attuned than were the left-wing choruses to the specifics of native American singing styles and the cultures which produced them. Some of the more familiar names in this group included Pete Seeger, Woody Guthrie, Burl Ives, Josh White, Aunt Molly Jackson, Richard Dyer-Bennet, Earl Robinson, the American Square Dance Group of New York City, and Alan Lomax. Lomax, moreover, was instrumental in furthering the collective success of most of the others because of his many commercial and New Deal political contacts, his position as head of the Archive of American Folk Song, his broad knowledge of traditional music, and his wholehearted zeal to get "the American sound to the American people."[12] It must be emphasized, however, that though these and other individuals in large part were responsible for the popularization of folk music in left-wing circles prior to and after World War II, they by no means shared a uniform political consciousness or acceptance of Communist ideology. Few in fact ever joined the party, some had no real political sophistication whatever. For many it frequently was less a matter of concrete partisanship than the relative availability of bookings and camaraderie among friends with the same musical interests that led them to perform for left-wing audiences.

Yet for some there was a more clear-cut commitment. The Almanac Singers, which included Pete Seeger, Lee Hays, Millard Lampell, Woody Guthrie, and others, sang folksongs and union and left-wing topical songs in folk style to nearly every radical group associated with the Old Left, on both American coasts and at many points in between, during a hectic year and a half of activity immediately before and following the United States' entry into the Second World War (1941-42).[13] Essentially, the Almanacs regarded themselves not as folksingers but as singing organizers whose primary job was to stimulate worker enthusiasm for union drives, collective labor activity, and anti-fascism. In keeping with traditional Marxist theory of the pre-Popular Front era, they tended to perceive the interests of the ruling classes and laboring masses as conflicting and mutually exclusive of one another. "There's the union people and the anti-union people," they wrote. "Decide which side you're on."[14] Seeing American cultural expression as pluralistic and divided between that fostered by the capitalist establishment and that produced by workers and their allies, the Almanacs for most of their existence rejected any thought of seriously attempting to function within the commercial entertainment media and, in effect, advocated the creation of a separate people's culture based on working-class artistic and aesthetic expression.

As far as the group personally was concerned, the folksong idiom was ideal for its purposes. The form was not strongly identified with bourgeois music institutions such as Tin Pan Alley or Broadway, but instead was a product of the American cultural experience associated with the rural lower classes. It conveyed straightforward, unpretentious, and sometimes class-conscious sentiments about every aspect of the people's life and struggles, and in many cases was comparatively adaptable to a mass singing context. As such, it had both a spiritual and an agit-prop significance. "Folk singing is a form of battle and a frontal movement to preserve our own people's culture," Lee Hays was quoted as saying.[15] Woody Guthrie observed, "The biggest parts of our song collection are aimed at restoring the right amount of people to the right amount of land and the right amount of houses and the right amount of groceries to the right amount of working folks."[16] An important byproduct of such reasoning was the inevitable blurring of any distinction between the terms "folk" and "workers" (or "people") and the largely interchangeable usage of these phrases and the concepts they represented.

The Almanac Singers were too few in number and lasted too short a time to have much overall effect on the entire radical labor movement of the early 1940s, but following the war some of their members and others attempted to carry out the essential goals of the group on a much larger and more systematic scale. The new organization was named People's Songs, Incorporated, and was composed of left-wing songwriters, singers, and other cultural entertainers grouped in a series of loosely knit chapters scattered around the country; its total membership eventually reached three thousand. The national leadership in New York was headed by Pete Seeger, Irwin Silber, Waldemar Hille, Lee Hays (briefly), Mario "Boots" Casetta, and others. Their broad goal was the creation of a singing labor movement. "The people are on the march and must have songs to sing," proclaimed the preamble to the first issue of the *People's Songs Bulletin.*[17] As a clearinghouse for progressive song activity, People's Songs was designed to "circumvent . . . the music monopoly of Broadway and Hollywood,"[18] in effect, by offering alternatives to the prevailing cultural outlets and content. The touchstone of all musical expression, as before, was to be the folksong idiom. In a general form letter designed to acquaint potential sponsors with the organization, it was stated:

> We have based our program largely in the rich and democratic traditions of American folk music. We feel that the whole American folk tradition is a progressive people's tradition. For that reason our comments, our new songs, our activities are, in great measure, rooted in the fertile soil of American folk music.[19]

Unlike the Almanac Singers, however, People's Songs contained many non-folksong oriented musicians from all parts of the jazz and popular music spectrums, so that while folksongs, folk-modeled topical compositions, and traditional rural music performance styles were the predominant base of the musical and cultural worldview of the group, there also was a considerably more diversified range of musical fare and interests represented in the organization.

For three years People's Songs supplied singers, entertainers, and songwriters to labor rallies, left-wing causes, and other agit-prop contexts; produced songbooks, workshops, and concerts; propagandized against the encroaching McCarthy-era political repression in the United States, and in its most sustained and intensive activity devoted most of 1948 to campaigning in song for Progressive Party candidate for President, Henry A. Wallace. In its early days, People's Songs proved to be a vital and dynamic new force on the progressive music front, and attracted admirers and endorsements from portions of the media well beyond the fringes of the Old Left.[20] But as the international Cold War and the domestic anti-Communist hysteria intensified after 1947, the organization eventually found its limited cultural and political entrees into the mainstream of American society closed off. Internal, long-term financial problems developed simultaneously, partly because of inexperienced management but also because of People's Songs' inability to attract sustained and substantial economic support from nearly all labor and most left-wing groups, including the Communist Party, to which it had access.

As a result, People's Songs was forced to close its doors early in 1949.

Its successor was People's Artists, Incorporated, a far more narrowly partisan organization directed by Irwin Silber, Betty Sanders, and a mixture of newcomers and holdovers from the People's Songs days. From 1949 to 1956, People's Artists attempted a limited continuation of People's Songs' program but, hemmed in politically by domestic Cold War pressures, it in reality functioned chiefly as the supplier of much of the folksong and other cultural activity of the rapidly dwindling Communist movement during the worst years of McCarthyism. Lacking a national chapter structure, its operations were confined principally to New York City and its vicinity.

People's Artists proved to be far more ideologically concrete in its worldview than People's Songs. In part this was because the former group had been dominated by Pete Seeger and others, now departed or in the background of the new organization, who tended to place generalized progressive activism through music ahead of the formulation of extensive abstract concepts about their overall direction and behavior. Too, it was the result of the isolation of the Communist left from the rest of liberal, much less general, public opinion during the most intense years of the Cold War when those remaining in the Movement were forced to intellectualize about their ideological convictions in order to justify to themselves and others the maintenance of an unpopular political position.

The very first issue of *Sing Out!*, originally People's Artists' radical folksong magazine, provided ample evidence for this new specificity in thinking. Its opening editorial offered a concise definition of "people's music," which neither the Almanac Singers nor People's Songs nor other individual or group attached to the Communist movement had ever outlined so concisely or well. The key paragraph read in part:

> What is this "People's Music?" In the first place, like all folk music, it has to do with the hopes and fears and lives of common people–of the great majority. In the second place, like that other music of which we have spoken–call it "composed," "concert music," or whatever–it will grow on the base of folk music. We propose that these two hitherto divergent lines of music shall now join in common service to the common people and that is what we shall call "People's Music." No form–folk song, concert song, dance, symphony, jazz–is alien to it. By one thing above all else will we judge it: "How well does it serve the common cause of humanity."[21]

The overtly ideological perspective of People's Artists likewise can be seen in such early *Sing Out!* articles as "Racism, Chauvinism Keynote U.S. Music," " 'Male Supremacy' and Folk Song," and "Can an All-White Group Sing

Songs from Negro Culture."[22] While heavily partisan in tone, many of these essays raised serious questions and made telling arguments against cultural abuses of American and Capitalist society. Sometimes, however, they lapsed into the sectarian excesses and pedantic convolutions of logic especially characteristic of the Communist left during its most isolated political phases:

> All forms of mass entertainment are . . . dominated by the ideology of male supremacy—and we must conclude, therefore, that this is a deliberately planned approach designed to help carry out the basic program of war, violence, and national chauvinism which are the cornerstones of monopoly-controlled culture.[23]

Through the mid-1950s, People's Artists sang, demonstrated, and wrote for peace, international good will (especially vis-à-vis Soviet and East European socialist countries), Negro civil rights, and the campaign to save the lives of accused atomic spies Julius and Ethel Rosenberg. It propagandized for an end to anti-Communist persecution by federal and private agencies, and excoriated turncoat, popular folksingers such as Burl Ives and Josh White who cooperated with Congressional investigating committees or issued "red-baiting" statements.

Ironically, however, the gradual dissolution of the McCarthy era contributed directly to the organization's decline. While the Old Left was almost completely cut off from the rest of American society, People's Artists was a major resource for left-wing cultural activity and entertainment. But when communication with outside artistic programs and talent once again became possible, People's Artists' bookings fell off. Internal tensions and a weak financial picture also complicated matters, and the steady attrition rate in the Communist movement as a whole during the 1950s, dramatically accelerated by Khrushchev's de-Stalinization speech and Soviet suppression of the Hungarian revolt in 1956, further undercut the working base of the organization. In late 1956, People's Artists' Executive Board voted to disband the group and to channel all future energy and funds into the production of *Sing Out!*, which, with a considerably modified political tone and heightened traditional music emphasis, eventually became the most successful and important folksong revival publication of the following decade. Few of the former People's Artists partisans participated in the management of the magazine's subsequent affairs, though, and for all intents and purposes with the demise of People's Artists the Old Left's active role in the popularization of American folk music was dead.

In view of the foregoing sketch of left-wing folksong activity during the Depression and World War II generation, what, then, was the Communist

Party's official position on folksongs and other traditions of the people during its viable years? The answer at first glance is deceptively simple; it had none. That is, while there were folksingers and others deeply interested in folklore who were members of the Communist Party, the party in general did not take any direct organizational interest in folk traditions or those adherents primarily concerned with them. Irwin Silber, a member of the Communist Party for fifteen years (1943-58) and a key figure in both People's Songs and People's Artists, observed in an interview with this writer:

> Now one would have the impression that the Communist Party sat around and figured [out] what to do with folk music. Bullshit! The Communist Party didn't know what to do with folk music . . . . Anything they [the leadership and most Party members] did consisted of a series of reactions to it, to the extent that they even thought about it.
>
> "Yes, let's have a folksinger at our meeting. That's what those people over there do. And it's somehow peripheral, but they're interested in it and they're party members, so let them do it." And from time to time, they would say, "Well, okay, what are you up to?" And somebody would come around and we'd tell him, and that was the extent of it. There was practically no attempt at trying to give direction, particularly, in our field of work.[24]

Silber's essential point is corroborated for the previous decade by no less a personage than Earl Browder, head of the Communist Party from 1932 to 1945 when he was ousted during a major internal political upheaval. Browder likewise told the author that during his years as leader of the party, the national organization never committed itself to the subsidy of any folksinger or other traditional artist, folklorist, or folk music group within the left. On those occasions when performers of traditional materials of one kind or another were paid by the party for their services at Communist functions, the district organizer or head of the local arrangements committee independently handled all the details, including the contractual agreements and money.[25]

It also seems clear, in retrospect, that during the more than two decades from 1935 to 1956 the great majority of left-wing sympathizers, even where they personally favored the popularization of folk traditions, did not seriously regard this cultural emphasis within the Communist movement and elsewhere as a major, concrete, tactical weapon in the people's arsenal. Folksongs and other folklore might be entertaining and might also describe much of the roots and aspirations of the masses, yet for most radicals they bore little relation to the realities of daily living in the urban and progressive milieus. At least some of the party leadership clearly felt that the ardor of the hootenanny revolutionists was misplaced.[26] Thus, although at times the party contributed to, even directly supported, various front organizations of writers, playwrights, musicians, and other cultural artists, it refused to subsidize folk performers or associated organizations. Nor was this for want of trying by some members of those organizations. During one of the recurrent financial crises of People's Songs, Irwin Silber approached officials in the upper echelons of the Communist hierarchy about securing funds for the group and was turned down flat.[27] The Almanac Singers were publicized so much in the pages of the *Daily Worker* that a friend of Pete Seeger's facetiously suggested the group must own the paper. "Yet we were orphans," Seeger recalls. "There was no [left-wing] organization that really made themselves responsible for us."[28]

At the grass-roots level of the movement, however, those few Communists who were especially concerned with the political and cultural implications of folksongs and other people's traditions did organize among themselves, and during the People's Songs era came to constitute an independent club[29] within the Communist Party. It was in this small unit at the lowest level in the Party hierarchy, spiritual successor to a much more loosely run and sporadic Marxist discussion group in the early 1940s, which involved some of the Almanac Singers, that specific attention was given to the ideological direction (though not the direct operation) of People's Songs and People's Artists. Silber recalls:

> Among the people in our club–there we would have big discussion about which directions we should move in and how . . . we who think of ourselves as Communists [should] apply our overall political philosophy to the particular field [folk and people's music] we were working in . . . . And we had great influence. In that sense the Communist Party played a very important role in directing the activities of People's Songs, People's Artists, and all the other organizations around it.

The Party Folk Music Club was formed in the late 1940s as one of several subdivisions of the Music Section of the Communist Party[30] (see the diagram on page 101 and the additional explanatory material in footnote 30). The Music Section along with many other branches of the Party's Cultural Division (writers, actors, and so forth) had existed as a special wing of the Industrial Division of the Communist Party prior to World War II and had been dissolved as part of a political reorganization during the war, only to be reconstituted again in 1947 after Browder's expulsion. At this time, musicians with common interests were grouped together as much as possible in clubs, according to their wishes. One of these was a new unit composed principally of individuals who were particularly concerned with promoting their political and cultural ideology through the use of and identification with traditional

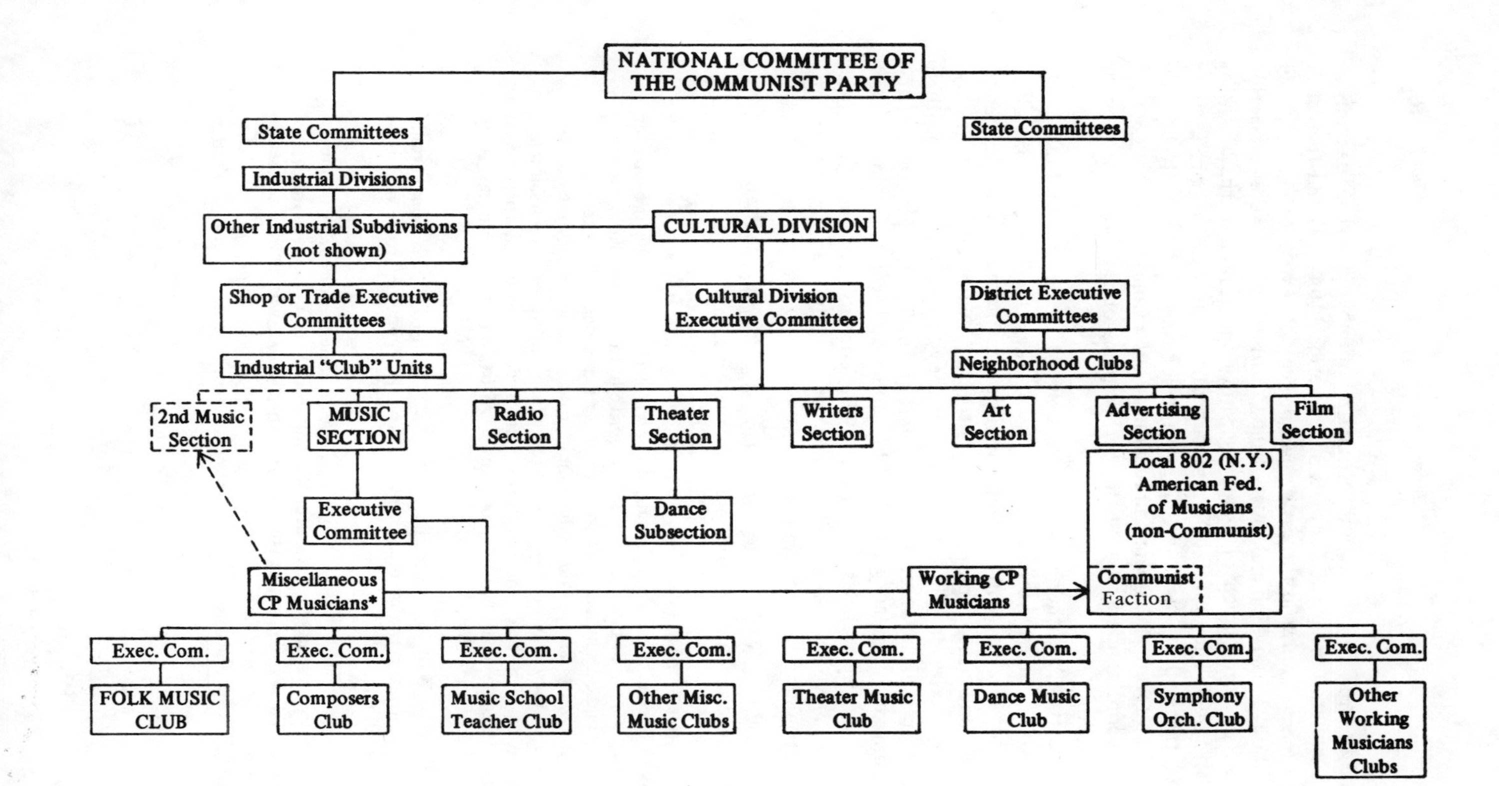

Diagram of the structural relationship of the Communist Party Folk Music Club to the rest of the Party hierarchy, 1947-ca. 1952. (Based on data supplied by Irwin Silber.)

*Became an independent Music Section in 1949.

music and the folk idiom. The Folk Music Club numbered perhaps as many as twenty members during the People's Songs period (1947-49) and thereafter shrank to ten or twelve in the early years of People's Artists (1950-52).[31] In 1952 the Folk Music Club and most of the Cultural Division were dismantled when the Party sent much of its membership underground at the height of the McCarthy era. The Cultural Division as a whole was restored once more in 1955, but the Folk Music Club never reappeared again, principally because too few of its former members still remained in the Communist Party. Those left were accordingly transferred into other parts of the Music Section or Cultural Division.

In theory, like other rank and file units of the Party, the Folk Music Club was supposed to meet once a week. At their meetings, the members would debate Marxism, current events, political theory, racism, social trends, art esthetics, and other topics which had little to do with folk music directly; but in the process, as Silber states above, they would try to define their Communist outlook on these and other matters, so that in the context of the People's Songs environment they could be applied to the latter's activities and music approach. Nevertheless, as the following conversation makes clear, the Communist Party Folk Music Club did not directly plan the policies or actions of People's Songs or People's Artists, nor did it ever try to:

> SILBER: The Communist Party Club did not go into any great detail about how People's Artists or People's Songs should be run. That would not have been appropriate. And we [the party Club] made it very clear that if it was a matter of [the] specific policy of People's Songs, that was for People's Songs to decide. If we simply imposed our will because there might have been some key people in the organization responsive to Communist Party discipline . . . this would be a mistake. We should not get that specific. In other words, in the Communist Party Club you should discuss the general [ideological] direction of the organization–a discussion which the organization itself might not even have. But . . . the Executive Committee of People's Artists would meet and decide what the policy of People's Artists was. No Communist Party Club would decide that.
>
> REUSS: Well, for example, what about [when] People's Songs would come out strongly against the [anti-Communist] regime in Greece or against the Marshall Plan?
>
> SILBER: That was a People's Songs decision, not the Communist Party's. Now that might have been Communist Party policy and individual people would say, "Yes, this is what we want," but it was never discussed in the Communist Party Club, "Now we'll try to get People's Songs to do this." It just didn't work that way . . . . There was no need for it . . . because whether

> the other people involved were members of the party or not, there was a general mutuality of political outlook . . . which is much more important than the fact that some of them were members of the party and some weren't . . . . I think if we [in the Club] had wanted to, we could have [arbitrarily decided People's Songs' policy]. There were enough of us in key positions to decide any way we wanted to. But it's almost like wearing two hats. The very same people might call two different meetings and they would discuss [matters] two different ways. And it was not as if the Party Club or the party on any level really figured out [People's Songs'] problems.

In many cases, moreover, there was substantial disagreement on the part of members of the Communist Folk Music Club over the specifics of ideology and the directions certain programs should take, and in numerous instances final conclusions were never reached.

While those in the Party Club worked on their own to shape a common radical sociopolitical outlook appropriate for their work in People's Songs and People's Artists, their efforts were ignored very largely by the rest of the Communist superstructure. As noted earlier, the party as a whole never contributed to either organization, and its leadership tended to regard the work of the left-wing folksingers in its midst as largely nonessential to the mechanics of revolutionary struggle, if not altogether spurious. Thus the only times the party bureaucracy interested itself in the work of People's Songs and People's Artists was when it ran checks on the political thinking and activities of its members in these groups. More often than not, these simply amounted to petty interference. On one occasion during the People's Artists period, someone in the Party Folk Music Club suggested that the songs chosen to appear in *Lift Every Voice* (The Second People's Song Book) be cleared in advance for approval by V.J. Jerome, the Communist Party's spokesman for cultural affairs on the National Committee, its top governing body. Jerome's only comment after a review of the book's proposed contents was to inquire why the book contained two Israeli songs but only one Soviet song. The Club's answer was that this was pure coincidence, but Jerome indicated his displeasure and ordered the balance redressed. Silber unhappily reviewed space, topical considerations, and other factors, and then notified Jerome that in order to include a second Russian song Woody Guthrie's "Roll On, Columbia" would have to be deleted. The latter's reply was, "It's not important. Take it out." It was.[32]

This type of incident occurred frequently on a larger scale all throughout the existence of the Old Left. As many historians and participants observed, party politicos generally maintained very little close rapport with the writers, artists, and other cultural workers under their jurisdiction, and often failed to comprehend many of the artistic problems and individualist natures of such people; as a rule, there was an absolute minimum of bureaucratic concern with purely esthetic matters. Silber remarks that most of the time it was a case of, "The party stands for this. Now what can you do to influence other people in your field in relation to this political program." Moreover, the top Communist leadership exhibited an almost total lack of confidence in the ability of its cultural workers to express left-wing ideology in their work independent of strict regimentation. This was most clearly demonstrated in 1946 when the *New Masses* published an article by Albert Maltz entitled "What Shall We Ask of Writers."[33] One of the better writers attached to the Movement in the 1930s, Maltz mildly suggested in the words of one historian that "a literary work must be judged on its artistic merits rather than on its ideology," and authors, "by their work, not by the committees they join."[34] Such statements were too much for the party leadership. Maltz was subjected to an avalanche of hysterical criticism and was forced to recant. Similarly, Irwin Silber recalls:

> I was a delegate to the National Convention of the Communist Party in 1957 after [the party had fragmented and divided bitterly in the wake of Khrushchev's famous speech attacking Stalin and Russian suppression of the Hungarian revolt]. And I served on a committee [which was] given the responsibility of drafting a resolution dealing with art and culture. And some guy from the National Committee was in charge of it.
>
> Well, he was terrified when in the course of the discussion we talked about announcing the need [for] artists to experiment in new forms and new ideas, and so on. He said, "We don't want all this experimenting going on .... That's not discipline. That just opens the door to all kinds of crazy things. It's a very dangerous concept you're putting forward there." We had a big battle about it.

But perhaps Woody Guthrie best underlined the absurdity, if not the dangers, of such monolithic and dogmatic stances. Shortly after Browder's explusion from the party in 1946, Guthrie was scheduled to appear before a Communist gathering. As he got up to sing, a party functionary cautioned him, "Don't say anything about Browder. He's a diversionist!" "What's wrong with a little diversion?" Woody shot back.[35] Parenthetically, it was because of such political unreliability that Guthrie's wartime application for membership in the Communist Party was never accepted.[36] Given this atmosphere, it is hardly surprising that the pre-War Almanac Singers and post-War People's Songs and People's Artists groups commanded at best only the moral support of the official Communist leadership and at worst (which was often) its disdainful neglect.

Ironically, too, some leaders and many rank-and-filers failed to take these radical folksong organizations as seriously as they might have because of their own unconscious duality of mind with regard to their personal revolutionary commitments. For unlike most of the movement's cultural workers, these units in fact occupied a fairly unique position within the Old Left after 1940 because of their relative lack of contact with capitalist art institutions, in substantial part through choice. Though there were some exceptions, most ardent left-wing performers and writers identified with the Almanac Singers, People's Songs, and People's Artists, possessed an in depth commitment to the projected working-class folk arts which also carried with it an implicit refusal to participate extensively in the cultural activities of capitalist or commercial establishments. This ideal was waived to some degree during periods of comparative cooperation between Communists and bourgeois governments, principally the World War II years, but in theory at least it was generally held that one either totally dedicated his energies to the workers, the unions, and the people, or by default, if not actively, he sided with the class elitists who exploited the masses out of their own self-interests. On the whole, few of the more politically conscious folksingers of the Old Left believed that true people's artists could be repeatedly successful commercially and at the same time relate to the class struggle. Popular singers like Burl Ives and the Weavers who on different occasions tried to maintain a foot in each camp, almost inevitably came to be viewed as having "sold out" or otherwise compromised their personal integrity. Of this dilemma and his early days in the movement, Pete Seeger recalls:

> I remember being continually intrigued by the problem of how a person is going to be an artist and make a living at the same time. Do you teach and then be an artist on the side? Do you work in a factory and be an artist on the side? Do you prostitute your art to make a living by it as, say, an advertising man, or work for Hollywood or radio? Do you try and do both? And it seemed impossible to me at that time to do both . . . . I could meet a man like Theodore Dreiser and everybody could say this man is a great artist and he also makes a living. But it was such an unusual thing that for me the idea that I could do it was completely out of the question. And I assumed that if I was going to be an artist, and be an honest artist, that I would always be broke.[37]

Such totality of commitment to the people's cause, however, seldom was evident in the statements and activities of the vast majority of other cultural workers in the Communist movement. Nearly all of the artists in adjacent fields—one estimate states 90 percent—were employed in various areas of the commercial entertainment world, bourgeois fine arts scene, or establishment media.[38] Such individuals sometimes also held responsible or prestigious positions within capitalist art institutions, and most so placed were ready to bask in their acceptance by and success in the latter as well. As a rule, they saw little or no contradiction between their cultural efforts for the bourgeoisie during the day and their left-wing political activities, ostensibly in the name of revolution, at night. Many, it is true, postulated the development of an independent workers' cultural expression, but, as Irwin Silber notes, most Old Left radicals were psychologically prepared to abandon the concept of a separate proletarian art as soon as interest in their work was shown by the Madison Avenue publishing houses, Broadway stage, or Hollywood film industry. "We were always fighting to get into the mass media," Silber recalls.

In short, the majority of Communist movement cultural workers, during the Roosevelt years and after nearly all middle class in their origins and income brackets, found it difficult to discount validation by the "System" as one of the prime measuring sticks by which to evaluate left-wing art. Making a full commitment to the class struggle, as so many Marxist writers and theorists demanded, in fact was far too threatening; for most radicals thus employed in the arts it would have meant breaking with their comfortable, sometimes affluent, existence, their positions within the commercial establishment, and many of the non-revolutionary middle-class values which unconsciously imbued their thinking. Thus, for example, when Irwin Silber assumed direction of the Music Section within the Cultural Division of the Communist Party in 1949, his first act was to assign Mao Tse-Tung's pamphlet *Art and Literature,*[39] dealing with the revolutionary commitment of artists, to all section units for reading and discussion. "Everybody read it as an abstraction," Silber remembers, "but it didn't have anything to do with their lives. [But] the whole point that we in People's Songs had was that this *was* our lives."[40]

Hence the crucial difference between the radical folksingers in the Old Left and much of the rest of the movement lay in the basic attitudes toward the folksongs, folk traditions, and derivative styles, forms, and expressions that all endorsed. To the former, the folk idiom was of fundamental importance, a touchstone and guiding light for all or most of their own cultural activity (this went so far in the case of the Almanac Singers that identification with the folk became a life-style reflected in varying degree in speech, dress, and mannerisms–sometimes comically misplaced–as well as songs).[41] Folk culture provided not only new mediums for propagandizing the class struggle, but also an entire avenue to a new art expression by and for the masses and apart from that controlled and sponsored by capitalism. As such, folklore, especially music, "represented a challenge to the established . . .

system," to use Silber's words. Hence its ideological importance to the radical folksingers and a few others was enormous.

On the other hand, to the majority of urban intellectuals in and about the party, folk traditions largely were window dressing, something in which to gild progressive art so as to provide another link, however tenuous, with the people. While from the 1930s on Communists and their sympathizers paid enormous lip service to the idea of folk-based working-class cultural expression, paradoxically, most were too ingrained with old middle- and upper-class prejudices weighted in favor of high art to seriously contemplate participating in the formulation and propagation of such a different esthetic perspective. An anecdote recalled by Irwin Silber illustrates this tendency succinctly:

> I remember going to a [Communist Party Music Section] convention before I became Section Organizer, where people talked vaguely about development in the field of music. [This was] in 1948 or '49, and maybe one hundred people were there. They talked how this or that was happening in music, about the symphony music field, serious composers, popular music. And I remember getting up in the middle of the discussion and saying, "You people don't know what's going on. You're talking about *their* culture. Nobody here has talked about the most incredible development of the last five years, that is what's happening with people like Pete Seeger, Earl Robinson, and the folksingers, and a new movement which is challenging the old accepted forms. You people . . . are snobs. You don't think of this as a serious music or a serious cultural expression. To you this is some sort of side issue, a periphery that is not serious music to be thought about seriously. You think of it as maybe some kind of vague agit-prop which we need on occasion. But now 'Let's talk about serious music. Let's talk about Aaron Copland and what he's up to, and is John Cage real or abstract–is he really revolutionary or is he counter-revolutionary'–and that's what you'll talk about. But you won't really deal with the things that have a chance to shape both musical ideas and general ideas in the form of music in this country." And this was the fact.

In many respects the left-wing folksong organizations were too radical, or at least different, in their worldview to be profoundly comprehensible to most people in the Communist movement. At the same time, one should not fault the majority of Old Leftists too heavily for failing to respond to traditional materials with an enthusiasm comparable to that of the Almanac Singers or People's Songs, or to accord folklore an equivalent importance in the proletarian struggle. Most northern Communists and allied individuals had little or no firsthand contact with rural American folksong traditions, and hardly could be expected to throw over their own urban art prejudices so easily. Culturally and psychologically, the gap in values, modes of artistic expression, and sociopolitical worldview was too great to bridge.

The radical folksingers of the 1940s and early 1950s thus were too limited in their appeal to be able to command much tactical support from either the party leaders or most rank-and-filers when the chips were down. Had the former been willing to invest more than a token interest in the Almanac Singers and People's Songs by supplying concrete aid in the critical moments of the lives of either, they thereby might have expanded the effective activities or at least might have prolonged the existence of both. Had more cultural workers in the Organized Left been able to overcome their ingrained predispositions favoring high art, and further contributed their talents to the above groups, the results might well have been the same. But such was not the case with People's Artists, for by the time this last group seriously began, the Communist movement itself was in its death throes as a viable political entity on the American scene.

University of Michigan
Ann Arbor, Michigan

NOTES

[1] *When Is Folk Music NOT Folk Music?* (Los Angeles: Fire and Police Research Association, 1963).

[2] *Congressional Record*, 88th Congress, 1st Session, Vol. 109, Part 13, 18221-18223.

[3] For example, Jere Real, "Folk Music and Red Tubthumpers," *American Opinion* 7 (December, 1964): 19-24; Herbert Philbrick, "Subverting Youth With Folksinging," *Your Church–Their Target: "What's Going On in the Protestant Churches"* ed. Kenneth W. Ingwalson (Arlington, Virginia, 1966), pp. 167-177; and Gary Allen, "That Music: There's More to It Than Meets the Ear," *American Opinion* 12 (February, 1969): 49-62.

[4] Noebel's articles have appeared in *Christian Crusade* magazine. See, for example, "Suffer Little Children," and "Columbia Records: Home of Marxist Ministrels" in the February and March, 1967, issues, pp. 7-9 and pp. 18-20, 28, respectively. *Rhythm, Riots and Revolution* (Tulsa, 1966) is an outgrowth of ideas first expressed in a pamphlet *Communism, Hypnotism and the Beatles* (Tulsa, 1965) by the same author.

[5] The major studies of American Communist interest in folksongs are R. Serge Denisoff, *Great Day Coming: Folk Music and the American Left* (Urbana, Ill., 1971), and Richard A. Reuss, "American Folklore and Left-Wing Politics: 1927-57," (Ph.D. diss., Indiana University, 1971) from which much of this article is drawn. For specific discussion of early left-wing considerations of folklore, see Richard A. Reuss, "The Roots of American Left-Wing Interest in Folksong," *Labor History* 12 (1971): 259-279.

[6] For particulars, see "The Roots of American Left-Wing Interest in Folksong," pp. 264-265.

[7] Text from the *Red Song Book* (New York. 1932), p. 22.

[8] For discussion of the "discoveries" of these individuals, see chapter 2 of Denisoff, *Great Day*, and chapter 3 of Reuss, *American Folklore and Left-Wing Politics.*

[9] *A Program For Proletarian Composers* (January 16, 1934), p. 5.

[10] "Cowell Performs Own Compositions in Piano Recital," *Daily Worker* (November 21, 1933): 5.

[11] This was proudly recalled years later by Earl Browder in an interview with the author, February 12, 1968.

[12] Alan Lomax interview, May 28, 1968.

[13] One sketch of the history of the Almanac Singers is R. Serge Denisoff, " 'Take It Easy, But Take It': The Almanac Singers," *Journal of American Folklore* 83 (1970): 21-32. See also the cited volumes by Denisoff and Reuss.

[14] "Hard Hitting Songs By Hard Hit People," *The Clipper* 2 (September, 1941): 7.

[15] Lillian Lowenfels, "One Million Americans Have Heard 'Almanacs,' " *Daily Worker* (September 2, 1941): 7.

[16] George Lewis, "America Is In Their Songs," *Daily Worker* (March 24, 1941): 7.

[17] *People's Songs Bulletin* 1: 1 (February, 1946): 1.

[18] Pete Seeger, "People's Songs and Singers," *New Masses* (July 16, 1946): 9.

[19] Unsigned mimeographed circular (n.d.) in the possession of the author.

[20] See, for example, "Hootenanny," *Time* (April 15, 1946): 71-72; "Roll the Union On," *Fortune* (November, 1946): 184; "Cultivating Songs of the People," *New York Times* 2 (August 25, 1946): 5; "People's Songs" (editorial), *The Christian Science Monitor* (March 4, 1947); and the citation of commendation by the New York Newspaper Guild reprinted in the *People's Songs Bulletin* 2:1-2 (February-March, 1947): 8.

[21] *Sing Out!* 1: 1 (May, 1950): 2.

[22] Irwin Silber, "Racism, Chauvinism Keynote U.S. Music," *Sing Out!* 2:5-6 (November and December, 1951): 6-7, 10, each month; Irwin Silber, " 'Male Supremacy' and Folk Song," *Sing Out!* 3: 7 (March, 1953): 4-5, 10; "Can An All-White Group Sing Songs of Negro Culture?" *Sing Out!* 2: 7 (January, 1952): 2, 14, a series of letters to the editors on said subject, which continued in several subsequent issues.

[23] " 'Male Supremacy' and Folk Song," p. 4.

[24] All material henceforth quoted from Silber is from my taped interview with him on April 2, 1968, unless otherwise noted. Silber's frank discussion of the ways in which the Communist Party interacted with People's Songs and People's Artists during the era under consideration was most helpful to my understanding of what transpired and how, and I gratefully acknowledge his help here. His insights into the dynamics of the Old Left milieu have heavily influenced my own interpretations in this essay. I have his permission to cite his past Communist affiliation.

[25] Browder interview.

[26] As an example, see George Charney, *A Long Journey* (Chicago, 1968), p. 51.

[27] Silber interview, February 29, 1968.

[28] Pete Seeger interview, April 9, 1968.

[29] The term "cell" was not used in the American Communist movement after the 1920s.

[30] The Music Section was divided principally between those musicians who worked regularly in bands, orchestras, and shows on a day-to-day basis, and those variety artists, composers, songwriters, sheet music pluggers, music scholars and theorists, and other miscellaneous music related personnel that functioned more on a craft basis. The former were almost exclusively concerned with union problems and their activities as Communist members of Local 802 (New York) of the non-Communist American Federation of Musicians union. The latter were more interested in the ideology of culture and other non-union related problems, and frequently complained that they could get no hearing for their own spokesmen in the Music Section, which was dominated by the working musicians. Consequently, in 1949, a second Communist Party Music Section was established for the craft musicians alone. Irwin Silber became its head a few months later. Silber estimates that in the late 1940s there were approximately 1000 to 1500 members of the Cultural Division of the Communist Party and 150 to 200 members of the Music Section.

It should be noted, however, that the diagram on page 101 is only an approximation of the Communist Party structure of these years, which actually was considerably more amorphous than indicated here. For example, Irwin Silber notes with regard to the Music Section: "In point of fact, it was never really that scientifically organized. While there was a folk music club for a while, and there were certain attempts to group people of common interests in other clubs, this was a very loose procedure; and aside from the folk music club, a person might be in one or another branch simply because Thursday nights were a more convenient meeting time than Tuesdays or vice-versa" (letter, August 9, 1970).

Also, the Cultural Division, while ostensibly national in scope, actually was limited in practical terms to the greater New York area and a small branch in Los Angeles, each under the jurisdiction of the Industrial Departments of their respective state Communist Party branches. Communist musicians, writers, and other artists living in parts of the country outside of these two cities thus belonged to neighborhood clubs rather than subsections of the Party's Cultural Division.

[31] These approximate figures are from the Silber interview. Not wanting to inadvertently identify individuals other than himself, Silber refused to state what percentage of the Club's membership participated in both People's Songs and People's Artists activities as opposed to those of one or the other. He does note, however, that after 1949 the Party generally reduced the size of club units for organizational and security purposes.

[32] Silber interview.

[33] February 12, 1946, pp. 19-20.

[34] David A. Shannon, *The Decline of American Communism* (New York, 1959), pp. 56-57.

[35] Lee Hays interview, August 16, 1965.

[36] As told by Marjorie Guthrie, Woody's wife, printed in Dave Johnson, " ' . . . Just A

Mile From the End of the Line,' " *Northwest Magazine* (Portland *Oregonian* Sunday Magazine) (February 2, 1969): 11.

[37] Seeger interview.

[38] Silber interview.

[39] New York, 1950. At the time, Silber assigned mimeographed copies, since the published edition had not yet appeared.

[40] Silber interview.

[41] Interviews with several former Almanacs.

THE STUDY OF ETHNICITY IN MODERN EUROPEAN ETHNOLOGY

Linda Dégh

The migration of peoples is a continuous and essential part of human history and is responsible for the distribution of ethnic groups throughout the world today. Population movements create nations, determine the existence of languages and cause depopulation and poverty in some areas and prosperity in others. Migration, group formation, dispersal, relocation, and integration are ongoing processes, and the ethnic conditions of population groups differ only according to their different rates of acculturation. Governments often manipulate ethnic groups either in their political aims, calling for a national unity and reconciliation of ethnic conflicts or in their policy of maintaining an artificial ethnic disparity, which usually results in open conflicts. Ethnic and national minority groups are consequently a central concern today in all nations of the world.[1] They are the concern of developing, modern nations that have to incorporate diverse ethnic cultures into a uniform system which forces the latter to give up claims for national independence in order to survive. They are the concern of small, modern nations governed by alien powers that have forced them to compromise. They are the concern of long established nations, large and small, with population groups that have adhered to different cultural values and thus over an extended period of time have developed group solidarity which causes power struggles to flare up periodically. They are the concern of the New World nations who have to cope with the desire of immigrant groups to retain their cultural identity while at the same time attempt to accommodate these groups into the dominant population. From the point of view of the power structure these concerns appear to be primarily political, but from the point of view of the ethnic groups they present educational and sociopsychological problems.

THE RELATIONSHIP OF NATIONALISM AND ETHNOLOGY

European ethnology, or folklore,[2] originated in the political struggles of various minority population groups for ethnic recognition through certain culturally distinctive features, even though they were politically affiliated with large empires. During the eighteenth and nineteenth centuries, specific forms of folklore and folklife played a decisive role in the claims of ethnic groups for national independence and became instrumental in the establishment of modern nations. Thus the independent schools of ethnography of the newly founded nations catered to the reinforcement of ethnic identity and the rise of national pride through the definition, propagation, and perpetuation of ethnic values.[3] A very similar political trend has stimulated and motivated the upswing of folklore research in the Third World today, as was made clear in the "Folklore and Nationalism, Politics, Ideology" session at a recent international conference on "Folklore in the Modern World."[4] Like the European pioneers–Justus Möser, Johann Gottfried Herder, the Grimm brothers, Wilhelm Heinrich Riehl, Št. Vuk Karadžić, Oskar Kolberg and so many others–Third World scholars see their work as a powerful weapon in the emancipation and independence struggle of their people. There is a difference, however, in the political background of Third World nations such as Bangladesh and that of modern European nations. Because Third World nations were formed primarily after the abolishment of colonial rule, their various ethnic groups have had to contend with a newly defined form of nationalism.

The resurgence of ethnico-political conflicts among the ethnic minorities of western nations today indicates that cultural pluralism remains an open issue. To a certain extent, as Michael Hechter has pointed out, "... ethnic solidarity might have a good deal in common with the phenomenon of political mobilization ... political movements arise to champion minority languages; cultural revivals, such as have occurred in Ireland, emerge to legitimate new cultural forms in the guise of old ones."[5]

It is obvious that the problem of ethnicity in its multiple manifestations is so complex that the study of the phenomenon demands multidisciplinary cooperation between the humanities and the social sciences. The folkloristic approach; that is, the intensive, fieldwork-based study of a people's interrelated social, intellectual, and material aspects of culture in their ethnic context, is one means of approaching the problem. The accepted terminology of national or regional schools of European ethnology is irrelevant because the academic and philosophic approach is the same.

ETHNIC STUDIES IN NORTH AMERICA

In the course of the last fifteen to twenty years American folklorists have begun to explore regional, ethnic, and immigrant cultural units and have made them an important field of research.[6] After several collecting expeditions it has become clear to most of them that past-orientation and item-concentration must be abandoned in order to open the way for a more timely focus on immigrant *processes*. Such processes include not only the adjustment and assimilation from immigrant to ethnic status, but also the sociocultural consequences of both ethnic and dominant values on the integration of new groups.[7]

The folkloristic problem of ethnicity in America differs considerably from that in Europe. While the successive waves of immigrants to the New World belonged to a great many ethnic groups, far more than those coexisting in any single modern European nation, almost none were strong enough to establish lasting ethnic communities that could create cohesive and specific cultural values. The two-step process of acculturation dissolved the ethnic enclaves in a very short period of time, usually within two generations.[8] In the first phase, the immigrant had to adjust externally in order to make his living and to compete in the new society. This consisted primarily of learning the language and of changing small, everyday habits that did not require making concessions but arose as absolute necessities. In the second phase, the immigrant's identification with the majority of the population arose as an inevitable internal change of values resulting from adherence to the new society.

Immigrants, as a rule, establish their ethnic communities only temporarily and later maintain their organizational framework symbolically. Thus their ethnic behavior remains rather marginal and in most cases has little to do with Old Country forms. This phenomenon can be easily explained by the fact that during the two successive processes, the Old Country patterns are washed away by the overpowering new experiences in the adopted new country. The immigrant does not bring along a perfect copy of the Old Country culture, but only some traits of it. He can bring along only what he has and because his social heritage is but a random fragment of some local variation of the culture of his class, it excludes many other important general aspects of the Old Country culture. Thus the peasant immigrant brought over what was the living culture of his home village as he knew it and he had rather poor information about other parts of his national culture. Furthermore, after entering ethnic enclaves, he gained reassurance from only a few members of his immediate homeland who belonged to the same age group and educational level and he had to adjust his inherited values to the rather vague pattern of the new national culture.[9] He also had to adjust to a variety of alien cultures in his immediate neighborhood, in addition to the dominant culture.[10]

The newness and complexity of this whole ethnic process is possibly more apparent in Canada where a bilingual, multicultural society has been officially recognized and where the time between mass migration and consolidation has been so brief (the immigrant generation still dominates) that the "Canadian" identity for the total population has not yet been established.[11] The North American folklorist, therefore, has to study this relatively short process in addition to the more crucial question: What part do pseudo-ethnic features, whether consciously or unconsciously maintained, play in general American folklore? Roger Abrahams at the "Folklore in the Modern World" conference reminded us of the need for a folkloristic method to study ethnicity in the culturally pluralistic United States.[12] Such a method would complement the research of other social sciences in an age in which there is a growing desire for ethnic recognition in individuals and groups, a search for ethnic identity, and a conscious exhibition of distinctive ethnic traits on the part of various population groups.

ETHNIC STUDIES IN EUROPE

Although politically explosive situations can reinforce ethnic consciousness in European countries, for better or for worse, the basic difference between European and American situations requires different folkloristic approaches in the study of their respective ethnic cultures. Ethnic groups in Europe are the result of an uninterrupted, slow and natural process involving many centuries, even millennia, during which they acquired sets of specific cultural features by which their ethnic identification could easily be made. European ethnic groups are vital and viable composite parts of national cultures whose strong historical ties and profound roots keep them alive even though they might be oppressed, relocated, transplanted or dispersed. During such periods of stress, they may adapt themselves to different multiethnic situations or they may settle in cultural islands far divorced from their motherland and enclosed within an alien nation, but they rarely disappear without a trace. Although an ethnic group might grow senescent, lose its language, and become absorbed by a stronger group, such a process is gradual and almost unnoticeable, affecting mostly the marginal population and not the core of the ethnic territory. In other words, in the study of European ethnic groups, we must consider them as historical formations and as parts of the cultural continuum so prevalent throughout Europe. That contemporary patterns of ethnic enclaves cannot be understood without their historical perspective was made particularly clear by the American anthropologist, Walter Goldschmidt, who commented after his European travels in 1958:

> Continental Europe is so generously sprinkled with reminders of cultural continuity . . . that it is more the wonder that sociological orientations are increasingly prevalent than that historical viewpoints should continue to flourish. These reminders are not merely the temples of war, religion and faded vainglory, but are also found in social institutions and antique customs that link the present age of atomic power to the distant past of Mediterranean civilization and pagan Europe. It is a contrast to America, where the temples represent a civilization completely foreign or are of recent date.

Goldschmidt concludes with the observation that "one can only explain culture in historical terms."[13]

Although historically and topographically limited, ethnic groups might be considered as very diverse entities in terms of the sizes of their populations and their systems of organization, statuses, and relationships. In Europe they are generally regarded as falling into two main formats: (1) as regional dialect components of a general national culture, and (2) as alien minority groups, language islands, or colonies within the nations.

In the first case, ethnologists investigate historical, geographical, ecological, and demographical facts, in addition to ethnographic field data, to account for the specific combination of cultural elements that characterize the ethnicity of a regional group.[14] Because ethnic groups have almost always developed by the merging and layering of diverse in-migrant ethnic variables as well as alien ethnic elements, ethnologists interested in dialect enclaves have placed particular concern on past waves of population movement. The cultural design resulting from such constant merging and layering of diverse groups has been found to be colored further by foreign elements in the immediate environment. It is often hard, if not impossible, to determine the boundaries of such groups because, as already indicated, outstanding features gradually tend to be washed away toward their borders. In regional ethnic group studies, researchers in the past have paid a great deal of attention to the so-called "ethnic specifics," that is, the local variations of the national stereotypes of the practical and expressive culture. As a result, they have found that the distinctive features of an ethnic group cannot be described by one or even more than one outstanding trait because the same trait might be of similar ethnic value among other groups under quite different conditions. What earmarks an ethnic culture is the specific combination and use of a complex of several traits. Scholars such as László Vajda have argued that the definition of the specific ethnic qualities of regional groups can result in the discernment of the national character of a whole people.[15] Such a purpose also motivated a number of folklorists to isolate regional variables in forms of folk literature. Folktale scholars in particular found that the regional subtypes of international tales often exhibit the configurations of the national stereotypes.[16]

In the second case, although alien ethnic colonies within larger nations were investigated in much the same manner as regional ethnic groups, the goal of the study became quite different. In fact, native ethnographers of the mainstream culture regarded uprooted ethnic groups beyond the borders of their homeland with nostalgia, whereas they were completely disinterested in the alien minorities that had in the meantime established themselves in the researchers' home neighborhoods. Scholars of powerful nations supported government policies in sustaining the ethnic loyalty of emigrant groups while envisioning at the same time their eventual resettlement; through their research they also supported discriminatory policies and enforcement of assimilation. This nationalistic narrowmindedness on the part of ethnographers not only created great gaps in scholarship,[17] but also helped to increase bitterness and hostility between minority and host folk groups who fell easy prey to aggressive nationalism.[18] These past-oriented, traditional ethnographers saw their emigrant colonies in terms of the Herderian *Volksgeist,* as the last remains of the national ideal. They viewed language islands as retainers of an archaic model from which the mother culture had deteriorated long ago and they yearned for a return to the halcyon state they believed such an ideal model represented.

THE SOVIET SCHOOL OF ETHNOLOGY

Among the history oriented ethnographic schools of Europe, the Soviet school most faithfully carries on the principles of nineteenth century pioneers by justifying folklore research with political goals. In a recent article, Bromley and Shkaratan, prominent Soviet scholars, stated that "most Soviet ethnographers are agreed that their science deals with ethnic entities."[19] Furthermore, they advance the opinion that "the core of ethnography's field of study consists in a study of the stable and characteristic features of ethnic traits whose sum give ethnic groups their inimitable character."[20] They then continue by describing ethnic entities in terms of subsequent stages of social evolution in each of which ethnic features manifest themselves in variable forms and intensity according to socioeconomic needs. They assume that ethnic processes are slower than socioeconomic changes and can, as a result, be discerned by direct observation of the everyday life of a contemporary folk, so that "research into the cultural features of ethnic entities has become the gist of the ethnographic approach to the present."[21]

Prior to Bromley's conceptions of the study of ethnics,[22] the Soviet school of ethnography had established its ideology and methodology in the service of national politics, consistent with the principles which resulted from the October Revolution of 1917. In the newly formed Soviet Union, ethnographers began to study and describe the multitudinous ethnic cultures in their quite diverse ethnic traditions, historical heritages, living conditions, and socioeconomic systems. Approximately thirty million of the population then lived in tribal, semi-feudal, agricultural, patriarchal, and nomadic-pastoral systems, and the government was faced with the problem of incorporating them into a modern industrial state. As S. P. Tolstov expressed it, the duty of scholars was to explore the origins and historical development of these ethnic groups to allow them to replace their obscure oral traditions, origin legends, and myths with factual folk histories.[23] Since many of the nationalities had not developed their written history or literature (in fact, they had no written language) it became the task of the ethnographers to revive the forgotten epochs of their history. In accordance with Lenin's minority policy, scholarly research was hence directed by the need to help underdeveloped minorities to make the leap virtually overnight from tribal conditions into the industrial age.[24] As Tolstov states, "The ethnohistoric monograph, the description of the origins and history of peoples, gradually became the basic type of scholarly study."[25] Two years later, S. A. Tokarev discussed the problem of "ethnogenesis-research" as a most crucial and difficult field and emphasized that the task was so complex that it necessitated the help of physical anthropologists, archaeologists, and linguists in the research.[26] However, he specified that such a research team had to be directed by an ethnologist whose concerns with specific ethnic traits enabled him to coordinate the field data of all related disciplines. The Soviet school of ethnography also raised the question of ethnic boundaries, which is currently viewed as one of the most important focuses of investigations attempting to define the specific characteristics of neighboring groups through comparative research.[27]

Like Soviet students of ethnogenesis, as well as other proponents of Marxist ethnography, most European ethnologists traditionally consider their discipline to be historically oriented.[28] The concept of "ethnos" or "ethnic group" as an entity for scholarly scrutiny was considered by its most outstanding proponents, the Russian emigrant, Sergei Shirokogorov,[29] and the German, Wilhelm Mühlmann,[30] as a continually changing product of historical conditions. According to Mühlmann, an ethnic group should be identified by shared and relatively stabilized cultural traits and by a real or assumed common origin.[31]

The members of an ethnic community can be distinguished from similar groups by external, physical features on the one hand and by cultural traits such as languages, customs, skills, and artifacts on the other. These traits should be commonly shared by the membership and should be essential for in-group interaction. In broader terms, other scholars deduced the specific ethnic features of a group from the sum of ethnographic field data. The Norwegian, Frederik Barth, summarized the term "ethnic group" as a population "which is largely biologically self-perpetuating, shares fundamental cultural values realized in overt unity in cultural forms, makes up a field of communication and interaction, has a membership that identifies itself and is identified by others as constituting a category distinguishable from other categories of the same order."[32] Other scholars stressed ethnic stereotypes developed by the membership of some ethnic groups in their critical evaluation of other groups.[33] More recently, Hechter has stated that ethnicity is composed of a set of specific culture forms: "observable customs, styles of life, and institutions, through which meanings are ascribed, goals are enumerated, and social life is regulated . . . " hence, " . . . ethnicity becomes indistinguishable from culture that originated in unique historical circumstances and processes."[34]

ETHNOLOGY AND THE NAZI IDEOLOGY

Following the First World War, the isolated ethnic enclaves beyond the borders of the motherlands became the primary targets for political propaganda issuing from the countries on the losing side of the war. A new resurgence of nationalism in Hungary demanded revision of the peace treaty that partitioned the former Austria-Hungary, the return of the lost territories, and the reduction to minority status of the population in the new succession states. Although Germany did not lose such large portions of its territory, the defeat crippled its economy and humiliated the national pride. With appeals to the founding fathers of *Volkskunde*, the great romantic nationalists, and the ideological heritage of W. H. Riehl, the discipline became a powerful weapon in the hands of Nazi folk and race theorists.[35] Among their targets were the German ethnic groups in southeast Europe. Beginning with the mid-twenties researchers and agents of the Reich visited the different ethnic areas and organized the single communities as German nationals, thereby awakening their consciousness of adherence to the mother country. Though at first this movement had a culturally imperialistic tendency, it later became a real imperialistic one.[36] Max Hildebert Boehm, the theorist of the research target of *Sprachinselvolkskunde*, made it clear that he viewed the German settler as a missionary, colonist, landlord and farmer, builder of cities, and carrier of material and intellectual progress for more than a thousand years, and that the settler's mission was to open up an additional German *Lebensraum* for the expanding nation. Boehm furthermore emphasized that the peculiar *Herrenbewusstsein*, the superior aristocratic attitude of the German peasant colonist toward his inferior environment, was manifested in his "awareness of the mission given to him by his people: drive toward the East."[37] Monographs were written by fieldworkers who explored southeast European German ethnic groups in support of this expansion ideology.[38]

In her recent critical evaluation of the movement, Ingeborg Weber-Kellermann stated that the unfortunate *Sprachinselvolkskunde* with its hybrid of "culture donor" and "lord-master" orientation is partly the cause for the tragedy of the southeast Germans. Weber-Kellermann furthermore pointed out that, contrary to the German concept of the petrified island, there is also objective research that presents a realistic picture of the interplay of interethnic contacts and intercultural exchange between the different groups. Like all social groups, ethnic groups also can be characterized by the dynamic process of adaptation and acculturation to the given living conditions.[39]

Weber-Kellermann is among the pioneers who succeeded in dissociating themselves from the ideological bias of German ethnic research that prevailed for at least one and a half decades after the end of the Second World War. The forced relocation of the southeast German ethnic groups to their *Urheimat* gave new impetus to the "back-oriented Volkskunde."[40] The new arrivals were questioned for their memories of the old culture which had to be "saved" from oblivion in the new environment of industrialized Germany. The teams of collectors, however, were far from objective; the *Jarhbuch für Volkskunde der Heimatvertriebenen*, established in 1956, greatly dramatized the ill fate of those who were expelled from their *Heimat*. Among many of their subsequent publications, as well as in works by other authors at that time, we can still read statements claiming that the archaic, isolated colonies did not adapt to the host countries.[41] Gottfried Henssen's introductory words to his *Ungarndeutsche Volksüberlieferungen* are rather typical of folklore collections of the period:

> From the folk groups that had to find a new home in Germany after the unfortunate outcome of the war, the Hungarian Germans acquire a special significance: the hard-headed "Schwabs" brought along a heritage of the best German quality that was in the course of several centuries passed from one generation to the other . . . Narrative and song stock that had been largely forgotten in the old motherland lived on among them in surprising richness and vigor, as it was strongly rooted in the life of their communities.[42]

A new generation of scholars had to grow up and take issue with the reconstructionism of traditional German *Volkskunde.* The new school, which criticized the old for its subjective preoccupation with materials gathered arbitrarily in opposition to an objective, problem-oriented focus on people, found a most stimulating setting in post-war Germany for experimentation with new methods.[43] Parallel to the settlement and acculturation of a great variety of German colonies and refugees from Prussia, researchers could observe step by step processes of change and integration, as observable in the present life of the new settlers. The change of the title of *Jahrbuch für Volkskunde der Heimatvertriebenen* into *Jahrbuch für Ostdeutsche Volkskunde* might symbolize the change in research interest of the group of scholars specializing in the German-ethnic cultures.[44] More recently Herbert Schwedt has raised the question of whether assimilation of the *Heimatvertriebenen* and the refugees into the mainstream culture has taken place.[45]

EUROPEAN ETHNIC STUDIES SINCE WORLD WAR II

Processes of change through the crossing of ethnic groups and the reorientation of ethnic values became the focus of research after the Second World War. As a consequence of the war, ethnic group relocation and exchange of minority populations between nations set minority groups into motion and stirred up internal migration as well.[46] No migration of this magnitude has occurred since the eighteenth century when groups of needy agriculturalists of different national origins were settled in the depopulated, fertile regions of eastern and central Europe which had been freed from Turkish occupation. Relocated ethnic groups offered a unique opportunity to observe accultirative processes in a virtual laboratory situation since the normally slow change that had taken centuries in earlier epochs was accelerated by compulsory resettlements and yielded new data in ethnic stratification. The team research conducted in the settlements of the relocated Bucovina Székelys in west Hungary started in 1948 and is still in operation. The research has produced numerous studies about the descendants of five settlements displaced from Transylvania in the late eighteenth century, resettled in 1941, and currently spread out in thirty-eight village communities.[47]

The study of interethnic relations has evolved as a special field in recent years. Following experiments concerning folklore exchange in bilingual areas within nations and along border zones,[48] teams of fieldworkers began to visit communities (single villages, cities, or areas) in which two or more nationalities coexisted, interacted, and overlapped. Of course, modern native ethnographers are greatly concerned with the diverse kinds of language colonies that live side by side within the territory of the mainstream culture because of their display of complex cultural stratification. Detached language colonies have combined autochthonous elements from the time of separation with those adapted from the dominant culture, and they have equally borrowed from the other coexistent alien ethnic groups. As such, the interchange of the inherited and the borrowed cultural elements resulted in the creation of a new version of the national culture model.

New techniques for studying ethnic groups have been developed in the preeminently multiethnic regions of southeast Europe, that is, Yugoslavia, Romania, Hungary, and Czechoslovakia. Several model studies have already been published and more are yet to come. For example, in the course of the last ten years a group of Czech researchers has investigated the folklore, culture, and language conditions of a Czech minority group in the Romanian Banat[49] and in the region of Daruvar (Yugoslavia).[50] Likewise, Hungarian and Slovak research institute members have studied Slovak villages in Hungary and Hungarian villages in Slovakia. Similar cooperative work is in progress in the ethnically mixed contact regions between Yugoslavia and Hungary.

These insights were utilized by the team of the *Marburger Studienkreis für Europäische Ethnologie*, with the support and cooperation of Romanian folklorists.[51] They selected a multilingual village for a community study, the aim of which was to examine interethnic relations in the process of sociocultural changes as it takes place in an ethnically mixed village of the Romanian Banat. The small community of their choice acquired its German majority in the early eighteenth century but also included Serbian, Romanian, Gypsy, and Hungarian populations. By the time of the study, from 1970 through 1971, different historical and political events had changed the population figures and reduced the German group to half the size of the Romanian. The continuing coexistence of the three main ethnic groups—Romanian, German, and Serbian—with their distinctive religious affiliations, made it possible to register empirically the change that took place within the lifetime of three current generations. The members of the research group focused their investigation in the village around the themes of labor, leisure, family life, school and education, and the observation of a calendar custom in the three ethnic groups. As a theoretical thesis for the study, it was postulated that:

> ... through the lasting encounter of ethnically distinct social patterns, processes of change of different intensity and speed will be kept in motion both in their structure and cultural manifestations. Consequently, despite their characteristic organization, ethnic groups cannot be described according to a set of traits because trait-combinations will always change according to the relevant socioeconomic context based on the given regional-historical situation.[52]

The east German colonies that survived resettling procedures after the Second World War have also continued to be attractive to folkloristic research. But the interest in the language islands has taken an entirely new turn. As already mentioned, Ingeborg Weber-Kellermann was among the most prominent critics of the aggressive political orientation of earlier studies.[53] After several field trips to the Swäbische Türkei in southwest Hungary in the fifties, she realized the necessity of cooperation among the specialists of neighboring countries to explore interethnic relations:

> The German people who have lived on their language islands for many generations, surrounded by a multi-ethnic environment have successively developed a loyalty to their homeland. The pillar of this loyalty is built up of the building blocks of [the universe comprising the] neighborhood, village community, the land and the market life in the nearby town.[54]

Furthermore, Weber-Kellermann emphasized that the visiting researchers grossly overestimated the significance of inherited folklore materials of the *Urheimat*, and that the colonists adhered more to their adopted *Heimat* than to their former homeland. A stock of tradition imported from the Old Country which had been left centuries ago represents only one, and not even the strongest, layer of the culture of the German colony. Even if there were a possibility of unwaveringly preserving old things for over ten generations, all this would prove is a remarkably durable conservatism.

All these researchers have emphasized that ethnic groups are to be considered as human groups whose lives together and whose ensuing cultural expressions are in constant flux. The ethnic group is an open system of social interactions and strings of cultural traditions which are in a constant dynamic process of growth and decay; always on the move.[55] The objective of the researcher, therefore, should be to recognize and describe the motivation and the mechanism that causes the changes in the ethnic pattern. In view of these perspectives on the study of interethnic contacts within multiethnic communities–observation of the process of interchange of ethnic elements, their spatial and temporal spread, the determination of ethnic boundaries and ethnic thoroughfares–the ways and means of intercultural borrowing between interacting groups can become one of the most fruitful fields in European ethnology.

Indiana University
Bloomington, Indiana

NOTES

[1] Tamotsou Shibutani and Kian M. Kwan, *Ethnic Stratification. A Comparative Approach* (New York: Macmillan, 1965).

[2] The different schools of folk culture research have used a variety of terms to designate their discipline, although their goals are similar. Nowadays German scholars especially reject the terms "*Volkskunde*" and "folklore" (its English equivalent) and argue for renaming the discipline "European ethnology," "cultural anthropology," or the "empirical study of culture." See Sigurd Erixon, "Ethnologie régionale ou folklore," *Laos* 1 (1951): 9-19; Linda Dégh, "Folklore and Related Disciplines in Eastern Europe," *Journal of the Folklore Institute* 2(1965): 103-19; Roland Narr, "Volkskunde als kritische Sozialwissenschaft," in *Abschied vom Volksleben*, eds. Klaus Geiger, Utz Jeggle, and Gottfried Korff (Tübingen: Tübinger Vereinigung für Volkskunde, 1970), pp. 37-73.

[3] Guiseppe Cocchiara, *Storia del folklore in Europa* (Torino: Einaudi, 1952), Part III, "Il folklore come strumento di politica e di dignita nazionale nel Romanticismo," pp. 209-303; Robert R. Ergang, *Herder and the Foundation of German Nationalism* (New York, 1931); Richard M. Dorson, section on Folklore and Nationalism, Politics, Ideology in "Folklore in the Modern World," *Folklore Preprint Series* 1:8 (1974), pp. 36-42.

[4] Held in Bloomington, Indiana, 28-30 August 1973. That session was chaired by Paulo de Carvalho-Neto.

[5] Michael Hechter, "The Political Economy of Ethnic Change," *American Journal of Sociology* 79 (1974): 1154.

[6] Richard M. Dorson, "Immigrant Folklore," *American Folklore* (Chicago: University of Chicago Press, 1959), pp. 74-165; *idem*, "Is There a Folk in the City?" in *The Urban Experience and Folk Tradition*, eds. Américo Paredes and Ellen Stekert (Austin: University of Texas Press, 1971), pp. 21-52; Linda Dégh, "Comments on Marcus S. Goldstein's 'Anthropological Research, Action and Education in Modern Nations, with Special Reference to the U. S. A.,' " *Current Anthropology* 9 (1968): 256-57.

[7] This process was outlined for the first time by Robert B. Klymasz in "Ukranian Folklore in Canada: An Immigrant Complex in Transition" (Ph.D. diss., Indiana University, Bloomington, 1970), p. 324; also in "From Immigrant to Ethnic Folklore: A Canadian View of Process and Transition," *Journal of the Folklore Institute* 10 (1973): 131-39.

[8] Milton M. Gordon, *Assimilation in American Life: The Role of Race, Religion, and National Origins* (New York: Oxford University Press, 1964); Otto Feinstein, ed., *Ethnic Groups in the City: Culture, Institutions and Power* (Lexington, Mass.: D. C. Heath and Company, 1971).

[9] John Kosa, *Land of Choice: Hungarians in Canada* (Toronto: University of Toronto Press, 1957), pp. 91-94.

[10] Linda Dégh, "Folklore Research Among Immigrant Groups," *Journal of American Folklore* 79 (1966): 554.

[11] According to Anthony H. Richmond's report, "Language, Ethnicity and the Problem of Identity in a Canadian Metropolis," Paper presented at the Ninth International Congress of Anthropological and Ethnological Sciences, Chicago, 1973.

[12] Roger D. Abrahams, "Folklore and Cultural Pluralism," Paper presented at the Folklore in the Modern World Conference, Bloomington, Indiana, 1973.

[13] "From the Editor's Desk," *American Anthropologist* 60 (1958): 6.

[14] A model of a brief description of regional ethnic groups within a nation is Károly Viski, *Etnikai csoportok, vidékek* (Budapest, 1938).

[15] László Vajda, "A néprajzi anyaggyüjtés módszere és jelentösége," *Ethnographia* 65 (1954): 1-19. The author sees ethnic specifics as the ultimate goal of ethnographic research. His conclusions were critized by two commentators, Tibor Bodrogi (pp. 581-92) and Lajos Vargyas (pp. 240-44).

[16] Just a few examples: Kurt Ranke, *Schleswig-Holsteinische Märchen*, 3 vols. (Kiel, 1955); Maja Bošković-Stulli, "Regionalna, nacionalna i internacionalna obiljeza narodnih pripovijedaka," *Filološki pregled* (1963): 83-93; Mihaj Pop, "Charactères nationaux et historiques dans le style des contes populaires," in *Fourth Ininternational Congress for Folk Narrative Research in Athens*, ed. Georgios A. Megas (Athens, 1965), pp. 381-90; Oldrich Sirovátka, "Zur Erforschung der nationalen Eigenarten des Märchens," *ibid*., pp. 517-26.

[17] For example, no systematic study was conducted among the diverse and now extinct communities of East European Jewry and no due interest was paid to the itinerant Gypsy tribes, coexisting with the native population in practically every European country.

[18] Robert W. Seaton-Watson, *The History of the Romanians* (Cambridge, England: Cambridge University Press, 1934); Robert A. Kann, *The Multi-National Empire*, 2 vols. (New York: Columbia University Press, 1950).

[19] Yu. V. Bromley and O. Shkaratan, "The General and the Particular in Historical, Ethnographical and Sociological Research," *Current Anthropology* 13 (1972): 570. See also the materials of two symposia in the ethnographical section of the Soviet-Hungarian Commission of Historians in *Népi Kultúra, Népi Társadalom* 5-6 (1971): 355-492.

[20] Bromley and Shkaratan, *ibid.*

[21] *Ibid.*

[22] Yu. V. Bromley, "On Typologizing Ethnic Communities," presented in a paper written for the Ninth International Congress of Anthropological and Ethnological Sciences in Chicago on September, 1973.

[23] S. P. Tolstov, "Sovetskaja škola v etnograffii," *Sovetskaja etnografija* 4 (1947): 8-28.

[24] I. Stalin, *Marksism i nacional'no-kolonial'nyj vopros* (Moscow, 1934).

[25] Tolstov, pp. 8-28.

[26] S. A. Tokarev, "K postanovke problem etnogeneza," *Sovetskaja etnografija* 3 (1949): 12-36.

[27] P. I. Kušner (Knyšev), "K metodologii opredelenija etnografičeskix territorij," *Sovetskaja etnografija* 1 (1946): 12-14; *idem*, "Metody kartografirovanija nacional'nogo sostava naselenija," *Sovetskaja etnografija* 4 (1950): 25-54.

[28] See "Historicism in Ethnology," in *Népi Kultura, Népi Társadalom*, pp. 201-369; Lajos Vargyas, "Miért és hogyan történeti tudomány a néprajz?" *Néprajzi Értesitö* 43 (1961): 5-20.

[29] Sergei M. Shirokogorov, *Ethnological and Linguistical Aspects of the Uralic-Altaic Hypothesis* (Peiping, China: The Commerical Press, 1931); and *idem*, *Psychomental Complex of the Tungus* (London, 1935).

[30] Wilhelm E. Mühlmann, "Ethnologie als soziologische Theorie der interethnischen Systeme," *Kölner Zeitschrift für Soziologie und Sozialpsychologie* 8 (1956): 186-205.

[31] *Ibid.*

[32] Frederik Barth, ed., *Ethnic Groups and Boundaries: The Social Organization of Cultural Difference* (Boston: Little, Brown and Co., 1969), pp. 10-11; Shibutani and Kwan, *Ethnic Stratification*, pp. 88-94, on the formation of ethnic stereotypes.

[33] William Buchanan and Hoadley Cantril, *How Nations See Each Other: A Study in Public Opinion* (Urbana, Illinois: University of Illinois Press, 1953).

[34] Hechter, "Political Economy of Ethnic Change," p. 1152.

[35] Wolfgang Emmerich, *Zur Kritik der Volkstumsideologie* (Frankfurt am Main: Suhrkamp, 1971), pp. 95-131, 100.

[36] *Ibid.*, p. 105.

[37] Max Hildebert Boehm, "Das Volkstum des Grenz- und Auslanddeutschtums," in *Handbuch der deutschen Volkskunde*, Vol. I, ed. Wilhelm Pressler, pp. 170-82; see also Grevens, *Der Territoriale Mensch: Ein literatur-antropologischer Versuch zum Heimat-phenomenön* (Frankfurt am Main: Athenäum, 1972), pp. 202-70; Christa Kamenitzky, "Folklore as a Political Tool in Nazi Germany," *Journal of American Folklore* 85 (1972): 231-33.

[38] Walter Kuhn, *Deutsche Sprachinselforschung* (1934); Rudolf Kriss, *Die schwäbische Türkei* (Düsseldorf, 1937).

[39] Ingeborg Weber-Kellermann, "Zur Frage der interethnischen Beziehungen in der 'Sprachinselvolkskunde,' " *Österreichische Zeitschrift für Volkskunde* 62 (1959): 19-47; *idem*, *Deutsche Volkskunde zwischen Germanistik und Sozialwissenchaften* (Stuttgart: Sammlung Metzler M79, 1969), pp. 82-83.

[40] Emmerich, *Zur Kritik der Volkstumsideologie*, p. 105.
[41] Johannes Künzig, "Urheimat und Kolonistendorf–ein methodosches Beispiel der gegenseitigen volkskundlichen Aufhellung," *Jahrbuch für Volkskunde der Heimatvertriebenen* 2 (1956): 103-40.
[42] Gottfried Henssen, *Ungarndeutsche Volksüberlieferungen: Erzählungen und Lieder* (Marburg: Elwert, 1959), p. 1.
[43] Rudolf Schenda, "Einheitlich–Urtümlich–Noch Heute: Probleme der volkskundlichen Befragung," in *Abschied vom Volksleben*, eds. Klaus Geiger, Utz Jeggle, and Gottfried Korff (Tübingen, 1970), p. 154; "Gegenstände zukünftiger volkskundlicher Befragung seien gegenwärtige soziale Probleme (die ohne Zweifel eine historische Dimension haben). Die Leitworte solcher Enquêten dürfen nicht mehr EINHEITLICH, URTÜMLICH, NOCH HEUTE, sondern müssen INDIVIDUUM IM SOZIALEN KONFLIKT, GEGENWARTSBEZOGEN und WAS MORGEN? lauten."
[44] Some of the numerous monograph studies on contemporary ethnography of East German relocated persons are: Josef Hanika, *Volkskundliche Wandlungen durch Heimatverlust und Zwangswanderung: Methodische Forschungsanleitung am Beispiel der deutschen Gegenwart* (Salzburg: Otto Müller, 1957); Georg R. Schroubek, *Wallfahrt und Heimatverlust: Ein Beitrag zur religiösen Volkskunde der Gegenwart* (Marburg: Elwert, 1968); Herman Bausinger, Markus Braun, and Herbert Schwedt, *Neue Siedlungen* (Stuttgart, 1963).
[45] Herbert Schwedt, "Ist eine Volkskunde der Heimatvertriebenen überflüssig geworden?" *Jahrbuch für Ostdeutsche Volkskunde* 17 (1974): 20-26.
[46] Gyula Ortutay, "Recent Internal Migration in Hungary and Ethnographical Research," *Hungarian Folklore* (Budapest: Akadémiai Kiadó, 1972), pp. 109-31.
[47] Summarized in Linda Dégh, *Folktales and Society* (Bloomington, Indiana: Indiana University Press, 1969), pp. vii-xi, 3-42.
[48] Karl Heinz Langstorff, *Lothringer Volksart* (Marburg: Elwert, 1953); Linda Dégh and Jaromír Jech, "Prispěvěk k studii interethnických vilvů v lidovém vypravování" *Slovensky národopis* 5 (1957): 567-608: Milko Matičetov, "Gefahren beim Aufzeichnen von Volksprosa in Sprachgrenzgebieten," in *Internationaler Kongress der Volkserzählungsforscher in Kiel und Kopenhagen*, ed. Kurt Ranke (Berlin: Walter de Gruyter, 1961), pp. 179-87; József Faragó, "Citeva date cu privire la povestitul bilingv in Europa rasariteana," *Revista de Ethnografie şi Folclor* 12 (1967): 277-82; *idem*, "Zweisprachige Märchenerzähler in Siebenbürgen," *Forschungen zur Volks- und Landeskunde* 13 (1970): 57-69.
[49] Vladimir Scheufler, Olga Skalníková, et al., "Kultura rumunských Čechu," *Český lid* (1962): 145-209.
[50] Divna Zečević, "Usmena kazivanja u okolici Daruvara," *Narodna Umjetnost* 7 (1969-70): 27-70; Iva Heroldová, Godišnji običaji Daruvarskih Čeha," *Narodna Umjetnost* 8 (1971): 199-245.
[51] Annemie Schenk and Ingeborg Weber-Kellermann, *Interethnik und sozialer Wandel in einem mehrsprachigen Dorf des rumänischen Banats* (Marburg, 1973).
[52] *Ibid.*, pp. 5-6.

[53] Ingeborg Weber-Kellermann, "Gedanken zu einer heutigen 'Volkskunde der Ungarndeutschen,'" *Néprajzi Értesitö* 40 (1958): 29-36.
[54] *Idem*, "Der Luzienstuhl im deutschen und ungarischen Volksglauben," *Hessische Blätter für Volkskunde* 49/50 (1958): 295-316.
[55] *Idem*, "Probleme interethnischen Forschungen in Südosteuropa," *Ethnologia Europaea* 1 (1967): 218-31.

THE *KALEVALA* AND FINNISH POLITICS

William A. Wilson

Folklore studies in Finland have from the beginning been intimately connected with the struggle of Finnish nationalists to achieve first cultural and then political independence.[1] Probably in no other country has the marriage of folklore research and national aspirations produced such dramatic results. At the beginning of the nineteenth century, the Finns, fragmented into several dialect groups and lacking the binding ties of a common literature and a written record of their national past, were ill-prepared to face the century of Russian rule and attempted Russification of their culture that lay ahead. Then in 1835 Elias Lönnrot published the *Kalevala*, the national epic based on the old heroic songs that Lönnrot and his compatriots had collected from the Finnish hinterlands and that Lönnrot had welded into a unified whole. In the following decades, a small band of scholar-patriots dipped deeply into this folklore as they forged a literary language, created a national literature and sought to reconstruct the prehistoric period when Finns had walked on Finnish soil as free men. The *Kalevala* and the cultural works based on it gave the Finns a newfound pride in their past, courage to face an uncertain future, and, above all, a feeling of self-esteem they had never known before. That their beleaguered little nation on the fringe of Western civilization had produced an epic comparable, in their own minds at least, to the great Homeric epics was to be a never-ending source of pride to the Finns. The *Kalevala* had become their book of independence, their passport into the family of civilized nations. A nation that had created the *Kalevala*, they repeatedly told themselves, was not destined to die. In 1907 the great lyric poet Eino Leino summed up the feeling of the times in these words:

> The national spirit which appears in it is the spirit of a free nation. . . . In reading it we feel ourselves to be free and independent. . . . From it there steps before us a nation which enjoys its existence. . . . It is no slave nation . . .

> nor is it an upstart nation, but rather a nation which has its own customs, traditions, gods and concepts of life. It is *old Finland*. . . . The Finnish tongue in the *Kalevala* sounds freely, brightly and victoriously. It gives a picture of a nation which is sovereign.[2]

That a decade later Finland was able to take advantage of unsettled world conditions and in actuality to become sovereign, was due in no small part to the feelings of cultural identity and national unity engendered by the *Kalevala*.

But in the years following independence both Finnish political ideology and the folklore research that underpinned it in many instances tended toward extremism. This development was due largely to two points of view which had by then gained widespread acceptance and to shifting national aspirations and commensurate adjustments in folklore theory. Both points of view had deep roots in the past, but in the volatile years between the world wars had emerged with renewed force.

The first of these was the firm conviction that the ancient *Kalevala* poems provided an untarnished reflector of the pristine national soul —the conviction that one ought to look to these poems, or to the *Kalevala* itself (which in the popular fancy was synonymous with authentic folklore) to discover what it really meant to be a Finn and to find historical models on which to build the society of contemporary Finland.

The belief that folklore was the abode of the mystical national soul was, of course, nothing new. It had been developed by Herder[3] and the German Romantics at the end of the eighteenth century and, at the beginning of the nineteenth, had been responsible for turning Finnish folklorists to nationalism and Finnish nationalists to folklore. Weakened momentarily in the 1870s and 1880s by the spread of empiricism and positivism, it had received new life at the turn of the century from the neo-romantic movement, which stressed feeling and intuition, and from the anti-positivism and loss of faith in reason that grew out of World War I. By the time independence had been won in 1917, every schoolchild had been taught again and again that Finnish folk poetry was a mirror for all that was one hundred percent Finnish. In the following years, if anything, the belief grew still stronger and continued as a means of influencing cultural-political thought. In 1921, for example, E. A. Saarimaa, a prominent educator, instructed his fellow teachers: "The national significance of our folklore . . . entitles it to a prominent position in the national literature studied in our secondary schools. But particularly the fact that our nation's individuality is best revealed in this poetry makes learning it important. The nation's soul is nowhere reflected so clearly as in its almost collectively created poetry. And one of the most important tasks of the secondary school is to acquaint the students with their own nation."[4]

The second point of view that made possible the political exploitation of folklore was the belief that folklore was to be handmaiden to the state—that the end of folklore research was service of the fatherland. Once again this belief found support in the teachings of Herder, who had argued that an individual could receive his fullest development only as an integral part of his particular nation and that service to that nation was the highest endeavor of man. Through the years preceding Finnish independence, this service had been expressed primarily in attempts to advance Finnish culture, to create a national literature, to elevate the vernacular tongue, and to draw nearer the common folk. But following independence, nationalistic endeavors took on a harsher tone. The milder spirit of Herder gave way to that of Hegel, and individuality yielded to national or racial loyalty.[5] The following oath read to initiates at the swearing-in ceremony of the Academic Karelian Society, the university's most influential and politically active student organization, reflects something of the changed spirit: "From this moment on you no longer belong to yourselves but to the Fatherland. You stand before an open door; on this side is everything which a weak human will consider worthwhile and desirable: *I, myself*. On the other side is self-denial: *The Fatherland*. You step through the door and shut it behind you with an unopenable bolt: *your manly oaths*."[6]

Sentiments such as this one soon began to echo in the statements of folklorists. For example, in a youth publication Valdemar Rantoja wrote: "Folklore research is with us in Finland a national branch of science whose task is to reveal the earliest development of the Finnish spirit and to create an ideological-historical foundation for our nation's independent life and for its historical duty."[7] And in a doctoral ceremony, in the militaristic tones typical of the time, Martti Haavio, one of the country's most brilliant young folklorists and, during the 1920s, a leading figure in the Academic Karelian Society, declared: "Only a free man can carry a sword, not a slave nor the servile minded. . . . In this land we have been chosen to fight on behalf of that culture which we received as an inheritance; indeed, to conquer new areas for it. Only so long as science in this land is free will there be a sword in our hands; only so long as there is a sword in our hands will science be free. And without free science that fatherland to whose service we have consecrated ourselves can never flourish."[8]

The trouble with this argument is that when a scholar has consecrated himself above all else to the service of his fatherland, the demands of his scholarship all too easily yield to the needs of that fatherland. He becomes a patriot first and a scholar second. In such instances, folklore continues to serve as a mirror for culture, but the image reflected depends on the political predispositon of the man holding the mirror. Such was frequently the case in Finland in the years following independence, as folklore study at times became not just a means of understanding culture, but also a tool for manipulating minds. Intellectual leaders and propagandists from both sides of the political spectrum interpreted Finnish epic poetry to fit their own views and then, in the name of loyalty to one's heritage, used this poetry to advocate diametrically opposed courses of political action—the political right to generate in the citizenry a militaristic posture and to argue for an expansionist foreign policy; the political left to counter the ideology of the right and to argue for a classless, communistic society.

FOLKLORE AND THE POLITICAL RIGHT

Folklore and Militarism

In preparation for "*Kalevala* Day" in 1917 (the annual commemoration of the publication of the epic) Eino Leino wrote in the popular press:

> To honor the *Kalevala* is to us Finns the same as honoring one's own deepest being; to come to know the *Kalevala* is the same as knowing the wellsprings of one's own spirit; to rejoice over the *Kalevala* is the same as rejoicing over the swelling, streaming sunshine of one's own breast, over faith in life and over fulfillment. If a Finn does not care to read the *Kalevala*, then that testifies that he does not care to glance at the pages of his own book of destiny; if a Finn does not like the *Kalevala*, then that testifies that he does not like anything nor anybody, for only one who loves his own primeval self can radiate love around him. But if a Finn ridicules the *Kalevala*, then that is a sin against the Holy Ghost.[9]

Though the *Kalevala* was never widely read, except in school assignments, Leino's words suggest the symbolical force the epic had achieved in the minds of the people. It was important simply because it was there, a spiritual monument to the greatness of ancient Finland. Thus ten months later, with independence now achieved, cultural leaders quite naturally looked to the *Kalevala* and to the more genuine old heroic poems from which it had been formed to seek guidance in determining what kind of nation independent Finland should become. The answer was clear: a strong militaristic nation, a great northern power.

This answer was based in part on the Finns' swelling pride, on their understandable desire, after centuries of foreign rule, to become masters of their own fate and to recapture that lost age of glory and heroism revealed to them by the *Kalevala*. But, perhaps more important, it was based on the national will to survive, on the firm conviction that only by becoming militarily strong could Finland hope to resist the malevolent powers emanating from the East. Following a divisive civil war in 1918, which many Finns blamed on Russia, and following the Peace of Tartu in 1920, which the political right, as we shall see, considered a betrayal of Finland's legitimate territorial interests in the East, there developed in the land a militant anti-communism and an unrelenting hate of the Soviet Union.[10] Russians were no longer Russians; they were "our hereditary foe" or, more often and more disparagingly, simply "Ruskis" ("Ryssät"). And they were denounced from all quarters in the most inflammatory terms. On "*Kalevala* Day" in 1923, for instance, Elias Simojoki, a theology student and later a Lutheran pastor, declared to Helsinki University students that to love their fatherland they would have to hate Russia:

> Hate of the Ruski was the power which made Finland free. Hate of the Ruski . . . is the Finnish spirit . . . . Do you know how to hate as one hates in blood wrath, as your forefathers hated? . . . Death to the Ruskis, whatever be their color. In the name of the blood spilled by our forefathers, death to the destroyers and spoilers of our homes, our kinsmen, and our fatherland. Death to the dividers of Kaleva's race, to the polluter of the Finnish nation. In the name of Finland's lost honor and her coming greatness, death to the Ruskis. On this "*Kalevala* Day," in the name of our fatherland's rising greatness and the awakening of our people, let a rousing cry of holy love and hate travel through the tribe of Kullervo and through our beloved birthland.[11]

Simojoki's intemperate blast was more extreme than most but still not atypical. Three days earlier Martti Haavio had told a university audience that "nothing good can come from Moscow–against Moscow we *must wage battle*."[12] And Haavio's friend, E. E. Kaila, wrote: "By the power of a strong national feeling and an active patriotism–hate of the Ruski–every individual and the entire society are to sacrifice themselves to this work, so that when the hour strikes we will not be caught napping but will be ready for battle on behalf of our national freedom, our state independence, and humane culture, ready for the battle and for victory."[13]

To stir up this martial spirit, to glorify fighting and reckless courage, and to convince their countrymen that they were capable of greatness, Finnish nationalists turned to the ideal world revealed in native folk poetry, and particularly to the militaristic world which the dean of Finnish folklorists, Kaarle Krohn, had recently discovered in the *Kalevala* poems.

At the turn of the century there had been little in Krohn's folklore theory and in his study of the *Kalevala* heroes that would lift the Finns' flagging self-esteem and spur them on to heroic actions of their own. Nurtured by the evolutionary and positivistic spirit of his youth and following, in part, lines laid down by his father Julius, Kaarle Krohn had argued in his great work *Kalevalan runojen historia (The History of the Kalevala Poems,* 1903-1910) that though a few of the *Kalevala* poems had mythological origins—the famous heroes Väinämöinen and Ilmarinen he considered to be gods of the water and air—the majority of them had clearly derived from medieval Catholic saints' legends which had arrived in Finland from the West. Beginning life in southwest Finland as small poetic "germ cells," the poems had migrated slowly across the land to the remote province of northeast (Viena) Karelia, sloughing off in the process original Christian names, which were replaced by those of the old pagan gods, and evolving all the time into the longer poems and clusters of poems which Lönnrot had eventually collected and shaped into the *Kalevala.* In none of this, then—the lack of a solid historical or mythological foundation for the epic poetry, the lack of an heroic age, the development of the poetry from borrowed rather than from indigenous materials, and the late blossoming of the poetry—was there much grist for the nationalists' mill. But as Finland began to struggle toward independence, Krohn began to change his theory. Indeed, few scholars have opposed the theories of other men with the vigor that Kaarle Krohn was in the ensuing years to oppose those that had once been his own.

From the end of the nineteenth century a spirit of resistance to Russian oppression had been developing in the land. Its first manifestation had been the 523,000 signatures (half the adult population) sent to the czar in 1899 to protest violation of Finland's constitutional guarantees. This petition was soon followed in 1902 by the refusal of three-fifths of the youths of conscription age to report for the draft, by the refusal of Finns in general to obey edicts they considered illegal, by the assassination of Governor General Bobrikov in 1904, and by the general strike in 1905, which in its beginning stages, at least, had been an act of unified resistance against the Russians. At the beginning of World War I, a number of young Finnish activists, having come to believe in the force of arms as the proper means to achieve political ends, sought military training in Germany while others of their number, for the first time seriously considering the possibility of political independence, had sought German assurances that in the event of Russia's defeat Germany would support Finland's bid for freedom.[14] These political activities and aspirations had been further augmented by neo-romanticism in art, music, and literature, which had once again focused attention on the *Kalevala* and the golden age of the past. The folklore-inspired productions of Eino Leino, Jean Sibelius, and Akseli Gallén-Kallela, the fervent patriotic sermons given in

1902 on the one-hundreth anniversary of Elias Lönnrot's birth, and the *Kalevala* celebrations held across the land in 1910 on the seventy-fifth anniversary of the publication of the epic all contributed to the Finns' sense of national self-esteem. And it was in the midst of this political climate in 1914 that Kaarle Krohn, in two short essays ("The Heroes" and "Kalevala and His Kin")[15] dramatically suggested that he had been wrong in his earlier *Kalevala* interpretations and that the ancient Finns really had had a famous past.

These essays were only preliminary steps to the major works to come, and in the intervening years the public waited somewhat anxiously to see what direction Krohn would take. Shortly before the March Revolution that would thrust Finland down the road to independence, J. R. Danielson-Kalmari, a leading historian and politician, declared in a speech at Helsinki university: "[Krohn] has presented the view that in the *Kalevala* we have before us much more historical material based on actual happenings . . . than we have ordinarily been accustomed to see. With great interest the Finnish people expect now, and have the right to expect, that *Kalevala* research will clarify this matter and show to what extent this new view is accurate."[16]

The Finnish people had not long to wait. The following year Krohn published *Kalevalankysymyksiä (Kalevala Questions*, 1918), which turned his former theories upside down and provided ample material from which the disciples of militarism could seek sustenance. Krohn now argued that the heroic poems had not begun life as insignificant poetic germ cells but as individually created artistic wholes which had often fragmented as they migrated from southwest Finland to Viena Karelia; that the original poems had not been composed in the Middle Ages but in the Late Iron Age (700-1100), during the warlike period corresponding to the Scandinavian Viking Age; and, most important, that the events described in the poems had derived neither from mythology nor from saints' legends, but from actual historical events. This meant that the principal heroes of the poems —Väinämöinen, Ilmarinen, Lemminkäinen—were real men, Finnish Viking chieftains who had once walked as free men on free Finnish soil and had with the sword won honor and fame for the fatherland.

To the end of his life, Krohn continued to write about his country's epic poetry, producing among other works his monumental *Kalevalastudien* (1924-1928) and remaining throughout unshakably committed to his new faith: once restored to their original forms through comparative textual analysis, the old poems would prove to be purely native poetry recounting the gallant exploits of fearsome Finnish heroes. A year before his death, Krohn wrote of old Väinämöinen, the greatest of these heroes, that he had been "a great man of good lineage," and "had been a battle-tested sea warrior, more skilled than his fellows in the use of the sword."[17]

To the academic community Krohn explained that his changed view had resulted simply from an honest assessment of "observed facts."[18] But that the change was also politically motivated and that Krohn, like so many others, was overwhelmed by the martial spirit of the times seems clear from even a cursory glance at his statements in popular publications.

In April, 1919, for example, in the leading nationalist paper *Uusi Suomi*, Krohn boldly defended his new historical view, gave a stirring account of the epic heroes–their consuming love of battle, their daring pillaging expeditions–and then, by quoting with obvious approval a statement by the Danish scholar F. Ohrt, suggested in conclusion that Finland's changed political situation had required a corresponding change in folklore interpretation:

> The formerly peaceful Finland has become militaristic, which during these unsettled times is good. *Kalevala* scholarship has followed the same road. Before the great war the notion prevailed that the *Kalevala* primarily depicted the thoughts and cares of a people living in peaceful circumstances, that the power of the word rather than of the sword was its ideal. Now from the *Kalevala* the clamor of warlike sea adventurers reverberates [and] golden hilts and dragon-crested ship prows gleam. The young people grown up in a Finland that has achieved its independence can in their imaginations return, project themselves back, to the folklore heroes and from them can gain inspiration for a common struggle.[19]

In 1923, in an essay prepared for the schools and the general public, he wrote: "After a century of scholarship . . . that daring supposition (the idea of the poems' historical validity) has changed to a scientific conviction at the very time when the Finnish nation has attained its external independence and has shown itself capable of both understanding and creating history."[20] To what extent he manipulated his data, either consciously or unconsciously, to inspire those creating Finland's new history is a question that lies beyond easy answer. It is perhaps best to take him at his own word. Shortly before his death he wrote: "At the time we were fighting for our independence there arose before my eyes an age following but similar to the Scandinavian Viking Age, when Finns, still independent, embarked on sea expeditions, appearing in turn on the shores of Sweden."[21] And for Kaarle Krohn that splendid Viking vision seems, to borrow a phrase from Robert Frost, to have "made all the difference."

Krohn died in 1933, but not until the end of World War II was his vision of a glorious past to fade from the minds of the Finns. Of the many scholars who helped keep it alive, two of the most influential were Jalmari Jaakkola and Martti Haavio. Though each departed somewhat from Krohn in their historical reconstructions, each, following him, believed epic poetry to be the key to the distant past, and each found revealed in that poetry a dazzling, heroic world.

Jaakkola, the first to hold the prestigious chair in Finnish history established at the University of Helsinki in 1932, was also one of the first professional historians to make the study of ancient history the study of folklore and thus lend further credence to Krohn's point of view. Just as the aurora borealis shimmered in the distant northern sky, so too, argued Jaakkola, did folk poetry provide a brilliant road back to the ancient Finns: "And that poetic flash, in spite of all its gilding, reveals a great reality which the tools of research can never penetrate as deeply as . . . the ancient Finnish heroic song."[22] In his major work, *Suomen varhaishistoria (Early Finnish History*, 1935) he stated in the preface that he intended to depict "the life of ancient Finland as it was reflected in the mirror of the period, the *Kalevala* heroic poetry." In the following pages, he brought vividly to life the different Finnish tribes who had lived and fought in Finland in those glorious years between 800 and 1100.

Easily the most brilliant and productive of Krohn's students was Martti Haavio, whose eloquent pen carried the message of folklore to a large portion of the populace. In a number of short articles and in two long studies meant for both scholarly and popular audiences–*Suomalainen muinaisrunous (Ancient Finnish Poetry*, 1933) and *Suomalaisen muinaisrunouden maailma (The World of Ancient Finnish Poetry*, 1935)–Haavio defended folklore as a mirror for culture in an eminently reasonable manner. Yet when he moved from general principles to specific descriptions of the Viking culture reflected in the heroic layer of poetry, he was carried away by the same enthusiasm for scenes of battle and conquest that had overcome his predecessors. "Our old poetry," he said, "relays to us information from the *Kalevala* culture, from the Finnish heroic age about which history is silent."[23] This heroic age "was restless and warlike, a Finnish society in which a spirit of battle held sway."[24] Of its heroes, Haavio declared: "Their carefree warrior-mentality is reflected in many passages in the poems; their yearning for fighting expeditions is sincere and often overwhelming."[25] After describing in considerable detail this warrior society, he exclaimed with a burst of pride: "Rich bounty, beautiful women, the honor of men, wilderness expeditions, pillaging expeditions, sea voyages, battles, blood revenge–there are some catchwords that capitally characterize the Finnish Viking Age."[26]

It is surprising that in a man like Haavio, essentially a scholar, scenes of conquest should evoke feelings of admiration, and that both he and his readers should find great cause for pride in having had ancestral heroes whose principal virtue seemed to be an overwhelming desire to wage fierce battle against their neighbors. Few can deny, however, that Haavio's eloquent rhetoric did tend to lend a rather pleasing prospect to the battle, pleasing enough, at least, to inculcate in young men ardent for glory what Wilfred Owen has called "that old lie, *dulce et decorum est pro patria mori.*"

Had Finnish folklorists simply been ivory tower academicians writing for other folklorists, their ideas would probably have had little impact on the general public. But they were not. Most of them were also political activists and folklore popularizers. They spoke at patriotic ceremonies; they helped prepare readers and folklore teaching guides for the public schools; and they wrote constantly for popular publications, including official and semi-official military journals.

One of the earliest of these articles and one that set the tone for many to follow was written by Väinö Salminen (a docent and later professor of Finnish folklore) and published in *Suomen Sotilas (The Finnish Soldier)* on "*Kalevala* Day" 1921. "One often hears the claim," stated Salminen, "that our forefathers did not admire heroic acts and warlike exploits, since these supposedly are not sung about in the ancient *Kalevala* poetry. That claim does not hold true. In the old poetry both the warrior's bearing and fighting capability are depicted with rapture." To prove this point and to provide Finland's modern young warriors with an inspiring model for action, Salminen described, in carefully selected detail, the feats of the hero Kullervo. A capital hero, Kullervo lusted after battle, proclaiming:

Soma on sotahan kuolla	It is sweet to die in war,
kaunis miekan kalskehesen.	Beautiful to die in the clashing of swords.

And when the call to battle sounded, he left for the fight with a gay, rejoicing heart. Such heroism, however, was not without its rewards, for Finnish warriors, Salminen melodramatically informed his readers, had always been much admired by the people, and particularly by Finnish maidens, who would gaze from their windows at passing young heroes and sigh:

Voi kun tuo minun olisi,	Oh, if he were only mine,
Suven syömättä olisin,	I would go a summer without eating,
aastajankin einehettä.	A year without food.

"From the Kullervo poems alone," concluded Salminen, "we see that war heroes and battle were not alien to the ancient Finns."[27]

The comments with which the editors of the journal introduced Salminen's article are as instructive as the article itself and clearly reveal the purpose for which it was published: "The most magnificent spiritual creation of our forefathers, the *Kalevala*, must not remain a stranger to a single Finnish youth. On this day, eighty-five years after the publication of our national poems, there is reason to recall in the columns of *The Finnish Soldier* what the *Kalevala* has to say particularly to the Finnish soldier."[28] In the following years Finnish folklorists would continue to argue that the *Kalevala* did indeed have much to say to the youth of the nation, and to its soldiers. Fourteen years later, for instance, Martti Haavio was still developing the same themes. In a "*Kalevala* Day" article in *Hakkapeliitta* (a publication of the Civil Defense Corps), he declared that "the heart of the *Kalevala* poetry is simply war poetry." Through this poetry, he argued, "we arrive in the midst of that age when Scandinavian Vikings in swift-sailing ships plowed the seas of the world, destroying, burning and plundering. Finnish society–our heroic poetry makes this perfectly clear–is a war society."[29] In another militaristic essay, this one published in *Laivastolehti* (*The Navy Journal*), Haavio discussed ancient Finnish heroes of the sea. Väinämöinen, for instance, was a great sea warrior and the society that had sung about him was a "Finnish war society in which the sea, war, and sea warfare were extremely popular, in which heroism was a virtue, in which a sea warrior merited the highest praise." The poems describing young Ahti, another bold and battle-hungry sea hero, were, exulted Haavio, "the clearest, the most human, and in my opinion the most beautiful of our heroic poetry."[30]

If the warlike spirit of the epic poems, then, was the true Finnish spirit, and if the epic heroes, the prototypes of Finnish character, were men of the sword, eager to take up arms to achieve their just ends, the lesson to patriotic Finnish youth was clear, "go and do likewise."

Folklore and Greater Finland

For most Finns, achieving their just ends meant simply becoming strong enough to defend their borders and to maintain their independence. But among some members of the political right, it meant not just defending borders but expanding them eastward.

When Finland became independent, East Karelia and Ingria, where most of the *Kalevala* poetry had been collected, remained in Russian hands. For years these regions had comprised a sort of Finnish holy land where artists, musicians, and literary men, not to mention troops of folklorists, had made pilgrimages to seek creative inspiration and to imbue themselves with the spirit of the *Kalevala*.[31] In 1920, at the Peace of Tartu, which the political right considered a cowardly betrayal of Finland's national interests, Finland and Russia agreed to keep existing borders, Russia's one concession being to grant East Karelia local autonomy. When the Bolsheviks failed to keep even this promise, Finland appealed to the Hague Court of International Justice and to the League of Nations, but to no avail.

The door had thus been nailed shut. A hue and cry of anger spread across the land, talk of holy war filled the air, and men swore sacred oaths never to sheathe their swords until their tribal brethren had been freed. The goal was to wrest Ingria and particularly East Karelia from Russia–by peaceful means if possible but by force if necessary–and to combine them with Finland proper into a Greater Finland (*Suur Suomi*), held together by the bonds of blood and culture.

The Greater Finland issue is far too complex for detailed discussion here. It deserves at least brief attention, however, because some of the same folklorists who admired their heroic ancestors' reliance on the sword were also among those militantly raising their voices in defense of an enlarged fatherland. For example, in 1919 Väinö Salminen wrote: "The Finnish race does not wish to seize foreign land. But from centuries of hard experience it has certainly learned enough that at long last it has categorically determined to take control in that area which has belonged to it from times immemorial."[32] In 1923, in a speech before the Estonian-Finnish University Club, Martti Haavio proclaimed: "[The Finnish race] must for all time knock down that pillar on which is inscribed *The Kingdom of the Ruskis*–and must erect one a thousand times higher on which is [written] IMPERIUM FENNICUM."[33] In 1935, in a harsh essay entitled "What Has the *Kalevala* To Say to Contemporary Youth?" Matti Kuusi, inspired by the heroic vision of Jalmari Jaakkola, declared: "It is understood that Finnish destiny is contingent upon this alternative, 'national destruction–national greatness. Either–or!' . . . only a desire for Finnish greatness can withstand the pressure of the Slavic desire for greatness. Thus an organic part of the youth's national ideology is belief in the coming liberation of the Finnish tribes beyond the border, Viena, Aunus, Ingria."[34]

From our perspective today, the Finns' desire to appropriate these areas, which bordered Leningrad and contained the Murmansk Railway, seems foolhardy. But one should recall that in its first years, at least, the Soviet Union was torn by civil war and by a struggle for survival. The Finns, sharing the prevalent belief that the Bolsheviks would soon be toppled from power, felt that in the subsequent realignment of Russia's borders Finland would have a more reasonable claim than others to East Karelia. Further, if the dream of a Greater Finland sounded like misty eyed idealism, so too had the dream of an independent Finland a century earlier. With that first dream now realized, the young men of the new republic set out with firm resolve to bring to pass the second. And in the propaganda campaign that developed, they once again found in folklore a most effective weapon.

The advocates of a Greater Finland based their argument on two major premises. The first was the belief that Finland, Karelia, and Ingria were ethnically one people and ought therefore to be one nation. There was much talk of achieving Finland's "natural borders," those which, as Väinö Salminen pointed out, God had intended for her.[35] The belief in nation-states as living organisms having gained considerable ground, it was generally felt that the divided Finnish tribes could never fulfill their destiny until they had become one nation. "The incorporation of all Karelia into Finland," explained Salminen, "is, frankly speaking, a condition of survival for the Finnish race and, at the same time, a condition of survival for the East Karelian nation."[36] This belief in ethnic unity was based on a common ancestry, on a common language, and, most important for our purposes, on a shared body of folk poetry.

Some Finns felt this poetry to be an ancestral inheritance from the misty past, from the period of Balto-Finnic unity when the Finns, Karelians, and Ingrians had lived together as one people and before they had migrated to their present homelands, taking with them their language and folk poetry. Others like Kaarle Krohn believed the poems had originated much later in Western Finland and then, through automigration, had moved slowly to the east and northeast where they had been preserved and reshaped by the Ingrians and Karelians. But whether viewed as a racial inheritance from primordial times or as collective creations resulting from their automigration, the poems came to represent for political activists the "binding tie" holding together the members of the Finnish race.

The symbolical significance that political activists found in this binding tie is illustrated well in an essay published by the Academic Karelian Society, the organization most devoted to the Greater Finland dream. "The *Kalevala*," stated the essay, "is the strongest witness of that affinity which holds sway between Karelia and the rest of Finland. It above all testifies that the Karelian nation and the Finnish nation are *one* nation .... The Finnish nation is not yet what it should be. Finnish nationality does not yet shape the Finnish state .... The duty of our present generation of Finns is . . . to work for the accomplishment of that goal which the *Kalevala* has initiated."[37] As the activists worked toward that goal, they turned also to narratives in the epic itself, and particularly to the story of "Lemminkäinen's Mother" to symbolize the hoped for establishment of Greater Finland. Lemminkäinen, killed by a treacherous enemy, cut to pieces and then thrown into the river Tuonela, was raked up from the river by his mother, put back together, and resuscitated. In like manner, Finnish patriots, supposedly stirred by the same kind of love that had moved Lemminkäinen's mother, were attempting to join together the divided parts of the "natural" Finnish body and bring it once again to life.[38]

The second premise on which the advocates of a Greater Finland based their demand for territorial aggrandizement was the belief that the publication of the *Kalevala* had prepared the way for Finnish independence and that the Finns, therefore, were now honor bound to bring independence to the Karelians and Ingrians, who had kept the old poems alive after they had faded in Finland proper. The following "*Kalevala* Day" editorial published in the influential newspaper, *Aamulehti*, is typical of the statements that echoed throughout the 1920s and 1930s:

> Without the *Kalevala*, Finnish national spirit and culture scarcely would have been able to rise to that strength, richness, and significance necessary for the birth of an independent Finland .... The Finnish nation must therefore remember the great debt of gratitude to Karelia and its singing folk who, through the *Kalevala* songs, have in a forceful manner indirectly influenced both the development of a Finnish national spirit and culture and, by the same token, the birth of a free and independent Finland .... On both sides of the state border the same tribe is still living, and on the Russian side it is still without that rightful political, national, linguistic, and cultural independence which it has prepared for Finland through the poems of the *Kalevala* .... The *Kalevala* obligates the Finnish people and state seriously to turn their attention to the plight of these border lands, to whom we owe a debt of gratitude for preserving the ancient spiritual treasure of our nation .... The badly oppressed Ingria, which has likewise been instrumental in preserving both the *Kalevala* poems and other folklore ..., also deserves our attention.[39]

Proclamations like this one often deplored the deprivations suffered by the surviving folksingers at the hands of the Bolsheviks. "The homes of these men," wrote Martti Haavio, "are presently being pillaged by oppressors; their boys and girls are presently slaves: there where the kantele and the Sampo anciently rang out, there sounds now a sorrowful lament. During these very days Ingria's singing villages are being emptied of their occupants; the sons of the double-headed eagle are raging frightfully in the dwelling places of the Finns, places where our wonderful folk poems once took refuge."[40] In like manner, E. N. Setälä, a professor of Finnish language and literature, and a prominent politician and statesman, declared in a stirring "*Kalevala* Day" address: "Listen, listen to the lament of Karelia from those everlasting backwoods, from the shores of wilderness lakes where the *Kalevala* songs once echoed .... The voice of that lament sounds over the Finnish land; it wrings our hearts."[41]

In this same address, Setälä referred to the Karelians as "the last border guard of Western civilization."[42] Some years earlier Kustavi Grotenfelt had similarily argued that Finland could fill its mission as Western civilization's vanguard "against the chaos of the East and against Bolshevism" only when it had attained its natural border.[43] Between the wars this position became entrenched in the thinking of the political right. Finland, it was believed, was destined valiantly to serve as the West's last outpost against Eastern barbarism, as "the steel wall," as Haavio put it, "protecting [the West] from Moscow."[44] This historical calling could be fulfilled, however, only if Finland were to become Greater Finland. The advocates of territorial expansion could thus appeal not only to narrow national interests but also to an unselfish concern for the welfare of Western culture.

In a public school reader published in 1930, Setälä complained to students that a "strict prohibition" stopped the Finns from crossing the border into the *Kalevala* song country of East Karelia and that only in their imaginations could they envision "that land of broad backwoods, of great lakes, and of the poems."[45] But in a little over a decade the Finns had actually crossed that border, not just in imagination but in fact. On November 30, 1939, Russia, having failed to win from Finland territorial concessions claimed necessary to protect the approaches to Leningrad, had attacked. In the short and vicious Winter War that followed, the Finns paid a terrible price in lost land and lost lives, but at the war's end (March 12, 1940) had managed to keep their independence intact. Fifteen months later, allied now with Germany, the country entered the conflict again, moving quickly into territory lost during the Winter War, and into East Karelia.

The Finns have always claimed officially that they moved across the border not to annex new territory but simply to establish a better line of defense. Whatever the case may be, there is no question that for many who lived this moment in history, the beginning of the war signaled the long-awaited realization of the Greater Finland dream, the restoration to Finland proper of the land that had preserved the *Kalevala*. An editorial in the Academic Karelian Society's principal publication proclaimed: "The moral justification for Greater Finland is irrefutable: it is based on the salvation of the Finnish race and culture from destruction by the East."[46] And Vilho Helanen, a long-time Society leader, declared: "Now is the day of the fulfillment of our great visions."[47]

The tone of statements such as these was set by none other than

Marshal Mannerheim, commander-in-chief of Finland's armies and one of the country's most powerful men. Three days after the war began he "summoned" his troops and fellow citizens to follow him in a "holy war against the enemy of our nation."[48] And two weeks later, as the army prepared for a major thrust eastward, he declared, in an emotional order of the day:

> In the War of Liberation in 1918, I swore to the Finnish and Viena Karelians that I would not sheathe my sword until Finland and East Karelia were free . . . .
>
> For twenty-three years [the Karelian provinces of] Viena and Aunus have awaited the fulfillment of this promise . . . .
>
> Fighters in the war of liberation, famous men of the Winter War, my gallant soldiers! A new day has dawned . . . . Karelian freedom and a great Finland glimmer before us in the powerful avalanche of world historical events.[49]

Whether Mannerheim, in spite of these words, was really committed to the Greater Finland dream is highly debatable. What he was committed to was the destruction of Bolshevism, which he despised. That he chose to allude to the dream, however, in order to rally the army and nation behind him in his struggle against the forces of the Kremlin demonstrates how firmly he believed that dream had seized the public imagination.

It was a dream, as we have seen, based solidly in folklore. And through these days of trouble and triumph, folklore continued to play an important political role, as the old arguments about ethnic unity and debts of honor were repeated with renewed fervor. As the Finnish armies moved intoxicatingly forward, Jalmari Jaakkola published a pontifical defense of the creation of a Greater Finland in the New Europe then taking shape and declared: "More clearly than any war or battle the *Kalevala* heroic poems show to both Finland and Europe that East Karelia belongs by spirit and nature to Finland."[50] In November, 1941, a Finno-Ugric Conference sponsored by the Finnish League and attended by numerous officials, including the President of the Republic, was held in Helsinki. In one of the several politically volatile speeches given at the conference, the well-known poet V. A. Koskenniemi, referring to the old folk poems, praised the heroic Finnish army for pushing the Finnish border eastward: "A great poetry created by a united race once found its way through the wilderness, from house to house, from home to home, across an artificial border; now the Finnish army of liberation has arrived at these same roads and paths and has opened new ones, in order to pay its debt of honor to Karelia, to the song country of our tribe."[51] Three months later, in the "liberated" village of Vuokkiniemi, where a century earlier Lönnrot had collected some of his best poems, a Finnish army officer, speaking at a "*Kalevala* Day" celebration, made the same point:

> Above all, of the great friends of East Karelia, we must mention Elias Lönnrot, who again and again crossed over the border into the parishes of Vuokkiniemi and Uhtua, collected from these backwoods areas ancient Finnish poems, and from them formed the *Kalevala*, the national epic of the Finnish people. We men of the Finnish army of liberation who last summer crossed the border to drive the Bolshevik oppressor from Viena Karelia and to return these areas to the Finnish race, crossed the border under the power of a sacred emotion. We remembered that we were nearing the villages from which the *Kalevala* poems were once collected. The Finnish troops, who have heroically driven the Russian enemy from Finland's old border, have walked the same paths that the collector of the *Kalevala*, Elias Lönnrot, once walked .... We Finns from beyond the former border wanted today, as we moved near the graves of the old Viena singers, to show them and the entire Viena lineage our delayed gratitude.
>
> To the singers of songs asleep in the grave, the Finnish soldiers want now to say: "We are here!" The rest of Finland owes a great debt of gratitude to this tribe. For Viena Karelia's part in the development of the Finnish nation toward an independent and virile society has been overwhelming .... The final result of this holy war is certain .... The Finnish land from the Gulf of Bothnia to the White Sea and from Lake Onega to the Gulf of Finland will rise to a new life.[52]

But the glory was short lived. Germany fell, and with it Finland. In the harsh peace terms that followed, the Finns' dreams of a Greater Finland faded forever.

FOLKLORE AND THE POLITICAL LEFT

During the first years of Finnish independence, the extreme left was less able to exploit folklore for political purposes than was the right. First of all, academic folklore study had always been in the hands of the nationalists, and it remained there after 1917; second, the Finnish government sharply curtailed the open publication of Communist propaganda; and third, following the Civil War in 1918, the most effective cultural and political ideologists had been forced to go underground or to seek exile across the border. Thus when the propaganda counterattack began in earnest in the 1930s, it took place not in Finland itself but among Finnish expatriates living in the land to which the political right looked with longing eyes–East Karelia.

Those who have attempted to play down the impact of the Greater Finland movement have generally argued that while its advocates made a lot of noise, they exercised little influence on the actual policies of the Finnish government. This assessment seems reasonably accurate, but it leaves out the crucial fact, as Wolf H. Halsti has pointed out, that they exercised considerable influence on the Soviet government.[53] The Soviets, of course, did not fear a Finnish invasion, but they did fear that one of the greater powers bent on destroying Russia would launch an attack on Leningrad under the pretext of aiding Finland.[54] A totalitarian state allowing no public deviation from official policy, Russia could not believe that the advocates of Greater Finland, considering the intensity of their propaganda, were speaking without government approval, and that Finland would not use the first available opportunity to move against Russia. Indeed, the Soviet Commissar for Foreign Affairs, Maxim Litvinov, once told a Western journalist that Finland had concluded a secret treaty with Germany and Poland to bring to pass the annexation of East Karelia.[55]

That the Communist leaders took Finnish folklore propaganda seriously is clear from the propaganda campaign launched in their own press during the *Kalevala* Jubilee Celebration in 1935, the commemoration in Finland of the centennial anniversary of the publication of the *Kalevala*. Few folklore celebrations, and certainly none in Finland, have ever matched the intensity of this event. *Kalevala* athletic events, *Kalevala* dramatic presentations, *Kalevala* radio programs, *Kalevala* concerts, *Kalevala* art shows, *Kalevala* festivals, and an endless array of fervent *Kalevala* speeches were held throughout Finland, all for the greater glory of the fatherland. At the gala festival held in Helsinki's new exhibition hall, the President spoke, the Minister of Education spoke, and the Speaker of Parliament, Kyösti Kallio, warmed the hearts of Finnish scholars by declaring: "In order to promote research aimed at throwing light on the past of the Finnish race, the Parliament, in session today determined to establish a two-million-mark fund for this research. On behalf of the Parliament it is my honor to wish success to this research."[56]

The Communists, of course, took quite a different view of this research. Press titles such as "Folklore and the Imperialistic Aims of the Finnish Bourgeoisie," "The Attempts of the Finnish Bourgeoisie to Force the *Kalevala* into the Service of Nationalism and Chauvinism," and "To What End has the Finnish Bourgeoisie Used and is Now Using the *Kalevala*?" make their attitude clear. "Thousands of Fascist students," cried one Communist publication, "have been sent throughout the land to arrange *Kalevala* celebrations, that is, to whip up anti-Soviet feeling . . . . The Finnish bourgeoisie have come to the egocentric conclusion that they can without hindrance soil and desecrate the best products of the people's creative ability and force them into the service of their plundering and national oppression."[57] Another wrote: "The Fascists in many ways demonstrate that from a cultural-historical perspective they haven't much to learn from the *Kalevala*. They are not organizing the *Kalevala's* centennial celebration because of the *Kalevala's* cultural-historical significance. Warlike impassioned speeches ... and provocative agitation against our Soviet land are a witness of that."[58] And a Leningrad paper published an intriguing cartoon which showed the old *Kalevala* hero Väinämöinen sitting with a bewildered look on his face while two uniformed Nazis pinned a swastika arm band on him. A third Nazi, arm raised in a *sieg heil* gesture, was handing him an automatic pistol. The caption read: "One or two more strokes and the old boy will be ours."[59]

To the Communists, the Finns' talk of freeing their racial brethren from Bolshevik oppression was simply a smoke screen behind which members of the Finnish bourgeoisie were masking their true intents of adding Karelian land and natural resources to Finland and thus further lining their own capitalistic pockets. On the basis of Finnish folklore, declared one Red newspaper, "Finland's timber capitalists and industrial magnates" claim that they have the right to appropriate the Karelians' land and to turn the Karelians themselves into "the slaves of the Finnish bourgeoisie."[60] Another wrote: "The nationalistic and chauvinistic wave which has in recent days become particularly strong is a definite preparation by the Fascistic bourgeoisie for the organization of a ... plundering expedition. The *Kalevala* Centennial Celebration will be used to intensify this struggle."[61] And still another exclaimed: "[The Finnish bourgeoisie is using the *Kalevala*] in the service of their Fascist dictatorship. With its aid Finnish Fascists attempt to fan the flame of nationalism and to seek sympathy, support, and justification for their plans to seize Soviet-Karelia."[62]

These statements show that the Communists had become fully aware of the symbolic importance of folklore in political propaganda and now realized that to counter this propaganda they would have to work out new interpretations of the old poetry. To emphasize this fact and to make the Soviet Karelians aware of "their cultural heritage," the Communists organized their own Jubilee Celebrations throughout East Karelia. On the same day that the cream of Finnish society met in Helsinki to commemorate the *Kalevala*, East Karelia's principal political leaders, many of them Finnish exiles, gathered in the regional capital Petroskoi to pay homage to the same epic. In his opening address Edward Gylling, Chairman of the People's Commissariat, decreed: "We have before us the especially important task of exposing the use of the *Kalevala* poems as the ideological foundation of the Finnish bourgeoisie's imperialistic ambitions, in the service of their Karelian-conquest enterprises and their daydreams of a Greater Finland."[63]

The man to whom this task of exposition fell was the prominent leftist ideologist Yrjö Sirola, one of the leading Social Democrats in Finland's pre-Civil War Parliament and, following his exile, an important politico and educator in East Karelia. In his youth, Sirola had studied folklore, and now in the *Kalevala* song country he took up the pursuit once again, studying the epic this time from a Marxist point of view. During the Jubilee Celebration in 1935, he gave an important "*Kalevala* Day" speech,[64] which was distributed widely through East Karelia, and wrote, with Ivar Lassy, the introduction to a Communist edition of the *Kalevala*.[65] These pieces formed the basis of a new ideological approach.

With intriguing duplicity, Sirola admitted from the outset that his purpose was political–he intended to use folklore to help advance the cause of communism; but at the same time he roundly criticized the Finnish nationalists for their own political interpretations, suggesting that only the progressive Communists were capable of properly understanding the old poems. "In the present circumstances of capitalism's period of decay," he moralized, "bourgeois science is not capable of moving ahead but prompts researchers artifically to reach conclusions which fit the dirty purposes of capitalistic imperialism."[66] The most unacceptable of these conclusions, claimed Sirola, were the notions that the folk poems had originated in Western Finland and had arisen from historical accounts of ancient aristocratic heroes.

Well aware that the theory of the origin of the poems in the West and their migration to the East had provided a convenient symbol in the struggle to unite these areas into a Greater Finland, Sirola claimed that the theory had been concocted by reactionary counter-revolutionists like Kaarle Krohn to justify the seizure of foreign land. Nobody denied, said Sirola, that the poems contained a few Western Finnish words, but these were a result not of migration, but of the Karelian singers' having visited Finland and having brought back to Karelia words they had learned on their trips. The poems themselves, however, were Karelian. They had been collected in Karelia; they had been collected from Karelians; and "without doubt" they had been created by Karelians. They did not link East and West. Thus "the Finnish bourgeoisie who so haughtily celebrate the *Kalevala* and make material and political capital from it, have [had] no part in the original poems from which the *Kalevala* was shaped."[67]

Nor had the supposed ancestors of these Finnish bourgeoisie, the warlike heroes of Viking Finland, had a hand in the creation of the poems. The poems quite obviously could not reflect the feudalistic society of Western Finland, as Krohn claimed they did, because they had not originated there. They reflected instead the social and economic life of ancient Karelia, and it was to this life, not the fantasies of bourgeois scholars, that Karelians ought to look for guidance.[68]

Like his counterparts in Finland proper, Sirola believed that folklore mirrored the spirit of the past, if not the actual events, and that it provided models for future action. As W. Edson Richmond has pointed out, romantic nationalism can masquerade as proletarian realism.[69] Certainly this was the case in Sirola's work. Finnish nationalists looked to folklore for a reflection of the national or racial soul; Sirola sought in folklore the soul of the proletariat, of the working class. But in each instance the notion prevailed that folklore surviving from the past revealed a world worthy of study and emulation.

And the golden world of the past that this study brought to the attention of the Karelians was not a society of gallant warriors but of peaceful workers, depicted in their daily round of activities, workers who tilled the soil, cultivated their crops, and built their homesteads "in groups," working always for the greater good of the community. This society, said Sirola, structured around the family, was actually a primitive, or prefeudalistic form of communism. And it was this society that the workers of modern Karelia were building once again:

> The Karelian people today, as they honor their folk poetry, stand amidst a tremendous socialistic construction work, which is changing the forests and lands into a new Sampo mill [the magic mill in the *Kalevala* that ground out good fortune to its owners] and is creating a new socialistic generation.
>
> The laments of slaves no longer echo through the lands of Karelia, but the victorious songs of a new socialistic construction work. Its Sampo is now the miraculous machinery of hundreds of factories and power plants, saw mills and stone quarries, railroads and canals, tractors and steamships.[70]

Having thus distorted the image, Sirola and his compatriots were now ready to ask their own youth, as right-wing ideologists had asked theirs, to capture the spirit of the *Kalevala* and to study the way of life reflected in it as they set out to build a better tomorrow.

Since the war, Communist leaders in East Karelia have on occasion continued to use folklore to serve their political ends, but in Finland itself the drama seems to have been played out. Folklore studies still prosper, but in a changed political climate and within new theoretical perspectives. In recent years there has been a renewed interest in Karelian studies but without the dreams of grandeur that once accompanied such endeavors. The voices raised in defense of Greater Finland have long fallen silent.

But the issues originally raised by those voices are still very much with us. Should the folklorist be content simply to study the folk and their lore, or should he use his research to bring about social, political, economic or religious change? Should he use the lore he collects and studies only to increase our understanding of and sympathy for the human condition, or should he attempt to use that lore to improve the lives of the people? Should he study folklore to understand his heritage, or should he attempt to shape the destiny of his ethnic group? Should he use folklore to study man or to control man?

With both nationalism and communism still major forces in world politics, with ethnic, sexist, and social movements gaining momentum in our own country, and with folklorists seeking increased state support of folklore study, these are not idle questions. Nor are they meant to be purely rhetorical questions. They have no easy answers.

My own view is that the folklorist's best course lies in always being a scholar first and a patriot or special pleader second—not because the cause one pleads is not worthy, but because his devotion to it too easily clouds his vision and allows him to see only that which serves his ideological ends. In any event, one hopes that those seriously seeking solutions to these questions will begin by examining the fruit that unions of folklore research and political ideology have borne in the past.

Brigham Young University
Provo, Utah

NOTES

1 For a more detailed discussion of the main arguments of this paper, see William A. Wilson, "Folklore and Nationalism in Modern Finland" (Ph.D. diss., Indiana University, 1974).

2 Eino Leino, cited in Martti Haavio, "Kalevalakultti," in *Kalevala: Kansallinen aarre*, ed. F. A. Hästesko and Martti Haavio (Helsinki, 1949), p. 264.

3 For a discussion of Herder's contribution to folklore studies, see William A. Wilson, "Herder, Folklore, and Romantic Nationalism," *Journal of Popular Culture* 4 (1973): 819-835.

4 E. A. Saarimaa "Kansanrunouden asema suomenkielisten oppikoulujen äidinkielen opetuksessa," *Virittäjä* 25 (1921): 1-2.

5 Matti Klinge, *Vihan velijistä valtiososialismiin: Yhteiskunnallisia ja kansallisia näkemyksiä 1910- ja 1920-luvuilta* (Porvoo, 1972), pp. 164-165.

6 Cited in Risto Alapuro, *Akateeminen Karjala-Seura: Ylioppilasliike ja kansa 1920- ja*

1930-luvulla (Porvoo, 1973), p. 94.

[7] Valdemar Rantoja, "Onko Kalevala tarua vai historiaa?" *Etelä-Pohjanmaan Nuorisoseuran Vuosikirja* (1938), p. 11.

[8] Martti Haavio, *Puheita vv. 1924-1958* (Porvoo, 1959), p. 13.

[9] Eino Leino, "Kansallisviikko: Kalevala kansan johtotähtenä," *Sunnuntai*, 25 February 1917, pp. 1-2.

[10] Max Jakobson, *The Diplomacy of the Winter War: An Account of the Russo-Finnish War, 1939-1940* (Cambridge, 1961), p. 16; C. Leonard Lundin, *Finland in the Second World War* (Bloomington, Ind., 1957), pp. 27-56; Klinge, pp. 57-112.

[11] Elias Simojoki, "Ryssänviha," *Ylioppilaslehti* 11 (1923): 68.

[12] Martti Haavio, "Suomen Heimo ja Moskova," *Ylioppilaslehti* 11 (1923): 60.

[13] E. E. Kaila, "Suomen kansan tehtävä," *Suomen Heimo* 1 (1923): 116.

[14] Eino Jutikkala, *A History of Finland*, trans. Paul Sjöblom (New York, 1962), pp. 227-249; Mauno Jääskeläinen, *Itä-Karjalan kysymys: Kansallisen laajennusohjelman synty ja sen toteuttamisyritykset Suomen ulkopolitiikassa vuosina 1918-1920 (Porvoo,* 1961), pp. 57-58.

[15] Kaarle Krohn, "Sankarit," in *Suomalaisten runojen uskonto* (Porvoo, 1914), pp. 301-347; "Kaleva und seine sippe," *Journal de la Société Finno-ougrienne* 30: 35 (1914).

[16] J. R. Danielson-Kalmari, "Puhe Ylioppilasyhdistyksen Kalevala-juhlassa 28. II. 1917," *Ylioppilaslehti* 5 (1917): 82.

[17] Kaarle Krohn, *Kalevalan kertomarunojen opas*, Suomalaisen Kirjallisuuden Seuran Toimituksia, no. 192 (Helsinki, 1932), pp. 141-143.

[18] Kaarle Krohn, *Kalevalankysymyksiä: Opas Suomen kansan vanhojen runojen tilaajille ja käyttäjille ynnä suomalaisen kansanrunouden opiskelijoille ja harrastajille*, 2 vols., *Journal de la Société Finno-ougrienne* 35-36 (1918), 1: 230-231.

[19] F. Ohrt, cited by Kaarle Krohn in "Runojemme sankarien sotaisesta luonteesta," *Uusi Suomi*, 30 April 1919, pp. 7-8.

[20] Kaarle Krohn, "Kertovainen runous," in *Suomalainen kansanrunous: Yleistajuisia tutkielmia koulutyön ja itseopiskelun avuksi*, ed. F. A. Hästesko (Helsinki, 1923), p. 35.

[21] Kaarle Krohn, *Kalevalan kertomarunojen opas*, p. 158.

[22] Jalmari Jaakkola, *Suomen varhaishistoria: Heimokausi ja "Kalevalakulttuuri"* (Porvoo, 1935), p. 442.

[23] Martti Haavio, *Suomalaisen muinaisrunouden maailma* (Porvoo, 1935), p. 420.

[24] Martti Haavio, "Suomalaisen sankarirunouden luonteesta," *Kalevalaseuran Vuosikirja* 16 (1936): 211.

[25] Haavio, *Suomalaisen muinaisrunouden maailma*, p. 420.

[26] Martti Haavio, "Suomalainen muinaisrunous," in *Suomen kulttuurihistoria*, ed. Gunnar Suolahti et al. (Jyväskylä, 1933) 1: 294; see also Haavio, *Suomalaisen muinaisrunouden maailma*, pp. 23-58.

[27] Väinö Salminen, "Kalevalan sankarit: Kalevalan ilmestymisen 85-vuotispäivän johdosta," *Suomen Sotilas* (1920): 150-151.

[28] *Ibid*., p. 150.

[29] Martti Haavio, "Sota ja suomalainen kansanrunous," *Hakkapeliitta* 10 (1935): 263.

[30] Martti Haavio, "Isänmaan meri sankarirunostossamme," *Laivastolehti* (1935): 292.

[31] There is a wealth of literature on the Finns' romantic attachment to Karelia. The best studies are two recent works by Hannes Sihvo: *Karjalan löytäjät (Helsinki, 1969)* and *Karjalan kuva: Karelianismin taustaa ja vaiheita autonomian aikana*, Suomalaisen Kirjallisuuden Seuran Toimituksia, no. 314 (Helsinki, 1973).

[32] Väinö Salminen, *Suomalainen Inkeri*, Sunnan Julkaisuja, no. 1 (Helsinki, 1919), p. 60.

[33] Haavio, "Suomen Heimo ja Moskova," p. 160.

[34] Matti Kuusi, "Mitä Kalevalalla on nykyiselle nuorisolle sanottavana?" in *Kalevala Suomen kansan omaisuudeksi* (Helsinki, 1937), p. 28.

[35] Väinö Salminen, "Itä-Karjalan kohtalo," *Suomalainen Suomi* 3 (1918): 87. See also Vilho Helanen, "Suur-Suomi on kansamme oikea ja lopullinen isänmaa," *Suomen Heimo* 6 (1928): 229-230.

[36] Salminen, "Itä-Karjalan kohtalo," p. 93.

[37] "Kalevala ja Karjala," *Suomen Heimo* 2 (1924): 26.

[38] According to Rauni Puranen, this parable was told frequently during the 1920's and 1930's–Personal Interview, March, 1966, Helsinki. See also "Kalevalan päivä–nykyisin juhlapäivä," *Suomen Heimo* 12 (1934): 42.

[39] O. A. Kallio, "Kalevala ja Karjala," *Aamulehti*, 28 February 1925, p. 2.

[40] Martti Haavio, "Suomalaisen kirjallisuuden vuosisatajuhla," *Suomen Heimo* 9 (1931): 50-51.

[41] E. N. Setälä, "Kalevala ja Karjala," *Kalevalaseuran Vuosikirja* 3 (1923): 11-12.

[42] *Ibid.*, p. 12.

[43] Kustavi Grotenfelt, "Itä-Karjalan puolesta," *Valvoja* 38 (1918): 440.

[44] Haavio, "Suomen Heimo ja Moskova," p. 159.

[45] E. N. Setälä, "Suomen suvusta," in *Uusi suomen kirja I: Yläkansakoulun lukukirja III*, ed. E. N. Setälä et al. (Helsinki, 1930), p. 196.

[46] Finno, "AKS: läisen ajatuksia," *Suomen Heimo* 19 (1941): 161-162.

[47] Vilho Helanen, "Välirauha on päättynyt," *Suomen Heimo* 19 (1941): 147.

[48] In *Puhtain asein: Suomen marsalkan päiväkäskyjä vuosilta 1918-44*, ed. Einari Kaskimies (Helsinki, 1970), p. 116.

[49] *Ibid.*, p. 120. For the history of this order of the day, see Kalle Lehmus, *Tuntematon Mannerheim: Katkelmia sodan ja politiikan poluilta* (Helsinki, 1967), pp. 55-62.

[50] Jalmari Jaakkola, *Suomen idänkysymys*, 2nd ed. (Porvoo, 1942), p. 27.

[51] In "Heimopäiväpuheita," *Suomalainen Suomi* 9 (1941): 397.

[52] Sakari Vapaasalo, "Vienan ja Aunuksen tie," *Suomen Heimo* 20 (1942): 141-145.

[53] Wolf H. Halsti, *Me, Venäjä ja muut* (Helsinki, 1969), pp. 169-171.

[54] Toivo Korhonen, *Naapurit vastoin tahtoaan* (Helsinki, 1966), pp. 52-62, 213-214.

[55] Jakobson, p. 17.

[56] Kyösti Kallio, "Eduskunnan tervehdys," *Kalevalaseuran Vuosikirja* 16 (1936): 60.

[57] A. Leppänen, "Kansanrunous ja Suomen porvariston imperialistiset pyrkimykset," *Punainen Karjala*, 22 February 1935: *Kalevala* Newspaper Clipping File, Manuscript

Archive, Finnish Literature Society, Helsinki.

[58] Mikko Lindberg, "Mihin Suomen porvaristo on käyttänyt ja nyt käyttää Kalevalaa?" *Vapaus*, 28 February 1935, p. 3.

[59] *Literaturnyj Lenningrad*, 26 February 1935: *Kalevala* Newspaper Clipping File, Manuscript Archive, Finnish Literature Society, Helsinki.

[60] K. Vento, "Suomen porvariston pyrkimykset alistaa Kalevala natsionalismin ja shovinismin palvelukseen," *Punainen Karjala*, 28 February 1935, p. 3.

[61] Leppänen.

[62] Lindberg, p. 3.

[63] Edv. Gylling, "Kalevalan 100-vuotisjuhla Kansallisella Valistustalolla eilen illalla, Tov. Edv. Gyllingin avajaispuhe," *Punainen Karjala*, 1 March 1935, p. 1.

[64] Yrjö Sirola, "Kalevalan 100-vuotismuisto," *Punainen Karjala*, 5 March 1935, p. 3.

[65] Yrjö Sirola and Ivar Lassy, eds., "Kalevalasta," *Kalevala*, by Elias Lönnrot (Petroskoi, 1935).

[66] Sirola, p. 3; Sirola and Lassy, pp. xix, xxiii.

[67] Sirola, p. 3; Sirola and Lassy, pp. xx-xxi, xxiii.

[68] Sirola, p. 3; Sirola and Lassy, pp. xii, xix.

[69] W. Edson Richmond, "Romantic-Nationalism and a Lesson for Today from Norway's Past," *Southern Folklore Quarterly* 25 (1961): 91.

[70] Sirola and Lassy, pp. xxiii-xxiv; see also pp. iii-xxiv and Sirola, p. 3.

THE POLITICAL USES AND THEMES OF FOLKLORE IN THE SOVIET UNION

Felix J. Oinas

In the Soviet Union the first decade after the October Revolution was the golden era of folklore research.* Since the party and the government were occupied with many urgent tasks, folklorists could pursue freely their research interests. Different trends, such as the historical school, formalism, and the so-called Finnish school, could thrive side by side. As a result, significant studies, perhaps the most significant folklore studies ever made in the Soviet Union (such as those by Propp, Žirmunskij, and others) were completed.

At the same time, folklore as a special art form was in its gravest crisis, since nothing less than its right to live, to exist, was at stake. The belief that folklore reflected the ideology of the ruling classes gave rise to a strongly negative attitude toward it in literary circles in the 1920s. The so-called Proletcul't (Proletarian Cultural and Educational Organizations) declared that folklore was hostile to Soviet people, because it reflected the *kulak* ("rich farmers' ") ideology. Numerous Proletcul't leaders called for the annihilation of folklore. A special Children's Proletcul't sought to eradicate folktales on the basis that they glorified tsars and tsareviches, corrupted and instigated sickly fantasies in children, developed the kulak attitude, and strengthened bourgeois ideals. The RAPP (Russian Association of Proletarian Writers), the heir of the Proletcul't, continued the same policy toward folklore. Its leaders considered folklore to be backward and suggested that it be uprooted.[1] The RAPM (Russian Association of Proletarian Musicians) joined the ranks of the enemies of folklore on the ground that the tunes of some folksongs were

*This study was supported by a research grant from the National Endowment for the Humanities, for which I am greatly indebted.

reminiscent of a certain prerevolutionary ballad.[2] The early post-revolutionary detractors of folklore were also enemies of classical Russian literature. This nihilistic attitude culminated in Vladimir Majakovskij's ecstatic cry, "We are shooting the old generals! Why not Pushkin?"[3]

Some leading folklorists, such as Azadovskij and J. Sokolov, raised their voices in defense of folklore. Both of them argued that folklore was not only concerned with the past but also reflected contemporary life. Sokolov's aphoristic phrase first formulated in 1926 had a wide echo: "Častuška, as well as many other folklore genres, is both a monument of the far past and a vigorous voice of our present." In the '30s Sokolov dropped the mention of častuška in this phrase, referring instead to folklore in general, thus giving his statement a broader validity.[4]

The voices of folklorists might have remained a cry in the wilderness had not the leading Soviet writer of that time, Maksim Gor'kij (Gorky), made a powerful appeal for folklore. Gor'kij gave a speech at the First Congress of Soviet Writers in 1934, in which, among other things, he discussed the relations between folklore and labor.[5] Gor'kij stressed (1) the close connection of folklore with the concrete life and working conditions of the people, for which reason its study should not be concerned with abstract mythic-religious ideas but must deal with concrete historical reality, work processes, and human relations, (2) the life optimism of folklore, which expresses the deepest moral and human aspirations of the masses and can have validity as the source of the world outlook of a people in its individual historical periods, and (3) the high artistic value of folklore. According to Gor'kij,

> The most vivid and profoundly conceived, artistically perfect hero-types were created by folklore, by the oral tradition of the working people. Hercules, Prometheus, Mikula Seljaninovich, Svyatogor, Dr. Faust, Vassilissa Premudraya, the ironical Ivan the Fool, always successful in everything he does . . . they are all perfect in their way, and in their creation, reason and intuition, thought and feeling were harmoniously combined. Such a combination is possible only through direct participation in the creative activities of labour, in the struggle for life.

Gor'kij's insistence that folklore belonged, first of all, to working people had far-reaching implications. As if by magic, it opened the eyes of the party leaders to the possibilities that folklore would have for the advance of communism. And from that time on, we can follow the conscious use of folklore for social and political purposes.

The first tangible result of Gor'kij's speech was the organization of large-scale folklore collecting projects, initiated and supported by the party functionaries. An extensive collecting expedition was organized by the Moscow oblast committee of the Communist Party on the initiative of L. M. Kaganovič, an intimate of Stalin. The program of this expedition, in addition to scholarly tasks, had other goals to pursue. The expedition had to collect both old and new folklore and had to establish which forms of folklore should be cultivated in the village for healthy Soviet esthetics. The collected material had to be polished and returned en masse to the people, so as to force out "various disgusting phenomena of thieves' and bourgeois poetry which had become grafted in various ways to the kolkhoz and workers' milieu."[6] The organization of the expedition to the Moscow oblast had an enormous significance in principle, since on its model numerous field trips were arranged to the peripheral areas of the Soviet Union. The collection activity became so all-encompassing and vigorous, extending over the whole country, that it was possible to speak of an all-Union folkloric movement. Local centers of folklore were founded in numerous districts and the collection of folklore was made obligatory for ethnographic organizations. The local intelligentsia, university students, and students of trade schools were mobilized for active collecting. Influential party papers, such as *Pravda* and others, published appeals for collecting as well as samples of collected materials. *Pionerskaja Pravda* made "pioneers" collect folklore and systematically published the collected materials. The newspaper *Kollektivist* in Tiflis attracted broad circles of collective farmers and workers to the task of collecting.[7]

The fieldwork conducted by folklorists served for both scholarly and political enlightenment. On the basis of instructions worked out by the Central Museum of Demography in Moscow, folklorists on their field trips had to give talks and lectures, arrange debates, and organize itinerant exhibitions for propagandizing kolkhozes. A typical collection event was undertaken jointly by an institute and the Union of Militant Atheists to the district Svetlojar in the Trans-Volga area. (By the way, it is believed that the city of Kitež had sunk into Svetlojar Lake to keep it from falling into the hands of the Tatars, hence the lake is considered holy.) During the fieldwork, the local people held their divine service on the lake while folklorists and atheists held discussions and lectures on the structure of kolkhozes and other problems of the day.[8] On their collection trips folklorists were required to keep a critical attitude toward the folklore material they encountered, since not all of it by any means warranted recording. They must not only reject songs and tales which were ideologically unacceptable, "reflecting the survivals of class-hostile ideology," but launch an active fight against them.[9]

Thus only the ideologically pure folklore, cleansed from casual and alien material, was taken down and preserved in the archives, and the purest of that could from there reach the publishers.

This ideologically unacceptable folklore includes thieves' and hooligan songs and the "cruel romances of the bourgeois type" and is usually performed and transmitted in streets and other places during "unorganized rest." In order to avoid this kind of interaction, care is taken that positive Soviet folklore be created and diffused in an orderly manner: during organized collective rest or in the course of various cultural events in clubs, houses of culture, reading huts, and at meetings of amateur circles.[10]

It appears from the preceding information that folklore scholars in the Soviet Union fill an entirely different role from those in the West. Azadovskij, for example, argues that folklore scholarship in the Soviet Union proceeds from the problems of social order, from the understanding of the tremendously effective role of folklore, which in one way or another shapes the consciousness of the people and either contributes to the growth of socialist construction or hinders it. Therefore, folklore scholarship could no longer be only an observer and recorder of facts, but had to combine the tasks of scholarly understanding with the urgent tasks of social education.[11]

Folklore in the Soviet Union has been used consciously for propagating the cultural construction and political education of the masses for one goal—the realization of socialism and communism. As early as in 1918, Lenin officially launched a comprehensive project for propaganda and agitation for socialism by means of art and "folk wisdom" (that is, folklore). What significance Lenin gave to art and folklore appears in the fact that he called this project "monumental propaganda" and through detailed letters and telegrams instructed A. V. Lunačarskij, the commissar of education, how to carry it out.[12] The utilization of folklore for propaganda purposes has also been duly emphasized by the Soviet folklorists. Jurij Sokolov writes:

> Never, in all the history of Russia, has the oral poetic word served the social aims so broadly and powerfully as in the Soviet period. Soviet folkloristics has helped to reveal the agitational and propagandist significance of folklore. And thereby, Soviet folkloristics has firmly allied itself with the practical tasks of our social life.[13]

And a group of folklorists echoes this thought:

> The popular tellers conceive their activity as agitational-propagandistic. They are popular agitators, people's tribunes, carrying their artistic patriotic word to the masses. Their works summon the readers and listeners to conscious work for the glory of the Fatherland.[14]

The pursuit of the correct direction and unblemished ideology of folklore depended on two groups: (1) on folklorists who had direct contact with folksingers and who were expected to give them guidelines for their creations and (2) on folksingers and tellers themselves who had to put these guidelines into practice. To these two groups we must add the party and government who had the supreme authority to control both the folklorists and folksingers.

First, the folklorists. In order to be able to give the right direction to the folklore being created and performed, folklorists had to have a clear idea of the specifically Soviet folklore that embodied Marxist–Leninist ideology. However, now and then they fell short of expectations and were accused by the party and government of espousing spurious ideas. For instance, in the mid-1930s folklorists were accused of being "still captives of old methodology, the roots of which were firmly entrenched in the ideology of the bourgeois society." This accusation came to the fore in connection with criticism launched against Demjan Bednyj's comic opera *Bogatyri* ("The Epic Heroes"), in which he depicted the bylina heroes in a derogatory manner. They were shown as representatives of the feudal aristocracy with all possible defects and vices, and the villains they fought were glorified as the "revolutionary element." This tendency to ridicule ancient heroes was suddenly found to be completely unacceptable, although Bednyj had been following the officially approved line still in force. Bednyj's and the folklorists' mistake was that they had not sensed the change of policy that was in the making behind the scenes. On order of a government committee, the opera was removed from the theater. A series of articles began to appear in *Pravda* and simultaneously in other leading newspapers, accusing the theater and especially the folklorists of falsifying the Russian historical past. Folklorists were condemned for their tendency to adhere to the tenet of the aristocratic origin of byliny and to deprive the working people of creative ability. These concerted attacks came from nonfolklorists, obviously under the direction of the party and government. Folklorists had no say in this matter, but the theory of nonaristocratic origin of the epic was imposed on them from the outside. Folklorists had willy-nilly to follow it in their own work and to make sure that these democratic trends were also followed by folksingers.[15]

Second, the performers (folksingers and tellers). We will ask: were the performers qualified to be the portrayers of all the progressive trends in Soviet society? Of course, they were not. Many of them belonged to the older generation and were totally or partly illiterate. They could sing some old byliny, ballads of unhappy love, and lyrical songs, but who cared for such stuff nowadays! The singers were in crying need of political education–first of all about intricacies of Marxism-Leninism and the burning problems of the day.

The all-Union and local party and scholarly organizations, in cooperation with folklorists, did everything possible to prepare the performers for their high calling. The master singers and tellers were invited to the regional or republic centers, to Moscow and Leningrad, where they visited museums, attended lectures, concerts, and theatrical performances, and familiarized themselves with the achievement of science and technology, literature, and art. Radios were installed in their homes, and subscriptions to newspapers and magazines and study aids were provided for them. They were presented with small home libraries. Like writers, they were sent on so-called "creative missions" (*tvorčeskie komandirovki*).[16] When Marfa Krjukova decided to write a long poem on Stalin, she was sent on a trip to the Caucasus in 1938, to give her an opportunity to see the places where Stalin had spent his youth and to talk with the persons who still remembered him.[17] The Olonec singer Mixail Rjabinin was sent to Moscow, where he visited historico-revolutionary museums to collect materials for his extensive life story of Lenin.

In the second half of the 1930s, the All-Union House of Folk Art (in Moscow) named after N. K. Krupskaja coordinated the work with performers. The House arranged conferences of singers, discussions of their work and of their artistic experiences, critical analyses of their performances, and competitions for the best works of folklore. In this endeavor, the All-Union House of Folk Art was assisted by research institutes of the all-Union and republic Academies of Sciences. The greatest masters among the singers, such as Marfa Krjukova, M. R. Golubkova, P. I. Rjabinin-Andreev, and F. A. Konaskov, were assigned writers and professional folklorists as tutors for the purpose of assisting them with facts and ideology. The tutors suggested suitable topics from newspapers, novels, or history, recorded the works the singers created, emended them, and arranged for their publication. The writer Viktorin Popov, Marfa Krjukova's tutor, accompanied the singer on her fact-finding trip to Caucasus; he gave her several biographies of Lenin, when she was preparing her "Lay of Lenin," and furnished books on Čapaev for her song about him. Popov admits that he helped Krjukova place certain events in their correct historical sequence, eliminate parts that had no direct relation to the basic theme, curtail superfluous repetitions that were too drawn out, and eliminate the peculiarities of the White Sea dialect.[18] Scholars who investigated Krjukova's songs had difficulty ascertaining how much the printed versions reflected the singer's own artistic intentions.

All the help rendered to performers was considered very beneficial.

When Jurij Sokolov, one of the most authoritative Russian folklorists, questions Popov's help to Marfa Krjukova saying, "Is such help justified [literally, legal]?", he answers: "Yes, it is justified."[19] According to Soviet folklore scholars, "This indefatigable care shown by the party and the government was to raise the level of folk creation and develop it still further. The systematic party leadership directed the productive talents toward the creation of works that were needed for all the people and helped the socialist construction."[20] How highly the Soviet government valued folksingers and narrators appears from the fact that several of them were elected full members of the Union of Soviet Writers (though some were illiterate) and, especially at the jubilee celebrations, were given the title of Honored Artist or awarded the Order of Lenin. Some were elected members of parliament. A medieval type bower (*terem*) was built by the government for Marfa Krjukova, a noted folksinger, in the village of Zimnjaja Zolotica on the shore of the White Sea, in 1939. The structure looked as if it were carried over from byliny: it had glazed stoves in the prince's chambers and small gates on carved porches, decorated with figures of horses and roosters. We are told that the folksinger preferred to continue living in her old hut and used the bower only for her guests.[21]

In addition to the performers of professional or near-professional status, there were many others who engaged in folklore activities. In the villages scores of younger people could easily improvise verses on any topic. Politically well informed, they hardly needed any special coaching, and their talent came in handy in the conditions of Soviet village life. Several of them developed, in the course of time, into respected folk performers.

As molders of the minds of the Soviet population, the folksingers and narrators had to propagate those ideas believed to have special significance during certain periods. Therefore the themes and topics of their creations frequently changed. In the 1920s and early '30s the party and government were especially concerned with the impression they had made on the populace. What better method could there be than to have the negative sides of the tsarist regime exposed and, by contrast, the great advantages of the Soviet order demonstrated? Best suited for this purpose were the so-called *skazy*, biographical narratives and memoirs told by folksingers and others about their own lives, about the events they had witnessed, and about the remarkable people they had met. These narratives were concerned with the sufferings of wives under their despotic husbands during the tsarist time, with the events of the revolution and the civil war, with life in the Red Army as compared to the tsarist army, and the like. Here, for example, is the story of a woman whose tyrannical husband in the tsarist time had humiliated her beyond measure:

> At my sister-in-law's wedding my husband got dead drunk. He got up, and he says, "And what does my foot want?" I already know his custom, I come out, I bow myself on my knees at his feet. But he says to me: "This is not enough! Throw yourself down flat before me like a fish!" My tears began to roll down. I threw myself at his feet like a fish. He had not thought that I was about to give birth! Looking upon me, all the people were disturbed, pitying me, with such an abdomen. But what was to be done, it was that government .... But now the Soviet government has pressed his wings down, like those of a little sparrow after rain. Now I am very well satisfied with the Soviet government.[22]

The performers cultivated extensively those folklore categories that had been neglected or ignored by the former regime, such as satires on priests and noblemen, traditions about revolutionary movements—especially those led by Razin and Pugačev—the folklore of serfdom, and the folklore of factory workers. Some of these themes later lost their initial lustre. This was the case with folklore about Razin and Pugačev, after Stalin, in his talk with Emil Ludwig, expressed his disapproval of such disorganized peasant uprisings.

The new folklore concentrated on themes of technological advances and socialist construction. Tractors, airplanes, and electricity, called "Il'jič's little lamp" (*lampočka Il'iča*), day care centers for children, bridges, and highways represented miracles for the common folk.

Beginning in the mid-1930s, great changes occurred in the Soviet society and the state, that necessitated shifts of emphasis in folklore. The major events were the collectivization of agriculture, changes in socialist work processes because of the Stakhanovite and shock work movements, and the adoption of the new "Stalin" constitution. Folklore was expected to whip up enthusiasm for all these developments.

A genre that was suited perfectly for such tasks was *častuška*, a short rhymed song, easily improvised, comparable to the German *Schnaderhüpfel* and Japanese *haiku*. Its characteristic features are its epigrammatic and frequently nonsensical character, extreme brevity, and marked rhythm. Because of its special form, častuška is essentially nontranslatable. Here are some examples:

On the Five-Year Plan:

> The Five-Year Plan is not a twig,
> it must not broken be;
> for the Five-Year Plan both little and big
> are ready to fight, you see.[23]

On women's liberation:

A wife is not a slave,
Things are equal now,
with your arms don't wave,
now a man must bow.[24]

On joining collective farms:[25]

All my close neighbors and the poor
people of the village have made
a choice—we are many, to be sure—
to join the kolkhoz family unafraid.[26]

About the Stakhanovite movement:

I read about Staxanov. He
is a true hero. I've been
with one desire: to be
like him, a Staxanov heroine.[27]

About the Stalin constitution:

Stalin, the happiness that you
have given us was never heard
before. Yet now our constitution sings it out, word for word.[28]

And the praise for Stalin:

Now at last we do live well,
comrade Stalin. We all agree
that you have lifted us from hell
and freed us from our poverty.[29]

In connection with the revision of Russian history after the denouncement of the ideas of Mixail Pokrovskij in 1934, there began a general propagation of Soviet patriotism. As Gleb Struve puts it: "A good Soviet citizen had to be a Soviet patriot. And patriotism . . . implied pride in Russia's past, in her military glory, in her territorial expansion, in her historical achievements, and in her military heroes."[30] This outburst of patriotic spirit brought to the fore in folklore, as in literature, the glorification of the Soviet governmental and military figures, such as Lenin, Stalin, Čapaev, Vorošilov, Budennyj, and others. The cult of Stalin acquired mythical proportions. Over and over again, folksingers showed that it was Stalin and nobody else whom Lenin had selected and designated to be his heir. The tenacious insistence on Stalin's heirship was necessary to dispel the legitimate doubts still prevalent on this matter in some quarters of Soviet society.

Soviet patriotism found its strongest expression in a new type of folksong, the so-called *noviny* "the new songs," as opposed to the *stariny* "the old songs." The noviny were a combination of byliny, historical songs, and laments. They imitated traditional folksongs, making use of their motifs and poetical devices, but employing contemporary life as their subject. Their protagonists were, according to the narrators themselves, no longer the ancient epic heroes, but the "new Soviet hero-innovators and defenders of the socialist fatherland," "the kolkhoz heroes and factory heroes."[31] Most often, the Soviet government and military leaders functioned as the heroes of this folklore.

In noviny the Soviet leaders are endowed with the same idealized qualities as Il'ja Muromec, Dobrynja Nikitič, and Aleša Popvič—bravery, resourcefulness, and self-sacrifice. Their adversaries are the "whites" (who correspond to the Tatars in byliny), headed by their leader Idolišče ("the most monstrous idol"). In Idolišče it is not difficult to recognize the tsar, the symbol of the old regime. Idolišče in the noviny appears as cruel, boastful, gluttonous, and cowardly. Thus the noviny have transposed the gallery of the old heroes and villains with their typical characteristics into Soviet reality and have assigned to them different roles. The best known novina singer was Marfa Krjukova from the White Sea region, one of the most talented of Russian folksingers.

In order to give an idea of noviny, we will briefly discuss Marfa Krjukova's famous novina "The Lay of Lenin,"[32] which was highly praised by Soviet folklorists. After the opening lines,

In those days, in former ones,
In those times, in olden ones,
Under Big-Idol Tsar of foul memory,
In Simbirsk, fine city on the Volga River . . .

the novina tells about the attempt of Lenin's brother Aleksander against the life of the Tsar. The attempt fails and Aleksander is executed. Mother sheds hot tears, from which the Volga waters "grow turbid." Lenin consoles his mother:

Grieve not, mother dear, do not sorrow.
We will, indeed, take a great vow amongst us,
A great vow for people's truth to battle! . . .
For I feel in me a great power:
Were that ring in an oaken pillar,
I'd wrench it out, myself with my comrades,
With that faithful bodyguard of mine—

I'd then turn about the whole damp mother earth!
Well am I trained in wise learning,
For I've read one magic little book [the Communist Manifesto],
Now I know where to find the ring,
Now I know how to turn about the whole earth,
The whole earth, our whole dear Russia.

The ring, with the help of which Lenin would turn about the whole earth, is a common folklore motif. It appears, for example, in the bylina about Svjatogor; Svjatogor (who is doomed to live in the mountains) states that if he would walk on the plain, he would fasten a ring to heaven, bind an iron chain to it, and drag the sky down to earth. This is exactly what Lenin wants to do.

The song goes on: arrested and exiled to Siberia, Lenin writes "express letters" instructing people how to carry on the struggle. With the help of Ivan, a Siberian mužik, Lenin succeeds in escaping abroad. There one night he hears a knock on the window and sees a fair maiden, called Nadežda (Krupskaja), who had come to join him and to be "a faithful wife, a faithful and unchanging wife."

During the heat of the revolution of 1905, Lenin takes leave of his wife, mounts a snow white horse and reaches the "steep mountains, famous Sparrow mountains." There he sees "heads rolling in the streets, people dragged to prison, exiled, and shot." Later the war breaks out. "Sly Yermania" (Germany) desires to conquer Russia. Tsar Nikolaška (Nikolaj II) drinks and brags, and his wife reveals military secrets to the Kaiser.

The beginning of the October Revolution is described in a style typical of the bylina:

On a morning it was, on an early morning,
At the rise of the fair red sun,
That Ilich stepped out of his little tent,
He washed his fair face
With spring water cold . . .
As he played on his birchbark horn,
The whole people heard him,
The whole people gathered and thronged.
They all thronged and gathered,
Up to that pillar the marvelous.
They gathered in a mighty force,
They took hold on the little ring, the magic one,
Hard it was to wrench the little ring,

With stout force they did wrench it,
Turned about glorious mother Russia land,
To another side, the just one.

Lenin now appoints "his friend Stalin as an aid," and Ivan, the Siberian mužik, as a people's commissar. Stalin manages to destroy the enemies.

Meanwhile, Lenin falls ill. We are told (against all historical truth) that Trockij's treason aggravates Lenin's illness, and he dies. The song now strikes lamentable chords:

It was not the fair sun has rolled
Beyond those famous Sparrow Mountains,
Nor beyond mother stonewall-Moscow . . .
Our fair sun has rolled down,
When into mother, into damp earth . . .
Was laid, indeed, Ilich our light . . .
Birds flew up then like falcons high to the skies,
Fishes then sank to the deep of the seas,
Foxes-martens scampered over the islands . . .

The motif of escaping fishes, foxes, and martens is taken from the bylina about Volx Vseslav'evič. In this bylina, the birds and animals, upon hearing the news of Volx's birth, flee.

The song ends with Stalin's giving his oath of loyalty to Lenin and with the erection of Lenin's mausoleum on Red Square, in which all the peoples participate:

Those [precious] stones all peoples carried up,
Each people brought one stone apiece.

The erection of the mausoleum in such a fashion is again a folklore theme, which is, for instance, disseminated widely among the peoples in Central Asia. In Russia it is usually connected with the establishment of a barrow, a mound, by a ruler (Ivan the Terrible) or a rebel (Razin, Pugačev, and others). Each soldier has to carry a handful or capful of dirt. The resulting mound is to serve as a demonstration of the might of the military leader and his army.[33]

As this brief outline shows, "The Lay of Lenin" is, as are also other noviny, a curious hodgepodge of genuine folklore motifs, communist propaganda, and distorted historical facts.

The noviny use the traditional bylina verse and the poetics characteristic of byliny. The constant epithets (*dobryj molodec* "good youth," *ruki belye* "white hands," *more sinee* "blue sea," and so forth), commonplaces, and other devices are a few examples. For a discussion of commonplaces used in noviny and in Soviet fairy tales, I refer to my essay "Folklore and Politics in the Soviet Union."[34]

Folklorists greeted the noviny enthusiastically as representing the "renaissance" of the epic. Jurij Sokolov wrote about Marfa Krjukova's noviny: "As a result, we have something new, original, independent, which in certain specific aspects . . . even recalls the 'ancient songs,' but as a whole is sharply distinguished from them, particularly by its great sustained lyric quality and by the free plan of its composition."[35]

In addition to noviny, folktales on contemporary themes were also created. Their heroes were the Soviet leaders and military men, members of collective farms, and workers. These tales, invented by the tellers, included only a few folklore motifs. The Soviet magic tales were mostly allegorical. The truth that some heroes were seeking turned out to be the October Revolution. The magic ring was the symbol of the scientific tasks that the polar explorers (*čeljuškincy*) had to solve, "the symbol of their scientific service to the people." Living and dead water was interpreted as the immortality and invincibility of the Soviet people.[36]

The "realistic tales" often exhibit an unnatural fusion of reality and unreality, as appears from the summary of a couple of tales by the Moscow oblast narrator V. I. Bespalikov. The tale "The Scarlet Flower" reflects the fights about kolkhozes. The kulaks make three attempts at the life of the chairman of a kolkhoz, a communist. Finally, they bury him alive. But the Order of Lenin pinned on his jacket grows as a red flower out of the grave and betrays the place of his burial. The grave is dug open and miraculously the hero is found to be still alive.[37] The tale "The Three Sons" was created to echo a newspaper account reporting the death of a frontier guard at Lake Ladoga and the temporary discharge of his duties by his brothers. In this narrative, the brothers enliven the youngest brother with the living water brought in an airplane by the middle brother, a pilot. When the enemies see him alive again, they have to conclude: "It appears that we can't ever destroy them."[38]

In the mid-1930s, a new lyro-epic genre appeared in the Soviet Union, letter-poems addressed to Stalin. Drafted jointly by folk performers and professional poets, they were amended at numerous meetings. After the final version had been adopted, it was sent to Stalin, accompanied by tens of thousands (in some cases even several millions) of signatures.

The writing of letter-poems was occasioned by important events in the life of workers or professional groups in certain oblasts, cities, factories, or kolkhozes. Such occasions were, for example, the observance of the new stakhanovite stage of the socialist construction by weavers of the city of

Ivanovo in 1936, the meeting of folk performers of Karelia in Petrozavodsk in 1939, when they were "enthused by their creative teamwork," and the commemoration by the workers of the Arkhangelsk oblast in 1940 of the twentieth anniversary of the liberation of the North from interventionists and White Guards.[39]

The letter-poems containing details of the most significant achievements of the groups were saturated with the highest imaginable tributes to Stalin. Though we may question their classification as folk tradition, they no doubt belong with the curious phenomena of the "Soviet folklore" that developed during the "personality cult" of the Stalin era.

When the Nazi menace increased at the turn of the 1930s and '40s, patriotic motifs in Soviet folklore became stronger. Heroism was extolled, the leaders lauded, and wreckers (*vrediteli*) and traitors debased. During the war, folklore, like literature, had to give its share to the war effort. At the initial phase of the war, when the situation was critical, high hopes for helping to save the Fatherland were attached to folklore. The notable singers and tellers, either alone or in teams, were sent to perform for the fighting men at the front and for collective farmers and soldiers in hospitals at the rear. How strongly the folksingers were filled with hatred for the enemy appears in the emotionally loaded symbolism used for the Nazis: "the fascist-snake," "the monster with the snake's heart," "the black raven" (or "the flock of ravens"), and such.[40] Folklorists made extensive collections of folklore with war themes and published them in front-line papers, major periodical publications, and numerous special collections. On Ždanov's initiative, a typical collection of patriotic songs (*Pesennik*) was compiled in the encircled Leningrad for the Red Army and 25,000 copies were printed.[41]

Even the Soviets' allies, the English and Americans, did not escape the folksingers' wrath. Satirical folksongs ridiculed Anglo-American ruling circles and their military high command for "their treacherous tactics which were designed to extend the war and assist German fascism."[42] The folksingers' targets were especially Lord Beaverbrook, "the low imperialist," and Winston Churchill, "the old fox." The songs revealing the "provocative policies" of the Allied were created in huge quantities, though hardly published during the war years.[43]

In songs about the war with German forces by Marfa Krjukova, even the ancient bylina heroes were brought to the Soviet scene. Thus, in one song Il'ja Muromec calls for the defense of the fatherland in the "last patriotic war," and in another, together with Dobrynja, Aleša, and other heroes, he fights in the ranks of the Red Army against the enemy to protect the Soviet frontiers.[44] This reminds us of an Old Russian war story of the thirteenth or fourteenth century in hagiographic style, "The Life of Aleksander Nevskij," in which the long-deceased saints Boris and Gleb come to the help of Aleksander in his fight against the invading Swedes. It is obvious that Marfa Krjukova got the motif of miraculous help from the hagiographic life of Nevskij, with which she had become familiar when she was creating her legend about Nevskij. On the other hand, she included the Novgorod bylina heroes Kostja Novotoržanin, Vasilij Buslaev, and others, in her own creation of the lay about Nevskij.[45]

Some historical figures of the last centuries are also brought into the Soviet war tales.[46] In a F. P. Gospodarev's tale, Ignat Nekrasov, one of the leaders of the revolt of the Don Cossacks against Peter the Great in 1707-08, is awakened by a little bird. He hastens to Stalingrad and begins fighting in the ranks of the Red Army, "and he does not lay to his grave, before the black city of Berlin has been taken by our people." In V. Ja. Syčev's tales, the revived generals Platov and Suvorov are made the main protagonists. Platov, who defeated Frenchmen during Napoleon's warfare, rises from his grave, since his "hands are itching" for battle, and advises scouts how to catch the Germans with the lasso. The Cossacks follow his advice, at first at Stalingrad and then elsewhere, and thus end the war. Suvorov, Catherine the Great's famous general, appears in a tale in Stalingrad and expresses his satisfaction with the victory of his grandchildren and great-grandchildren over General Paulus.

During the years following the war, the glorification of Stalin continued on a large scale, acquiring the scope of real oriental worship. Both the folklorists and folksingers endeavored to coin the highest imaginable attributes for this "leader of the nations," "father of the peoples," and "teacher and friend of all workers." The deification of Stalin was accompanied by the flourishing of Soviet patriotism and the glorification of Russian superiority in all fields of human endeavor. These tendencies found their official sanction in the literary policy pursued by Ždanov beginning with 1946. Ždanov's so-called "anti-West witchhunt," which fought against cosmopolitan and comparative tendencies in Russian culture in general, affected the folklore scholars more than the folksingers. The comparative-historical works of several leading folklorists (Propp, Žirmunskij, Azadovskij) were condemned and their authors made to recant.[47] These works had followed the trends that had been officially approved to that time.

When the nightmare of Stalinism finally passed with Stalin's death in 1953, and especially with his condemnation in 1956, folklore got rid of its worst constraint. Folklorists now felt free to criticize the great exaggerations and gross mistakes of folklore research in bygone years, such as the thesis of "the flourishing of Soviet folklore," the propagandizing of pseudo-folklore as genuine folklore, and the artificial grafting of the genre of noviny onto folklore.[48] They pointed out that it was not suitable for the noviny to use the bylina imagery that expressed the esthetic ideas of the far past for their depiction of the Soviet present. "The show of the Soviet reality immured in the poetic forms of the twelfth-fourteenth centuries, sounds like a parody, does not reveal the (essence of the) theme, but vulgarizes it."[49] The so-called Soviet fairy tales were said to be products of individual creation and to have no relation whatsoever to Soviet folklore. They "have not become the property of the people and therefore there is absolutely no reason to consider them as Soviet folklore. They are simply unsuccessful literary works."[50] Folklorists were sincere in their self-criticism concerning the idealization of Stalin: " 'The tragic guilt' of many Soviet folklorists was in that they, yielding to the influence of the propaganda of the personality cult (that is, the efforts at deifying Stalin), tried to present the matter in such a way as if the whole nation glorified Stalin from all its heart and created these idyllic, conflictless, gala words about the 'happy life'. . ."[51] Folklorists unanimously agreed that the "personality cult" had brought to the fore many creations that had scarcely any connection with folklore. They were joined by the singers, who vociferously repudiated and rejected much of the propaganda material they had created "on order" and had called "folklore." From now on, no folklore on Stalin or other contemporary leaders was created or studied.

The following years have brought about a general relaxation among the folklore scholars and folksingers alike. Folklorists have turned their attention to serious scholarly problems. The excited debate on the nature of Soviet folklore in 1953-55 and again in 1959-61 that activated almost all the folklorists,[52] and the discussion of the specifics of folklore genres that followed, could have happened only in this atmosphere of temporary promise and hope.

Folksingers, relieved from the obligation of singing praises to the leaders, were subject to somewhat less pressure from the party and government than before. However, they were not encouraged to sing for the mere joy of singing, but for the benefit of their country, for the propagation of the social and political ideas and of the construction work. Here are. for example, themes of songs sung at the end of the 1950s in a Ukrainian village: the unity of the people with the Communist Party; the Soviet fatherland, free reconstruction work, fight for peace and friendship of nations; matters of work in factories, mines and kolkhozes; building of an hydro-electric plant; a tractor operator who was a two-time hero of socialist work, a famous milking woman, and workers of a machine-building plant. The youth sang of tilling the virgin lands, of the members of the Komsomol who, following the party's summon, went to work at Donbas, of the youth festival, of launching earth satellites, and of other topics. Finally it is mentioned that lyrical love songs, satirical songs, and humorous songs also were sung.[53]

These folksong topics give little opportunity to the singers to spread the wings of their fantasy and to excite their listeners. That is obviously the reason why fieldworkers have been reporting a lack of interest in folklore in the countryside. They point out that folklore (obviously the classical type) has been preserved only among the older and, to a lesser degree, among the middle generation. Among the youth merely the častuška is being practiced. "The singing culture of the youth is developing," as Emel'janov notices, "on the non-folkloric basis."[54]

This remark about the "non-folkloric basis" refers evidently to the amateur artistic activity in its broadest sense, the activity that has found a strong echo among the younger generation. There are several reputed folklorists who are advocating the broadening of the notion of folklore to include the amateur activity of the masses. For example, Čistov suggests that folklore should embrace "all the literary-artistic culture of the Soviet people in all the richness of its forms and aspects, which can appear orally or in writing, can be composed by a professional writer or a member of the amateur literary club, can arise as an individual or collective work, can be printed in books, journals, newspapers, wall-newspapers, can be presented on the radio, in movies, on stages of the houses of culture, in reading rooms, clubs, can be recorded on gramophone records, presented at youth evenings and mass outings."[55]

The majority of folklorists have so far been successful in denying folklore status to this broad amateur activity. In connection with the disappearance of numerous classical genres, great shifts are bound to occur in Soviet folklore in the very near future, and several aspects, if not all, of amateur artistic activity may well be promoted to the status of folklore.

Indiana University
Bloomington, Indiana

NOTES

[1] V. I. Čičerov, "Russkie učenye ob otnošenii nardnogo tvorčestva k defstvitel'-nosti," *Voprosy narodno-poetičeskogo tvorčestva* (Moscow, 1960), p. 34.
[2] Y. M. Sokolov, *Russian Folklore* (Hatboro, Pa., 1966), pp. 623-24.
[3] Maurice Friedberg, *Russian Classics in Soviet Jackets* (New York, 1962), p. 12.
[4] Ju. M. Sokolov, "Priroda fol'klora i problemy fol'kloristiki," *Literaturnyj kritik* 1934, No. 12, pp. 133-34.
[5] See Felix J. Oinas, "Folklore and Politics in the Soviet Union," *Slavic Review* 32 (1973): 46-47.
[6] M. K. Azadovskij, "Sovetskaja fol'klorisika za 20 let," *Sovetskij fol'klor* 6 (1939): 8.
[7] *Ibid.*, pp. 8-9.
[8] E. V. Gippius and V. I. Čičerov, "Sovetskaja fol'kloristika za 30 let," *Sovetskaja ètnografija* 1947, No. 4, p. 36, fn. 19.
[9] *Ibid.*, p. 37.
[10] G. Samarin, "O edinstve literatury i fol'klora," *Voprosy literatury* 1959, No. 2, p. 172.
[11] Azadovskij, p. 12.
[12] V. Potjavin, "Leninskaja ideja propagandy sredstvami fol'klora," *Russkaja narodnaja poèzija* (Fol'klorističeskie zapisi Gor'kovskogo gosuniversiteta, 1961, No. 1), pp. 138-40.
[13] Sokolov, *Russian Folklore*, p. 141.
[14] A. M. Astaxova et al., *Očerki russkogo narodnopoètičeskogo tvorčestva sovetskoj èpoxi* (Moscow and Leningrad, 1952), p. 523.
[15] For a detailed discussion of these questions, see Felix J. Oinas, "The Problem of the Aristocratic Origin of Russian *Byliny*," *Slavic Review* 30 (1971): 513-22.
[16] See Oinas, "Folklore and Politics," p. 52.
[17] Ju. M. Sokolov, "Osnovnye linii razvitija sovetskogo fol'klora," *Sovetskij fol'klor* No. 7 (1941), p. 50.
[18] Sokolov, *Russkij fol'klor,* p. 677.
[19] *Ibid.*
[20] A. M. Astaxova et al., p. 196.
[21] Nikolaj Leont'ev, "Volxovanie i šamanstvo," *Novyj mir* 29:8 (1953): 232, fn. 1.
[22] Sokolov, *Russian Folklore*, p. 685.
[23] Ivan A. Lopatin, "What the People Are Now Singing in a Russian Village," *Journal of American Folklore* 64 (1951): 186.
[24] *Ibid.*, p. 187.
[25] The following four songs were translated by my colleague, Professor Willis Barnstone.
[26] Astaxova et al., p. 234.
[27] *Ibid.*, p. 241.
[28] *Ibid.*, p. 245.

[29] *Ibid.*, p. 235.
[30] Gleb Struve, *Russian Literature under Lenin and Stalin, 1917-1953* (Norman, Okla., 1971), pp. 277-78.
[31] Astaxova et al., pp. 223-24.
[32] The following excerpts from this novina in English translation are quoted from Alexander Kaun, *Soviet Poets and Poetry* (Berkeley and Los Angeles, 1943), pp. 185-91.
[33] Vera K. Sokolova, "Istoričeskaja ustnaja proza i dejstvitel'nost'," *Narodno stvaralastvo–folklor* 1969, Nos. 29-32, pp. 315-16.
[34] Oinas, "Folklore and Politics," pp. 50-51.
[35] Sokolov, *Russian Folklore*, pp. 676-77.
[36] Astaxova et al., pp. 320-23.
[37] *Ibid.*, pp. 234, 323.
[38] *Ibid.*, pp. 280-81.
[39] *Ibid.*, pp. 242-43, 220-21.
[40] Leont'ev, p. 242.
[41] Gippius and Čičerov, p. 50.
[42] Astaxova et al., p. 444.
[43] *Ibid.*, pp. 444-45.
[44] See Oinas, "Folklore and Politics," p. 53.
[45] Also other Slavs have brought ancient heroes and mythical beings to the present scene. The Czech poet Petr Křička's collection *The Song of the Sword* (*Píseň meče*, Prague, 1946) is based entirely on the material drawn from Russian and South Slavic epic songs and other traditions. The hero of the song "The Plower–Bogatyr" is the peace loving Russian bylina hero Mikula, who plows the kolkhoz fields with a "maple-wood plow" and repels the attack of the enemy with an "elm-wood cudgel." In the song "The Banquet" the Russian rivers have a feast at the Sea tsar's, in honor of the Mother Volga, which at Stalingrad "met chest against chest the evil dragon and strangled its twelve heads." (S. Nikol'skij, "Russkij fol'klor," *Sovetskaja ètnografija* 1949, No. 4, pp. 217-18; see also Leont'ev, p. 241).
[46] Astaxova et al., pp. 430-32.
[47] For details, see my "Folklore and Politics," pp. 53-55.
[48] B. N. Putilov et al., "Fol'kloristika," in V. G. Bazanov, ed., *Sovetskoe literaturovedenie za 50 let* (Leningrad, 1968), p. 277.
[49] A. Nečaev and N. Rybakova, "O nekotoryx problemax fol'kloristiki," *Sovetskaja ètnografija* 1953, No. 3, pp. 136-37.
[50] Oinas, "Folklore and Politics," p. 56.
[51] V. Gusev, "Dve diskussii," *Russkaja literatura* 1962, No. 4, pp. 188-89.
[52] *Ibid.*, pp. 186ff.
[53] Samarin, p. 169.
[54] L. I. Emel'janov, "Makar'evskij rajon," *Russkij fol'klor* 6 (1961): 137; cf. also pp. 139-140.
[55] K. V. Čistov, "O nekotoryx problemax fol'kloristiki," *Sovetskaja ètnografija* 1954, No. 2, pp. 108-09.

FOLKLORE POLITICS IN THE SOVIET UKRAINE: PERSPECTIVES ON SOME RECENT TRENDS AND DEVELOPMENTS

Robert B. Klymasz

Only he who believes in the people and delves into the source of the people's living creativity will take and hold power.

–V.I. Lenin in 1917[1]

INTRODUCTION

To postulate the enormous impact of politics on the folklore and folkloristics of the Soviet Ukraine is hardly a difficult matter when one notes that that country's recent history includes a revolution, two world wars, territorial unification, such concomitant by-products as famine, civil strife, purges, and, finally, even a president whose not inconsiderable academic pursuits included the study of folklore.[2] The details and vast dimensions of these experiences have been documented and evaluated elsewhere.[3] As far as folkloristics are concerned, however, the crucial manner in which official Soviet culture policy permeates and conditions this particular field of Ukrainian scholarship and related activities remains largely a terra incognita.[4] The direction and scope of the relationship is reflected in the following statement on the goals of the humanities and social sciences in the Soviet Ukraine today, as prepared in 1967 by I.K. Bilodid, one of the Ukraine's leading academicians and philologists:

> The most important task . . . is: to conduct a systematic, aggressive battle against anti-communism; to give a solid criticism of the contemporary bourgeois philosophy, sociology, historiography, law and economic theories of the apologists of capitalism; to expose the falsifiers of the ideas of

> Marxism-Leninism, of the history of the development of society; to give a decisive rebuff to the manifestations of rightest and "leftist" revisionism and of national narrow-mindedness both in theory and in politics.[5]

In terms of folklore, a similar message can be discerned in the following excerpt from a pamphlet on "The Educative Significance of Ukrainian Folklore" that was issued in 1960 by the "Society for the Dissemination of Political and Scientific Skills":

> Soviet proverbs praise highly the devotion to the socialist Motherland, friendship among nations, collectivism, the communist ideal, Leninist principles, Bolshevik modesty, and other moral-political qualities of the people of our socialist society.[6]

Unfortunately, official efforts to measure up to these ideals and to regulate or control folkloristic trends in the Ukraine have been generally frustrated by the Soviet Union's perennially sensitive nationalities problem. The position of Ukrainians as the largest ethnic minority along with the implications of such status vis-à-vis the Russian majority are factors that aggravate and intensify attempts to generate a new and mythically perfect "Soviet man." The concepts of "melting pot" and *e pluribus unum* require no elaboration here although it is important to note that the overt and at times ruthless imposition of such policies in the Soviet Union has tended to favor the more powerful Russian segment of the Union's population, to inflame the explosive nature of the so-called "Ukrainian question," and unavoidably to influence the subsequent course of Ukrainian folkloristics.

With the preceding paragraphs for its backdrop, the present paper marks an attempt to underline specific recent phenomena in the Soviet Ukraine's folklore-and-politics syndrome. The bulk of the discussion is based on certain key publications, as well as three visits to the Ukraine over the past fifteen years, and some personal conversations and correspondence. The author alone is responsible for the English translation of all excerpts originating in Ukrainian and Russian language sources. My efforts to arrive at an evaluative synthesis are only tentative and perhaps somewhat biased; however, I feel no compulsion to apologize for the latter.

PERIODIZATION AND DEVELOPMENTAL FOLKLORISTICS

In 1958, F.I. Lavrov showed how attempts to isolate, distinguish, and highlight features of the Ukrainian folklore complex were actively discouraged and suppressed during the pre-Soviet era in his diligently documented survey of the oppression and persecution of Ukrainian folklore by the censors in tsarist Russia.[7] On the other hand, a compatriot of his, the well-known dissident of the 1960s, Ivan Dzyuba, has also pointed to the paradoxical fact that it was before the revolution and during the period of anti-Ukrainian tsarist policies in the nineteenth century that the epoch-making, monumental folklore collections of P. Čubyns'kyj, M. Drahomanov, V. Antonovyč, Ja. Holovac'kyj, and others first made their appearance.[8] A sequel to Lavrov's work and one that would uncover the correlation between intolerance and productivity in the Soviet era of Ukrainian folkloristics remains unwritten. Nonetheless, the general drift of events is discernible, thanks in large part to I.P. Berezovs'kyj's pioneer monograph on "Ukrainian Soviet Folkloristics" published in 1968 under the auspices of the Ukrainian Soviet Academy's Ryl's'kyj Institute for the Arts, Folklore and Ethnography in Kiev.[9]

Berezovs'kyj's periodization of Ukrainian Soviet folkloristics is composed of three consecutive stages of development: (1) 1917 to the mid-1930s, (2) the mid-1930s to the mid-1940s, and (3) the post-World War II period. Unfortunately, Berezovs'kyj's characterization of certain aspects in each of the three periods ignores or treats superficially certain facts and processes that remain potentially embarassing to the Soviet regime today. For example, the extraordinary maturation and productivity of Ukrainian folklorists in the first period is belittled by the author's uncritical and noncommittal roll call technique of listing names and titles without rehabilitating or evaluating the theoretical and methodological problems posed by this creative era in Ukrainian Soviet folkloristics. The subsequent decimation of Ukrainian folklore studies by the Stalinist regime in the 1930s[10] is understandably (but not justifiably) bypassed in Berezovs'kyj's discussion of the second period, which he treats simply as a transitional and corrective phase in the development of Ukrainian folkloristics. In contrast to the initial period of supposedly bourgeois dominated permissiveness, we are shown how the Party paved the way, as it were, for the triumph of Marxist-Leninist dialectics in folklore research just as in all the other sciences in the Ukrainian Soviet Republic. In effect, however, the victory was Pyrrhic in nature since it signaled the start of an unprecedented sterile period in quantity and quality of output. This dearth of serious folklore scholarship goes unnoticed by Berezovs'kyj although not a single Academy publication in the field of folklore appeared between 1933 and 1937,[11] and although the authorities found it necessary in 1939 to import a prominent Russian folklorist (none other than Jurij M. Sokolov himself!) to head and revive the Ukrainian Academy's moribund Ukrainian Folklore Institute officially founded three years earlier in 1936.[12]

The third stage in Berezovs'kyj's developmental scheme for Ukrainian

Soviet folkloristics, the post World War II period, continues up to the present day, although the data suggests that it would be more credible for 1953 (the year of Stalin's death) to mark the cutoff date for the third stage and the start of a fourth period, which, since the mid-1950s, has begun to atone for the situation by exhibiting a marked increase in the number of folklore publications and a growing tolerance for apolitical folkloristics both past and present. The new sobriety is reflected in Berezovs'kyj's goals for contemporary Ukrainian folkloristics, which include the following features:

> ... the systematic accumulation of scientific information that is as complete as possible; the constant exchange of knowledge; the systematic study and creative assimilation of the best accomplishments of world scholarship; raising the culture [?] of scientific research; elaborating the methodology for the concrete-sociological study of folklore, and so on. An inextricable constituent part of this task is raising the level of bibliographical work and the creation of suitable indices and finding aids of various kinds.[13]

TRENDS, DILEMMAS, AND APPLIED FOLKLORE

An important trend in contemporary Soviet Ukrainian folklore scholarship is its focus on Ukrainian folklore within and in relation to the larger framework of Slavic folklore and folkloristics. Linguistically, historically, and folkloristically this emphasis is certainly justifiable and warranted.[14] If viewed from a narrower, political point of view, however, one can readily discern how easily the well established concept of pan-Slavic studies and scholarly pursuits can serve as political propaganda to support and bolster the Kremlin's call for fraternalism and solidarity among the socialist countries of Eastern Europe. Although the notion of a united Slavic world under a single socialist sun has yet to result in the publication of a collection of Slavic folklore from the Warsaw Pact countries per se, it is an easy matter to cite a string of thematically related works that form a series of rather unimaginative, superficial, and tendentious surveys of Ukrainian-Russian, -Polish, -Czechoslovak, and -Bulgarian folkloristic relationships.[15] A similar concern for the Slavic socialist folklore heritage is reflected in the Ukrainian Academy's initiation in 1965 of a special, but somewhat unexciting, annual hardback journal devoted to Slavic literary studies and folkloristics (*Slov'jans'ke literaturoznavstvo i fol'klorystyka*).

While studying and fostering Ukraine's folkloristic ties with traditions in countries that are politically aligned with the Soviet regime, Ukrainian folklorists appear generally reluctant to study the folklore of non-Ukrainian ethnic groups in the Republic or to discuss and consider important current trends in Western folkloristics in any objective or sympathetic manner. Instead, Western folklore scholarship usually figures as the butt of somewhat paranoiac and offensive harangues in the Ukraine's popular bimonthly journal of folklore and and ethnography, *Narodna tvorčist' ta etnohrafija ("Folk/People's Creativity and Ethnography").*[16] The journal's lead articles appear in the form of unsigned party pronouncements on topics that are presumably of considerable importance to the folklore world in the Soviet Ukraine, and there is even a special section ("Against Bourgeois Ideology") for those specialty essays of criticism and attack.[17] The demeaning and parochial task of serving as the Soviet Union's leading watchdog in matters relating to folklore politics is certainly not as pronounced in current Russian folkloristics and can, with some validity, be seen as a measure of the degree to which Ukrainian Soviet folkloristics still remains politically suspect and unreliable in the eyes of party bureaucrats.

The insular and defensive stance assumed by folklorists in the Soviet Ukraine today has still another aspect that is mirrored, for instance, in M.M. Pazjak's bibliographical survey of Soviet Ukrainian publications in the field of folklore for 1972.[18] Except for possibly a single fresh collection of field materials,[19] the bulk of the twenty or so items considered by Pazjak represents bigger and better retrospective compilations of specific folksong cycles, reprintings, and, in general, works that distinctly avoid contributing to the solution of problems that are crucial in world folkloristics today. The nature of this bias and the rationale for devoting so much energy to rehashing and refurbishing the achievements of the past were defined several years earlier by the Russian folklorist, V.E. Gusev, a leading advocate of the Marxist approach in Soviet folkloristics:

> In exchange for the various theories of folk creativity, each reflecting the historical limitations of bourgeois folkloristics in various ways and in varying degrees, there has come a new scientific methodology with its concrete-historical dialectical approach to facts, with its sober evaluations of contrastive phenomena in the field of folklore, with its historical optimism in defining perspectives on the development of the spiritual culture of the laborers . . . .
>
> It is necessary to relearn the whole totality of facts relating to the conditions of existence of the popular masses at various stages in the history of society, to investigate how these conditions formulated aesthetic views and their reflection in various forms of folklore throughout the history of art from its genesis to our days . . . .
>
> Soviet folkloristics emerge from the Leninist behest to study the artistic creativity of the popular masses "from the social-political point of view." In

> our days this point of view is defined by those historical goals which the Soviet people establish under the guidance of the Communist Party—especially by the contemporary tasks of the ideational and aesthetic education of the laborers.[20]

In the interests of "historical optimism," then, the new Soviet Ukrainian folkloristics is programmed in a way that supports the ongoing reconstruction of the past, gives it a strong and well defined diachronic bent, and underscores the preeminence of the laboring masses in all matters that pertain to artistic creativity. With regard to this latter trend, however, the elevation of the working classes to the level of a supreme, collective wellspring of inspiration for the more sophisticated forms of cultural expression in the Ukraine (such as the fine arts, belles lettres, the theater, opera, symphonic music, and so on) has made the Ukrainian Soviet intellectual highly suspicious of all party moves that imply the forced "folklorization" of these other fields of artistic endeavor. Viewed by some as a form of cultural genocide, this particular aspect of folklore politics in the Soviet Ukraine is vividly exemplified by the excessive homage paid to verbal lore as a force that has prompted the so-called "democratization" of Ukrainian literature in its various forms.[21] In this connection, it is indicative that no reference is made to the distinction between folkloristics and literary studies (as jointly formulated, for example, in 1929 by the prominent Slavicists, R. Jakobson and P. Bogatyrev),[22] that writers and literary trends whose productions have little overt concern with folklore are denigrated or completely ignored, and that authors of unique genius are canonized by the state as "people's" poets, writers, and artists. Besides resulting in a distortive view of Ukrainian folklore and literature, this open policy of folklorization has been used on occasion to trap and expose those groups and individuals whose active pride in the folkloric heritage of the Ukraine was deemed overly nationalistic and thereby contrary to the ideals and goals of the state. The dual and potentially insidious aspect of this phenomenon has been underlined in the following excerpt from an eyewitness account of Ukrainian music under the Soviets:

> Therefore, on the one hand, folk-ethnographic art and, in general, Ukrainian national culture, finding itself in the hands of communist ideologists, served as a propagandistic tool; and, on the other hand, it was a means to attract the Ukrainian element to active participation, a means for its encouragement and, in the final result, for its destruction.[23]

FAKELORE, PRUDERY AND INCARCERATION

In contrast to the pervasive focus on the folksong tradition, it is somewhat disconcerting to note the extent to which the Ukrainian folktale corpus has been neglected in recent Ukrainian folkloristics. The publications that do appear invariably fail to meet Western standards for comparative annotations in terms of analogues or parallel texts and do not include numbered references to specific international or even national tale types or motifs—evidently to avoid the contaminating influence of the decadent Finnish school and its bourgeois cosmopolitanism.[24] Similarly, the party's campaign against the country's churches and traditional religious life is reflected in the total absence of folkloristic works relating to Slavic or ancient Ukrainian mythology, on the one hand, and in special compilations of antireligious stories, jokes, and anecdotes on the other.[25] In this same regard, the classic winter folksong cycle has been officially purged of its inextricable religious stratum relating to the Nativity in favor of a newer and more acceptable outlook:

> Heaven and earth, heaven and earth
> Rejoice today –
> The laboring masses throughout the world
> Are celebrating their freedom.[26]

The crass politicalization of traditional material includes the total lack of any reference whatsoever to erotic lore[27] and the circumvention of the varied insights into folklore and folklore processes offered by such apolitical approaches that are normally associated with formalism, psychoanalysis, sociology, structuralism, and, as mentioned above, the historical-geographical techniques of the Finnish school. An example of the party's open intolerance of non-Marxist-Leninist folkloristics is its long-standing effort to discredit the work of a rather special team: Myxajlo S. Hruševs'kyj (1866-1934) and his daughter, Kateryna Hruševs'ka (1900-1953).

It was noted earlier that M.S. Hruševs'kyj authored several major works of considerable importance for Ukrainian folkloristics and that, as president of the Central Council of the short-lived Ukrainian parliament from 1917 to 1918, he stands as a rare if not unique example of a head of state who also applied his talents to research in the field of folklore.[28] Modern Soviet sources brand him as a bourgeois nationalist and specify, among other things, that Hruševs'kyj did not comprehend or appreciate the "law of class struggle." His politically dubious reputation was unavoidably passed on to his daughter, Kateryna, who is responsible for what is still the most important work on the Ukrainian epic tradition, the *dumy*.[29] To a large degree, Hruševs'ka's complication and analysis mark a kind of culminating point in the nation's long-standing romance with its epos, as the ideal place to search for the noble, heroic and glorious moments in its history. In any case, the two volumes that together make up the work have been accused by Soviet critics of favoring the *gesunkenes Kulturgut* school of interpretation and, as a result, they have been blacklisted now for almost half a century.[30] A bibliographical rarity, the books are virtually unavailable, although a reprint edition is currently being prepared by Harvard's Ukrainian Research Institute. Berezovs'kyj's outline critique of K. Hruševs'ka's work in 1968 included the following, ostensibly scientific justification for this harsh reception:

> First, the author did not clearly perceive the demands of the historical study of popular creativity and did not consistently realize this principle. This was reflected in her grouping of works not by the concrete events reflected in the epos, not by stages of the historical evolution of the people, but usually according to theme and the general features of the specific milieus reflected in the texts ("*Dumy* of the Slaves," "*Dumy* about the Sea," "*Dumy* about the Steppes," "*Dumy* about the Knighthood," "*Dumy* about the Xmel'nyc'kyj Period").
>
> Second, K. Hruševs'ka overly categorically declared that the *dumy* are works of professionals (among whom she included beggars), overemphasized the role of the professional tradition in the development of the heroic epic underlining that some *dumy* emerged under the influence of this tradition; she said that the creators of the *dumy* do not necessarily have to be the eye-witnesses of or participants in the concrete historical events. In comparison with the works of F. Kolessa who underlined the popular origin of the *dumy* and their especially close ties with life and with the collective experience of the masses, the investigation of K. Hruševs'ka, particularly in the part in which she considered the problem of the genesis of the *dumy*, lost out from the methodological point of view.[31]

Hruševs'ka's work on the *dumy* was her last contribution to Ukrainian folklore scholarship. Deemed unreliable in the eyes of the Stalinist authorities, she was arrested in 1937 and deported to a concentration camp.[32]

More than any other chapter in the history of Ukrainian Soviet folkloristics the case of K. Hruševs'ka serves to illustrate the extremities to which the politicalization of folklore and folkloristics can lead. The quarrel here is not with the Soviet recognition of folklore as a potent instrument for social change, or with the state's preference for a single trend in Ukrainian folkloristics, but with the annihilation of other trends and the arbitrary imposition of a single standard for excellence in scientific research and investigation. These are the strictures that have made Ukrainian folkloristics under the Soviets a field only partially credible and a discipline deprived of its full potential. Recent achievements,[33] however, do indicate that a turning point is within reach. The signs are rich with promise, and one can only hope that the direction of change will serve to promote the formulation of a fresh and politically unencumbered *veritas* that exceeds all expectation.

Canadian Centre for Folk Culture Studies
National Museum of Man
Ottawa, Ontario
Canada

NOTES

[1] M. T. Ryl's'kyj et al., eds., *Ukrajins'ka narodna poetyčna tvorčist'* ("Ukrainian Folk/ People's Poetic Creativity"), Volume 1 (Kiev, 1958), p. 25.

[2] This was Myxajlo S. Hruševs'kyj (1866-1934). Several of his works are of importance for Ukrainian folkloristics, especially his survey of verbal creativity from the thirteenth to the seventeenth centuries (his *Istorija ukrajins'koji literatury* ["History of Ukrainian Literature"], Volume 1 [Kiev, 1923]).

[3] See, for example, the following English-language monographs: Yaroslav Bilinsky, *The Second Soviet Republic: The Ukraine after World War II* (Rutgers University Press, 1964); George S.N. Luckyj, *Literary Politics in the Soviet Ukraine, 1917-1934* (Columbia University Press, 1956); and Robert S. Sullivant, *Soviet Politics and the Ukraine, 1917-1957* (Columbia University Press, 1962).

[4] In the preparation of this paper the following works were of special interest: Ilhan Başgöz, "Folklore Studies and Nationalism in Turkey," *Journal of the Folklore Institute* 9 (1972): 162-176; Richard M. Dorson, "The Question of Folklore in a New Nation," *Journal of the Folklore Institute* 3 (1966): 277-298; M. Carole Henderson, "Folklore Scholarship and the Sociopolitical Milieu in Canada," *Journal of the Folklore Institute* 10 (1973): 97-107; B. Krawciw, "People's Way of Life, Folklore, and Art under the Soviets," *Ukraine: A Concise Encyclopaedia* 1 (University of Toronto Press, 1963), pp. 422-429; Felix J. Oinas, "Folklore and Politics in the Soviet Union," *Slavic Review* 32 (1973): 45-58; Vlajko Palavestra, "Tradition, History and National Feeling," *Journal of the Folklore Institute* 3 (1966): 267-276; and Chun-chiang Yen, "Folklore Research in Communist China," *Asian Folklore Studies* 26-2 (1967): 1-62.

[5] I. K. Bilodid, "Suspil'ni nauky (vstup)" ("The Social Sciences [Introduction]"), *Istorija Akademiji nauk Ukrajins'koji RSR* ("History of the Academy of Sciences of the Ukrainian SSR") 1 (Kiev, 1967), p. 297.

[6] Ju. P. Stupak, *Vyxovne značennja ukrajins'koho fol'kloru* ("The Educative Significance of Ukrainian Folklore") (Kiev, 1960), pp. 28-29.

[7] F. I. Lavrov, "Cenzumi utysky ta peresliduvannja ukrajins'koho fol'kloru v cars'kij Rosiji," in M.T. Ryl's'kyj, pp. 171-204.

[8] Ivan Dzyuba *Internationalism or Russification? A Study in the Soviet Nationalities Problem* (London, 1968), p. 144.

[9] I. P. Berezovs'kyj, *Ukrajins'ka radjans'ka fol'klorystyka. Etapy rozvytku i problematyka* (Kiev, 1968). See also V. Petrov's all too brief review in *Narodna tvorčist' ta etnohrafija* ("Folk/People's Creativity and Ethnography"), No. 1, 1969, 94-95.

[10] See, for example, pertinent references in N. Polons'ka-Vasylenko's historical survey of the Ukrainian Academy from 1918 to 1941, *Ukrajins'ka akademija nauk (Narys Istoriji)* 2 vols. (Munich, 1955-1958).

[11] This can be verified by consulting *Vydannja Akademiji nauk URSR 1919-1967. Suspil'ni nauky. Bibliohrafičnyj pokažčyk* ("Publications of the Academy of Sciences of the Ukr. SSR 1919-1967. Social Sciences. A Bibliographical guide") (Kiev, 1969).

[12] See P.M. Popov's biographical account, "Vydatnyj radjans'kyj fol'kloryst Ju. M. Sokolov" ("The Leading Soviet Folklorist, Ju. M. Sokolov"), *Narodna tvorčist' ta etnohrafija*, 1958, No. 3, 23-33.

[13] Berezovs'kyj, p. 328.

[14] See, for example, the following works: Francis Dvornik, *The Slavs Their Early History and Civilization* (Boston, 1956); Roman Jakobson, "The Kernel of Comparative Slavic Literature," *Harvard Slavic Studies* 1 (1953): 1-71; Kazimierz Moszyński, *Kultura ludowa słowian* 2 vols. (Kraków, 1934-1939); Lubor Niederle, *Manuel de l'antiquité slave* 2 vols. (Paris, 1923-1926); and many others.

[15] See, for example, the following publications: M. Hajdaj, *Čexoslovac'ko-ukrajins'ki vzajemyny v sučasnij fol'klorystyci (1918-1960)* ("Czechoslovak-Ukrainian Relations in Contemporary Folkloristics (1918-1960)") (Kiev, 1963); V.A. Juzvenko, *Ukrajins'ka narodna poetyčna tvorčist' u pol's'kij fol'klorystyci XIX st.* ("Ukrainian Folk/People's Poetic Creativity in Polish Folkloristics of the 19th Century") (Kiev, 1961); M.I. Kravcov, ed., *Mižslov'jans'ki fol'klorystyčni vzajemyny* ("Inter-Slavic Folkloristic Relations") (Kiev, 1963); N.S. Šumada, *Ukrajins'ko-bolhars'ki fol'klorystyčni zv'jazky (Period bolhars'koho vidrodžennja)* ("Ukrainian-Bulgarian Folkloristic Ties (The Period of the Bulgarian Revival)") (Kiev, 1963); H.S. Suxobrus, *Ukrajins'ko-rosijs'ki fol'klorni zv'jazky v osvitlenni vitčyznjanoji nauky peršoji polovyny XIX st.* ("Ukrainian-Russian Folkloric Ties in the Light of Domestic Scholarship in the 19th Century") (Kiev, 1963); and others.

[16] Abbreviated in Soviet sources as *NTE*, the journal is shared as the joint official organ of the Ukrainian Academy's Ryl's'kyj Institute for the Fine Arts, Folklore and Ethnography *and* the Ministry for Culture of the Ukrainian S.S.R. The *NTE* has had a rather motley career and is currently criticized in the West for its marked *Heimatskunde* bias and generally low level of scholarship (see Natalie Moyle's review of *NTE* for 1970 in *Recenzija; A Review of Soviet Ukrainian Scholarly Publications* 1 (1971): 73-80). An indication of the *NTE*'s popularity is reflected in the following comparative circulation figures for *NTE* and two leading Soviet Russian periodicals with kindred interests: the

first issue of *NTE* in 1973 was printed in 12,500 copies (up from 5,000 copies for its first issue in 1957); volume 13 of the annual *Russkij fol'klor* ("Russian Folklore") (1972) was printed in 3,000 copies (up from 1,500 copies for volume 8 in 1963); the sixth issue for *Sovetskaja etnografija* ("Soviet Ethnography") in 1973 was printed in 2,415 copies.

[17] See, for example, the following from *NTE*: V. Je. Husev, "Pro ponjattja j sut' fol'kloryzmu v umovax kapializmu i socializmu" ("About the Concept and Essence of Folklorismus in Conditions of Capitalism and Socialism"), *NTE* 1973, No. 5, 41-45; V. Ju. Kelembetova, "Pro dejaki naprjamky v sučasnij buržuaznij ethnohrafiji" ("About Certain Trends in Contemporary Bourgeois Ethnography"), *NTE* 1973, No. 6, 31-40; T.K. Kyčko, "Rasyzm - ideolohija sionizmu" ("Racism - the Ideology of Zionism"), *NTE* 1973, No. 5, 35-40; V.V. Tančer, " 'Masova kul'tura'–znarjaddja duxovnoji ekspansiji kapitalizmu" (" 'Mass Culture'–Capitalism's Tool for Spiritual Expansion"), *NTE* 1974, No. 1, 32-46; L.M. Zemljanova, "Prohresyvna pressa SŠA u borot'bi za peredovu fol'klorystyku" ("The Progressive Press in the U.S.A. in the Fight for an Advanced Folkloristics"), *NTE* 1961, No. 2, 72-79; and others.

[18] M.M. Pazjak, "Fol'klorystyčni vydannja 1972 roku" ("Folkloristic Publications of the Year 1972"), *NTE* 1973, No. 2, 88-92.

[19] Orest M. Hyža, *Ukrajins'ki narodni pisni z Lemkivščyny* ("Ukrainian Folksongs from the Lemko Region") (Kiev, 1972).

[20] V.E. Gusev, *Marksizm i russkaja fol'kloristika konca XIX načala XX veka* ("Marxism and Russian Folkloristics from the End of the 19th to the Beginning of the 20th Century") (Moscow, 1961), pp. 173-177.

[21] Pazjak, p. 90. In this same connection one should note also the ongoing publication of a special series of individual popular compilations of folksongs collected by various Ukrainian literary figures *(Ukrajins'ki narodni pisni v zapysax pys'mennykiv)* as well as the following monographs: V.H. Bojko, *Poetyčne slovo narodu i literaturnyj proces. Problema fol'klornyx tradycij v stanovlenni ukrajins'koji radjans'koji poeziji* ("The Poetic Word of the People and the Literary Process. The Problem of Folkloric Traditions in the Making of Ukrainian Soviet Poetry") (Kiev, 1965); A.A. Nazarevskij, *Iz istorii russko-ukrainskix literaturnyx svjazej. Starinnye knižnyze legendy i ix svjazi s russkim i ukrainskim fol'klorom* ("From the History of Russian Ukrainian Literary Ties. Ancient Book Legends and Their Ties with Russian and Ukrainian Folklore") (Kiev, 1963); and M.T. Ryl's'kyj, *Literatura i narodna tvorčist'* ("Literature and Folk/People's Creativity") (Kiev, 1956). A similar bias with regard to the field of music is reflected in the recent work of I. Ljašenko on national traditions in music as a historical process *(Nacional'ni tradyciji v muzyci jak istoryčnyj proces* [Kiev, 1973]).

[22] R. Jakobson and P. Bogatyrev, "K probleme razmeževanija fol'kloristiki i literaturovedenija" ("On the Problem of Distinguishing between Folkloristics and Literary Studies") in Roman Jakobson's *Selected Writings* 4 (The Hague, 1966), 16-18. (The theses outlined in the article were originally formulated in Prague in 1929 and published in *Lud słowianski* 2 [1931]: 229-233.)

[23] Hryhory Kytasty, *Some Aspects of Ukrainian Music under the Soviets* (New York, 1954), p. 57.

[24] The rationale behind the Soviet aversion for the Finnish method was succinctly described by Richard M. Dorson in his article on "Current Folklore Theories," *Current Anthropology* 4 (1963): 97.

[25] For example, see the following collections: *I pip i ks'ondz i rabyn. Ukrajins'ki narodni atejistyčni pisni ta prykazky* ("The Pastor, the Priest and the Rabbi: Ukrainian Folk/People's Atheistic Songs and Proverbs") (Kiev, 1957); and the Academy publication compiled by M.S. Rodina and F.D. Tkačenko, *Narod pro relihiju; zbirnyk fol'klornyx tvoriv* ("The People about Religion: A Collection of Folkloric Works") (Kiev, 1958). Similar Ukrainian folkloric items are found in a collection published by the State Publishing House for Political Literature in Moscow: *Narod o religii. Na materialax russkogo, ukrainskogo i belorusskogo fol'klora* ("The People about Religion from Russian, Ukrainian and Byelorussian Folklore Materials") (Moscow, 1961).

[26] O.I. Dej, *Koljadky ta ščedrivky. Zymova obrjadova poezija trudovoho roku* ("Carols and New Year Songs. The Winter Ritualistic Poetry of the Working Year") (Kiev, 1965), p. 631.

[27] Soviet Ukrainian sources ignore, for example, the following materials that are of direct interest to Ukrainian folkloristics: Sigmund Freud and D.E. Oppenheim, *Dreams in Folklore* (New York, 1958); V. Hnatjuk, "Die Brautkammer. Eine Episode aus dem ukrainischen Hochzeitbräuchen," *Anthropophyteia* 6 (1909): 113-149; V. Hnatjuk, "Ein erotisches ukrainisches Lied aus dem XVII Jahrhundert," *Anthropophyteia* 6 (1909): 344-347; V. Hnatjuk, "Parallelen zu einem magyarischen Volkslied," *Anthropophyteia* 6 (1909): 347-352; P. Tarasevskyj, *Das Geschlechtleben des ukrainischen Bauernvolkes* 2 Vols. (Leipzig, 1909-1912).

[28] See note no. 2, above.

[29] Kateryna Hruševs'ka, *Ukrajins'ki narodni dumy* 2 Vols. (Kiev, 1927-1931). The first volume was extensively reviewed by V.N. Peretc in *Etnohrafičnyj visnyk* ("The Ethnographic Herald") 7 (1928): 73-132.

[30] The Soviet aversion for K. Hruševs'ka's work is noted in Polons'ka-Vasylenko, Vol. II, pp. 74-75, 196, and by O. Pritsak in his review of the bibliographic guide cited in note no. 11, above, in *Recenzija. A Review of Soviet Ukrainian Scholarly Publications* 1 (1970): 35-36.

[31] Berezovs'kyj, pp. 130-131.

[32] Polons'ka-Vasylenko, Vo. II, pp. 74-75.

[33] Of special significance in this regard are the currently accelerated efforts to select and reprint the "acceptable" folkloristic works of deceased scholars such as I. Franko, V. Hnatjuk, M. Hrinčenko, F. Kolessa, and K. Kvitka.

A SONG ABOUT THE COLLAPSE OF THE NOLI GOVERNMENT IN ALBANIA

John S. Kolsti

A song recorded in the Albanian Highlands in 1937 tells of the return of Ahmet Zog to Albania in 1924 and the collapse of the Fan Noli government. It was taken down by Albert Lord in the Albanian Highlands in 1937 from a non-Moslem singer,[1] Gjok Pjetri of Kastrati. While most of the songs Lord collected are in Albanian decasyllables and mostly exceed five hundred lines (one contains over two thousand), the song about Fan Noli and Ahmet Zog is short, containing only two hundred lines. It deals with events which took place a little over ten years before Lord recorded them. In this paper we shall examine the song's historicity to determine to what extent the singer's political biases and prejudices affect its content, and we shall also analyze the singer's style to follow his ability to compose regular octosyllabic (or decasyllabic) verse in Albanian. Let us turn first to the problem of versification.[2]

THE SONG

The song begins with a typical formula invoking the name of God and adds that there is no other king like that of the Albanians:

Lumit Zot i kjofshim fal
Mbretin t'onë kerkush se ka

The introductory lines are octosyllabic; by line 5, however, the singer falls into a rhyming pattern using the participial ending *-ue*, moving from the longer 4-6 line typical of the Albanian epics back to the 4-4 line of the ballads:[3]

Ahmet Begun e kishin tradhëtue
Kishin sjellë vodat me votue

Disa vota ja kishin ndalue
Ahmet Begu ish idhnue
Prej Shqipnies kish dal e shkue

In line 10 the singer ends his line with the noun *Serbie*; the next six lines rhyme as follows:

kan hi	(verb)
Zotni	(noun)
Madhni	(noun)
te ri	(adj.)
e mi	(adj.)
Shqipni	(noun)

After six octosyllabic lines he switches in line 16 into longer style; but he repeats the line, rearranging his formulas to end the verse with the verbal form *çue*, and once again falls into the style of the ballads:

Per mem çue dhe nji herë ne Shqipni
Dhe i herë ne Shqipni mem çue
General gradat i due
Tjerat vet kam me i fitue . . .

This switching back and forth between octosyllables and decasyllables continues throughout the whole song. A good example of this is the singer's use of two substitution systems to express the idea of assembling the clans:

Hot e Grude me mi bashkue (29)
Mem bashkue Plave e Guisnje

In line 86 the singer "splits" the six-syllable formula *Plave e Gusinje,* beginning the line with the verb form *mbledhim:*

Mbledhim Plave e Gusinje

Another example which demonstrates the different substitution systems occurs in line 130 and 131. The longer line ends in a six-syllable unit after the caesura: a noun object is followed by the auxilliary verb and the participial form. The next verse is shortened[4] by the omission of the object in the second half of the line:

Ne Tiranë	/	giylet i kish leshue
Merr Fan Noli		(letrën) e kish kendue

In the performance of this short song the singer formulated approximately seventy-five percent of his lines in octosyllables; the remaining lines apparently were recited in the style of the epic songs.[5] Regardless of the length of the lines, the singer frequently fell into patterns of rhyme and assonance. In fact, approximately sixty-six percent of his lines end in this manner, verbal forms accounting for just over one half of these lines. In one such pattern eight lines end in the familiar participial desinence *-ue*. After a single-line break in this string another thirteen lines continue the rhyme. While this verbal pattern is very useful to the singer, he is not incapable of maintaining the rhyme by employing totally different formulaic expressions. This occurs in line 54 and 55:

Mbasi ti i ke lejue
Shka asht Shiptar desin per mue (pro.)

The fact that the singer is experienced enough to rhyme lines using different formulaic patterns and (however awkward) of varying length emerges in his conclusive invocation:

Kjoft e rrnoft bashk me Shqiptar
Kjoft e errnoft mbret e Zogu i Pare (200)

The same practice of maintaining rhyme while switching from one style of versification to another may be found in songs recorded during the second World War. Four lines from a Partisan song recorded in 1942[6] clearly demonstrate this tendency among some Albanian singers—a tendency the bilingual Ugljanin so strongly resisted:

Vjenë ushtria nga Luznia,
Vjenë ushtria për mjedis Luznisë,
Për me dalun n' at fushë t' Alisë,
Me djek kullat e gjithë parisë.

To sum up, we may say that the singer recorded by Lord in 1938 does in fact belong in the oral tradition of the Albanians. His two hundred line song reveals that he is skilled in producing both octosyllabic and decasyllabic verse, willing to employ both for the purpose of producing or continuing a rhyme pattern. Of all the singers recorded by Lord during his field trip in Malsi, Gjok Pjetri is the only one to have this particular trait. Had Lord been looking for more such material he no doubt would have found it. As it is, he did record *per kujtim*[7] a song curious not only because of its hybrid style but also because of its content. Let us now turn to the problem of folksong as history, keeping in mind the obvious Geg prejudices that this song reflects.

THE STORY

Song No. 15 in the Lord Collection is titled "The Song of the Flight of King Zog I to Yugoslavia." A much more appropriate title would be "The Song of the Return of Ahmet Zog from Yugoslavia." The singer, in praise of his king, describes how Zog and his followers among the Moslem Albanians in Yugoslavia return to Albania, with the full support of the Yugoslav government headed by Pašić. Zog, leading his mercenary army, successfully reaches the Albanian capital, Tirana, and proceeds to shell the town, forcing the local government officials to flee the "liberating" army in total disgrace. The officials, after they have pilfered money from the state treasury, are driven by their chauffeurs to the coast where they board vessels to flee to Italy. Having saved Albania from the government of Fan Noli, a "nobody,"[8] Zog gains control of the government and sets about the task of healing the wounds caused by needless political bickering among the Albanians. "That's the kind of person he is," concludes the singer.

Was he? Is this particular song of any historical value at all, or is it simply a propagandistic tool, or faulty product in the singer's workshop? The song about Fan Noli and Ahmet Zog is, unfortunately, a combination of all three factors: in spite of the factual errors and the obvious political bias, the singer does stress the role of the leader of the Serbian Radical Party in the return of Ahmet Zog to power in Albania—an event that marked the end of parliamentary government in Albania in the 1920s and checked, temporarily, the emergence of western educated, anti-feudal, primarily Tosk critics of the political power of the Moslem beys. Let us turn to the song itself to see how Pjetri viewed the circumstances surrounding Zog's return from exile in December of 1924.

The Story (lines)	Historical Background[9]
Introductory Invocation (1-2)	
Fan Noli and Ahmet Zog have quarreled. (3-4)	In 1921 Colonel Ahmet Beg Zogu and Col. Bajram Curri successfully blocked Yugoslav-supported attempts by a Geg (Catholic) chieftain to establish the "Republic of Mirdita" in the Highlands. But "settling of accounts" between Bajram Curri and Zog resulted in Zog's troops "defending" the Tirana government from the insurgents. With his troops in power in the capital Zog was able to declare martial law. His strong-arm tactics resulted in Fan Noli's resignation of his post as Foreign Minister in Xhafer Ypi's government. Zog used his cabinet post as Minister of the Interior to con-

solidate his military and political base in the country.

The election fraud enrages Zog, who was cheated of some votes. (5-8)

Fan Noli led a coalition of anti-Zogist elements–which included Bajram Curri, Col. Rexhep Shala, the military commander of the Shkodra district, and Tosk agrarian and political radicals–which deprived Zog of a clear-cut majority in the elections of December, 1923. The consequences of an assassination attempt on Zog's life two months later, not the outcome of the elections, finally forced Zog out of office as Minister of the Interior and as Prime Minister.

Zog leaves Albania and goes to talk with Pašić in Yugoslavia. (9-11)

Zog's bitter enemy Avrem Rustemi was murdered by Zog's Mati clansmen. The vendetta-style killing resulted in an armed rebellion against Zog, led by Bajram Curri and Col. Rexhep Shala who was dismissed by Zog after he had countersigned a manifesto inviting Parliament to meet in Shkodra in protest to Zogist terror. Zog was forced to fly to Belgrade. His prospective father-in-law, whom Zog had just recently appointed as his "successor," and who represented the feudal landlords who bitterly opposed changes in the social and political system handed down after five hundred years of Ottoman rule, fled to Mussolini's Italy.

Zog confers with Nikola Pašić. He asks support for a military venture against the Fan Noli government: specifically, he requests permission to recruit Kosovars for the attack on Tirana, adding that he will pay them out of his own pocket. Zog explains that he has no need of Yugoslav troops. (12-36)

Zog's dealings in Yugoslavia, both in Belgrade and among the Kosovars, lasted approximately six months. Pašić feared the possible effect of Fan Noli's reform movement among the Albanians inside Yugoslavia. The "Red Scare" propaganda of the Pašić government was directed not only at Bishop Noli, but also at irridendist leaders among the Gegs, including Bajram Curri, who had been active against the Yugoslavs two years before Zog's exile.

Pašić agrees to allow Zog to recruit his volunteers and promises him that his mercenaries will be given access to roads leading across the border into Albania. He cannot give him any of his own troops, he adds. Pleased with this arrangement, Zog bids Pašić farewell. (37-57)

Zog had asked for and was provided not only with Yugoslav officers but also with troops from the remnants of Wrangle's White Russian Army. He had good reason to be pleased with his dealings with Pašić.

Zog reports on his conversation with Pašić to some of his supporters, who swear allegiance to the future king of the Albanians. They in turn inform Cena Beg of the plan to invade Albania, an invasion that Cena Beg is to help lead. (58-118)

Border incidents increased in intensity as the date for the full-scale invasion of Albania neared. Zogist elements were active all along the border, from Montenegro to Greece. The major assault was to be in the south, in the Dibra area, where Zog's pro-Yugoslav brother-in-law, Cena Beg Kryeziu, was based.

The invasion begins when Cena Beg leads his three thousand volunteers across the Dibra Line into Albania on Christmas Eve. Tirana is reached and shells fall on the city. (119-130)

Approximately ten thousand troops, including heavy artillery, crossed the Albanian border December 10-13. Serious resistance was not met by the invaders who reached Tirana on Christmas Eve. Fan Noli's achievement of balancing the national budget was all for nothing as one military unit after another severed its allegiance to the Tirana government, with clan loyalties[10] once again undermining any attempts to create a strong, centralized government.

An ultimatum is delivered to Fan Noli, who loses control of the situation. He summons Rexhep Shala, and the decision is made to have chauffeurs drive them to Durrës[11] from which they board a vessel for Italy. All Albania is astonished by their fleeing to a foreign land. (131-160)

Seeing that the military situation was hopeless, Fan Noli and his supporters abandoned Tirana and fled to the coast. With the approach of Zogist forces from the Greek front, Fan Noli made his escape to Italy, as Shefqet Vërlaci, Zog's prospective father-in-law, had done six months earlier.

At midnight Zog enters Tirana too impatient to wait until Christmas morning. He makes a speech in which he condemns the government officials who left their offices in disarray and who robbed the state treasury before fleeing abroad,

Zog entered Tirana with little more notice than when he had left it in June: the country was not being subject to one crippling revolution after another as various political parties were "settling accounts" with each other. Tirana had not even forging the name of Zog I on their edicts. He proclaims an amnesty[12] of thirty days for his fellow Albanians to return home, so long as they stay out of politics in the future. He wants state funds to go towards helping the poor, not towards financing campaigns to crush any political opposition, for "such a man is Zog I." (161-198)

yet attained its position of superiority over other Albanian cities both north and south. Instead of an amnesty, Zog crushed his long-time foe Bajram Curri in Malsia in March, 1925.[13] In the same month Luigj Gurakuqi, who had prepared the manifesto of the previous June, was assassinated in Bari, Italy. Political opposition to Zog's terroristic policies found no home in Mussolini's Italy. Zog, who had, through the Parliament, proclaimed Albania a Republic and himself as President in January, almost immediately after his take over, had also returned Fan Noli's favor by pronouncing the death penalty on him *in absentia.*

By September of 1928 Zog's power was such that he had himself proclaimed King of the Albanians, just halfway through his seven-year term as President.

"Long live King Zog I among the Albanians!" concludes the singer.

(199-200)

Zog's rule was to last just six more months after this song was sung. Zog's political and economic concessions made to the Italians from 1925 on were to result in an ultimatum sent to Tirana from Mussolini and the invasion of Albania by Italy on Good Friday, April 7, 1939. Zog and his followers fled to Greece; and Sefqet Vërlaci headed the new government which abolished the Constitution of 1928 and passed the crown to King Victor Emmanuel III of Italy.

The brief historical summary, reconstructed both from Albanian and non-Albanian writings covering this period, suffices to show, not surprisingly, that Ahmet Zog, the heroic figure in this historical narrative poem, is far removed from the young military officer with the rank of colonel who, in the space of a few years, employing terrorist tactics inside the country while balancing the external threat posed by Yugoslavia and Mussolini's Italy, managed to have himself proclaimed King of the Albanians. The singer's view of history, it is obvious, is blurred by his loyalty to one of the most powerful Moslem beys in Albania and his hostility towards the Harvard educated founder of the Independent Albanian Orthodox Church. The singer himself seems to want to "settle accounts" with this "nobody" who still represents for him the potentially dangerous intellectual stratum of Tosks (and Gegs) who, in 1938, would soon find themselves in a life and death struggle against Fascist Italian and, finally, Nazi German invaders. The death blow to the singer's world was just a matter of a few years in the future. It is interesting to speculate how the singer might have been able to repeat his song theme for theme to sing of the "disgraceful" flight of King Zog I to Greece, after the state treasury had been "pilfered!"

THEMATIC ANALYSIS

The thematic structure[14] of the singer's song is fairly simple, as the general outline below will show. What is curious, however, is the fact that Zog, except for his appeal to Pašić in one conversation, his report to his men in another, and his proclamation of amnesty at the end of the song (where the singer finds occasion to praise his king), has little else to do with the song. Most of the action themes developed beyond a single line or two revolve around Fan Noli and, to a lesser extent, Cena Beg. This fact may be seen at a glance in the following outline.

Main Themes	lines	
Introduction	1-7	
Travel	9-11	Zog from Albania
Conversation	12-37	Zog
	38-54	Pašić
Travel	55-58	
Conversation	59-75	Zog
	76-105	Juke
	106-114	*halal*, or farewell blessing
Assembly-Battle	115-130	Cena Beg
Ultimatum	131-139	Fan Noli
Assembly-Travel	140-160	Fan Noli and Rexhep Shala
Travel	161-164	Zog to Tirana
Amnesty	165-196	Zog
Conclusion	197-200	

The outline shows that approximately three-fourths of the lines in the song involve conversations, including Fan Noli's reading of the ultimatum.

Zog's appeal to Pašić is elaborated in the conversations which follow it, a convenient device for lengthening a song. Most interesting in these conversations, from a purely thematic viewpoint, is the *halal* blessing described by the singer in lines 106-114. These lines, perhaps more than any others, remind the reader of the longer epic songs; the singer expresses the farewell exchange between his heroes fully in the style of the Albanian and Bosnian epics. He obviously is capable of incorporating not only substitution systems from the different styles of singing he has heard but the themes as well. Interesting too, is the reading of the ultimatum by Fan Noli: the singer has not described, to say nothing of elaborating, Zog's writing or sending of the letter. Indeed, even the word "letter" is missing from the theme.

It is worthy of note, finally, that the singer throughout the conversation in his songs adds his own opinions or interpretation of the events being described, be it through the figure of Musa Juke in the hotel room in Belgrade or Zog himself addressing the population of Tirana. If the song is uneven, or "irregular" (as Ugljanin would complain) at the formulaic level, we may ascribe this to the ideas the singer is working into his song, which otherwise falls into the category of historical not traditional, or epic, folksongs.

The song, for all its poetic and historical shortcomings, nevertheless adds an important note to the significance of Lord's collection of Albanian folksongs in the 1930s. Publication of his materials, as well as Albanian collections containing the same singers recorded years later,[15] will only help to demonstrate the richness of a heritage of oral tradition that is still alive among the Albanians. Songs political or historical in content, regardless of the socioeconomic world-view of the performer, merit as much attention as the traditional ballads and epics. Just as little attention must be paid to what Ugljanin has to say about the art of oral composition as to the "accuracy" of the so-called "historical songs." Similarly, songs recorded since the war deserve as much attention today as the songs which have fortunately survived from the past.

The University of Texas
Austin, Texas

APPENDIX

No. 15 THE SONG OF THE FLIGHT OF KING ZOG I TO YUGOSLAVIA

Praise be to God, there is none like our king. However, a split occurred in Albania: Fan Noli and Ahmet Beg quarreled. Ahmet Beg was cheated. When the election was held, he was deprived of some votes. Ahmet Beg became distressed. He quit Albania and went to Servia (10). He went to see Pashiç and said to him: "I am glad I find you well, sir." "Welcome, you highness," (he answered). "I have come to make friends with you" (Ahmet Beg then said). "You know I have quarreled with my friends. Send me back into Albania, even back into Albania with the rank of general. I will attend to the rest myself: no one is going to rule over me (20). I do not want your soldiers; I have no need of their assistance. I have only one favor to ask of you: I want only my fellow Albanians in the districts of Luma and even to the border which are under your control to help me get into Albania. For I intend to return to Albania to assemble Hot and Grude, and Plave and Gusinje (30). I will take volunteers, and pay them all, so I can return to Albania. I will send these Albanians back to you. If you do me this good turn, I will be your friend forever." Consider what Pashiç said to him: "You have to come to see me as a friend. May God help you. You have been of great service to Albania (40); I will do you this small favor. I cannot give you my troops; but I will assemble Hot and Grude, even Hot and Grude and Montenegro. I can give you Plave and Gusinje, and also Diber on this side of the border. When you have the three thousand volunteers I will open the roads for you. You speak to them, you highness; because I cannot compel them (to cross the border)" (50).

Ahmet Beg was pleased, and he said to Pashiç,[16] "Since I have your permission, all true Albanians will die for me." Ahmet Beg rose to his feet, even rising to his feet and extending his hand to thank Pashic. He went to a hotel to report to Musa Juke and a few others, including Zef Serreqi (60). "I have come to an honorable agreement with Pashiç. But listen to me, my brothers. I have no need to seek fame, but wish only to rescue Albania; for Fan Noli is a nobody who will ruin Albania within one year. Let us now as true brothers join in a vow to die for the Fatherland. Rise now to the task (70) and inform all Albanians that Hot and Grude, which are on the Montenegrin border, are ours, that they are rallying to our Party and will make our Party strong." Musa Juke spoke up (and said): "Do not worry, King of the Albanians; for if you keep your word and have good luck, you will soon reach Tirana. (80) I myself will assemble Hot and Grude, even Hot and Grude and Montenegro. With Zef Shuke sworn to our cause, we will quickly move into Albania. We will send word to Cena Beg and assemble Plave and Gusinje and the neighboring districts. Two or three thousand men will be assembled, to be commanded by Cena Beg. When the Diber front is reached (90) I will open fire and we will surround the whole of Albania. And on the other front Zef Shuke will command Hot and Grude, and from the Hot flank will open fire from four directions." This is how the Albanian heroes allied themselves. They shook hands with Zog, agreeing to make their move when seven days and a week pass (100). "Either we will perish or we will return to Albania. May you rule over Albania; may you rule over the Albanians, together with us proudly by your side." The heroes stood up and parted shaking hands in a farewell blessing, as is the custom of the Albanian heroes. "We do not know if we shall live or die once we enter the battle (110). Perhaps our fate is to die and never to see each other again in this life. But however many Albanians are left will be ready to die for their king." The heroes then parted, having set the date to start the attack in order to destroy the opposition. Cena Beg was alerted to assemble the clans (120) and to march to the Diber line.

Cena Beg rose to his feet and assembled three thousand men. He set out for Diber. He reached the Diber line, even crossing the Diber line on Christmas Eve to lend aid to the Albanian people. He began to shell Tirana, even dropping shells on Tirana (130). Fan Noli received (an ultimatum): "Give me back my position: you cannot usurp my post. I was the one who created Albania, spending my wealth for it, and I intend to save Albania. When I received my schooling all I studied was Albania." Fan Noli was distraught. He rose to his feet (140) not knowing what course to take. He summoned Rexhep Shala, even summoned him and said: "Zog the First has routed us. I have no other choice, Rexhep, but to give in to him. He intends to make himself king and will not give up Albania before he dies." The two of them rose to their feet and summoned all the chauffeurs (150). All the nobles gathered, climbed into automobiles and made straight for Durres. They boarded a ship and set sail for Italy. All Albania looked on in amazement. Men with self pride who regarded themselves as true Albanians opposed them. "Why did they flee to another country?" (they asked) (160).

On Christmas Eve, at midnight, Zog reached Tirana: he who was called Zog the First could not wait for the night to pass. Then Zog spoke as follows: "I am dumbfounded by these officials who left their offices, even leaving them wide open, without any consideration for the fatherland. They made off with the treasury (170) and still call themselves Albanians. They squandered funds in every direction, forging orders with the signature of Zog the First. To those who call themselves Albanians and who desire to return to Albania I will grant amnesty. I will restore their former rights: we shall die as brother Albanians, as brave and loyal Albanians. We need not emigrate (180). Why leave for foreign countries? Why depend on foreign kings? Since we call ourselves true Albanians we should work together in Albania."

That is what Zog the First is like. He bears no ill will against any Albanian. He granted a thirty day amnesty to those desiring to come back to Albania, so long as they left their politics behind (190). "No one can oppose me," (he said). "I will only have to waste money; and it is a shame to waste the Fatherland's money when our peasants are poor. What use to them is our squabbling for power?"

Thus he became a sovereign king, the sovereign Zog the First. Long may he live together with the Albanians! Long live King Zog the First!

(I am from Malsia. I have never attended school, and I can't read or write. May you remember me by my song of our king sung to the lahuta.)

Gjok Pjetri
September 8, 1937
Pjetroshani, Kastrati

NOTES

[1] See appendix for the translation of this song, ms. 15 of Lord's unpublished collection. The Lord Collection is in Widener Library, Harvard University, Cambridge.

[2] Lord has edited and translated songs recorded in the field with the Milman Parry in his *Serbo-Croatian Heroic Songs*, 2 vols. (Cambridge and Belgrade: Harvard University Press and the Serbian Academy of Sciences, 1954). Conversations with Ugljanin have also been included in those valuable volumes.

In *The Singer of Tales* (Cambridge: Harvard University Press, 1964), Lord has made a study of Ugljanin's art of oral composition both at the thematic and formulaic levels.

[i] These conversations appear in my unpublished dissertation, "The Bilingual Singer," (Harvard University, 1968). Ugljanin, who had continued to sing in Albanian long after he had gained notoriety in Albania as a singer of Bosnian epics, viewed with some disdain the Albanian ballads, or "women's songs," he consented to demonstrate for Parry, "translating" them (to use his word) into Serbo-Croatian octosyllabic verse! Ugljanin's comments, in my opinion, help explain why scholars like A. Schmaus and Stavro Skendi (see his *Albanian and South Slavic Epic Poetry* [Philadelphia: American Folklore Society, 1954]) make erroneous comparisons between songs and singers in Albanian and Serbo-Croatian, to the detriment of the oral tradition among the Albanians. This is expecially surprising when both use data supplied by a bilingual singer perfectly capable of repeating both epic songs (in decasyllables) and ballads (in octosyllables) in both languages. For Ugljanin, the problems caused by Parry's interpreter's line of questioning are not related to any "translating" of formulas across linguistic lines (something which I concluded at the end of my study, does not take place at all during an actual performance), but instead to the unheard-of thought of rendering in one style of singing songs which belong to the other, regardless of the language involved.

[3] The 4-4 line and the 4-6 line are syllabic in Serbo-Croatian. Their counterparts in Albanian are not: their rhythm is like that of the Serbo-Croatian epic songs and "women's songs," but the syllabic count is highly irregular, something Ugljanin was quick to point out. Something, too, that Lord noted about certain "irregularities" in Ugljanin's own performances in Serbo-Croatian.

[4] Since not much else is known about this singer, it may be incorrect to say he "shortens" his lines to produce octosyllabic verse. It is correct to say this of Ugljanin, however. who accomplished just this for Parry in both Albanian and Serbo-Croatian.

[5] Although the Lord Collection was not orally recorded, as was Ugljanin's singing in Albanian, it is not too difficult to distinguish between the shorter and longer lines in the various songs, there being few such problems in the traditional songs which make up most of the collection.

[6] See No. 93 in Arsen Mustaqi's anthology, *Këngë Popullore Historike* ("Historical Folk Songs") (Tirana: Universiteti Shtetëror i Tiranës, 1968), p. 153.

[7] The singer's comments about himself and his singing the song *per kujtim* "as a remembrance" are given at the end of the appendix.

[8] Fan Noli was hardly a "nobody," as evidenced by his numerous literary and

scholarly achievements, including a stuay of the music of Beethoven and the French Revolution, a history of George Castrioti, or Skenderbeg, and translations of Shakespeare and Edgar Allen Poe into Albanian. When I was introduced to him in Boston, Massachusetts, I was struck by his small size: to all generations of Albanians living in America he was truly an awesome figure, as recent Albanian scholarship is demonstrating, as witnessed by the research being conducted by Prof. Koço Bihiku at the University of Tirana.

[9] For a brief biographical sketch of both Fan Noli and Zog see L.S. Starvianos, *The Balkans Since 1453*, pp. 717f. Good coverage of the period is provided in Joseph Swire's *Albania, The Rise of a Kindgom* and Stefanaq Pollo's *Historia e Popullit Shqiptar* ("History of the Albanian People").

[10] Of general interest on this point is Ian Whitaker's, "Tribal Structures and National Politics in Albania, 1910-1950," reprinted from *A.S.A. Monographs* 7 (London, 1968).

[11] This flight from Tirana in a motorcade reminds one of a somewhat similar departure by the Greek Metropolitan Jakopos from Korcha approximately three years earlier, when the Albanian government had just survived Yugoslav-supported insurrectionists among the Catholic Gegs of the Mirdita Clan in the north, and pressure from the Greeks and Grecophone Albanians in the south. It is precisely in this period that Ahmet Zog began to usurp power in the Xhafer Ypi cabinet, a move aided by Fan Noli's resignation as Foreign Minister.

[12] A general amnesty had been proclaimed in 1921 after the "Sacred Union" had secured the territorial integrity of Albania. Zog, it turned out, was not as lenient toward his political enemies. After the death of Bajram Curri and the assassination of Luigj Gurakuqi, he maintained the policy of granting more and more economic and political concessions to Italy against the advice of his brother-in-law, Cena Beg, whom he had appointed Minister of the Interior. Cena Beg was assassinated in Prague in the fall of 1927. Pro-Italian supporters of Zog, including Musa Juke and Zef Serreqi, to say nothing of Vërlaci, helped turn Zog towards Mussolini, waging internally a campaign of terror against a new threat to the government: namely, a growing Communist movement among Tosk (e.g. western educated Enver Hoxha) and Geg intellectuals.

[13] Songs of Bajram Curri may be found in recent anthologies of Albanian folksongs. In Dhimitër Shuteriqi's anthology of Albanian literature, *Antologjia e Letërisisë Shqipe* appears a poem by Fan Noli (p. 253), which eulogizes Bajram Curri's death in his mountain hide-out, a castle-like cave radiantly illuminating the heavens for the liberation of Albania, a catacomb. Even Ugljanin would have appreciated the force of Fan Noli's final verses typical of the "Albanian songs" he tried to demonstrate for Parry:

> Me zjarr' shenjt u ndrit kjo shpellë
> gjer në qiejt u ngrit Kështjellë
> për çlirimin' e Shqipërisë,
> Katakomb' i Dragobisë.

[14] For an analysis of thematic structures of oral epic songs see David Bynum, "A Taxonomy of Oral Narrative Song" (Ph. D. diss., Harvard University, 1964). Bynum, in his thesis, used data taken from Serbo-Croatian materials. I found his approach

excellently suited to Albanian data in the Lord Collection.

15 For example, manuscripts collected by Q. Haxhihasani in the Archives of the Folklore Commission, which contain a song of Musa the Highwayman by Sokol Martini, recorded 14 years after the singer recited the story for Lord. Haxhihasani's version has been published in his *Kenge Popullore Legjendare* ("Legendary Folk Songs") (Tiranë: Instituti i Shkencave, 1955), pp. 273 ff. The song is No. 40 in the Lord Collection; it contains 170 lines. (I have translated the songs in the Lord Collection and hope to publish both Lord's and Parry's materials in Albanian in the near future.)

16 The Albanian spelling for Pašić (Pashich).

FOLKLORE STUDIES AND NATIONALISM IN TURKEY

İlhan Başgöz

Interest in folklore began in Turkey in the second half of the nineteenth century when the need was felt to forge a national language which could be understood by the majority. The language used by the Ottoman intellectuals and men of letters, especially in their writings, was composed largely of the vocabulary and the grammatical rules of Arabic and Persian. This domination was increased by the contribution of religious and educational institutions to such a degree that the common people did not understand the language of law, official writing, or literature. The Ottoman intellectuals and writers were not affected by this communication gap so long as the function of literature remained pleasing the court with eulogies and praise of wine and the pleasures of love.

The Tanzimat reforms, which were introduced in 1839, inaugurated a functional change in Ottoman literature. A new generation of writers who were in contact with the West, especially France, and admired the economic, social, and educational institutions of Europe, soon realized that literature played an important role in the development of these institutions. They returned to Turkey and followed Western models, introducing novels, short stories, plays, and journalism, which had been unknown in the Ottoman past and which now carried a message to the common people. Through these new forms writers hoped to enlighten the people in order to gain their support for social and political changes. Their success, however, in influencing people by means of literature was limited, simply because only a few people understood the language of their writings.

Thus the necessity of reforming the language and of facilitating language teaching appeared in this background in the 1860s. Ahmet Midhat Efendi (1884-1913) posed the problem in this way:

> Our literary language is not the language of one nation. It is not Persian, Arabic or Turkish. The masterpieces of our literature cannot be understood by an Arab or Persian. We also cannot claim that it is our literature, because we do not understand it either. Are we getting to be a nation without a language? No, because our common people have a language which they understand. Let us replace theirs with our literary language, and create a national language out of it.[1]

To create a literature using the language of "common people," which was pure Turkish and unspoiled by foreign influences, made the Tanzimat writers interested in folklore and folk literature. İbrahim Şinasi (1826-71) wrote a play in 1859 using language simple enough to be understood by the uneducated masses in İstanbul.[2] Three years later he published a collection of four thousand proverbs.[3] Another writer, Ziya Pasha (1829-80), declared that "our genuine language and literature are the ones living among the people. Our national poetry and verses are still alive among the minstrels and the common people."[4] Many other poets, novelists, playwrights, and the intellectuals joined the movement between 1860 and 1900. In order to popularize his novels, Hüseyin Rahmi (1864-1944) employed the narration techniques of the shadow theatre performers and of the traditional storytellers.[5] Ahmet Midhat Efendi composed short stories based on the proverbs taken from Şinasi's collection in order to teach morals to the people,[6] and Abdülhak Hamid (1851-1937) filled one of his plays with local expressions and proverbs.[7] Finally, at the turn of the century, Mehmet Emin (1869-1944), using extensively the metric system of folk poetry and the themes expressing national feeling, won the title of "national poet."[8]

Despite their practical interest in the language and literature of the folk, the intellectuals of this period did not recognize the value of folklore as a whole. For example, Namık Kemal (1840-88) condemned the folktale as a genre completely out of touch with reality and nature, a genre which fails to describe morality, tradition, or the feelings of individuals, all of which are necessary elements of all art forms.[9] Süleyman Faik expressed his opinions on the same matter in this way: "They are the product of lazy people and just lies which were listened to by simple-minded folk."[10] When the famous Hungarian folklorist Ignácz Kúnos visited Turkey in the 1880s and revealed his program to collect Turkish folklore, the Ottoman writers advised him to engage in a more serious subject.[11]

The emergence of Turkish nationalism marked a new era in the attitude of intellectuals toward folklore. Nationalism, which had shaken the nineteenth century history of Europe, did not become an important force in Turkey until the First World War. In this delay the heterogenous structure of the Empire and the attitude of the ruling class toward Muslim-Turks played important roles. National consciousness among minorities, such as Greeks, Bulgarians, Albanians, and Arabs, might speed the independence movements that would destroy the Empire, so nationalism was strongly opposed. Furthermore, a nationalism based on Turkish culture was unimaginable for Ottoman intellectuals; the term "Türk" was associated with peasant ignorance and stupidity. As the Turkish people in the Empire were never viewed by the rulers as a national unit in which political power rested, but as subjects whose main duty was to fight, national pride was hardly able to develop among them.

The rulers and the intelligentsia, two power groups capable of creating a national spirit and developing the Empire into a national Turkish state, identified themselves primarily as Moslems and Ottomans. They felt offended when they were called Turks. When one of these writers wrote a poem that was understood and appreciated by the folk, his response was, "What a mistake I made. I see the common people enjoying my poetry."[12]

Studies in pre-Islamic Turkish history and language in Europe, the nationalism and independence movement among minorities in the Ottoman Empire, the failure of the 1908 reform, a last call for Ottoman unity, and the influence of German imperialism—all contributed to the emergence of Turkish nationalism. The attack of the Arabs against their Moslem brothers, the Ottomans, during the First World War, was the final blow to the forces which were still resisting nationalism.[13] Finally the Turks realized that they must have a separate identity beyond being Moslem.

Ziya Gök Alp (1876-1924), the father of Turkish nationalism, formulated its principles at that time. His message emerged at an opportune moment and became a rallying cry for Turkish intellectuals who were trying to create a national consciousness from the remains of the collapsed Empire. Gök Alp searched for Turkish identity in national history, literature, and language. In his system, these three cultural elements are viewed as the main sources to unify the Turkic peoples and to replace Ottoman culture with an unspoiled natural culture of the Turks. In order to reach the true, national culture everything Ottoman should be refuted. Ottoman culture and institutions played an important negative role in Gök Alp's ideology: the role of scapegoat. In attacking the Ottomans Gök Alp said:

> Fifteen years ago there were two languages side by side in Turkey. The first, known as Ottoman, was recognized officially... The second, limited almost entirely to speech among people . . . was considered the argot of the common people. Nevertheless, it was our real and natural language... In

> similar fashion there were two prosodic systems... The second was the meter used by the Turkish people in which the popular poets wrote very lyrical poems. These poems were the natural result of inspiration and creativity. The same dichotomy exists also in our literature. Turkish literature consists of popular proverbs, riddles, tales, ballads, legends, war stories, epics, anecdotes, and folk plays. The proverbs are maxims of the people, who also created riddles. These are the sincere works of the Turkish people.[14]

Gök Alp then poses this question:

> Why is everything Turkish so beautiful and everything Ottoman so ugly? The answer is that the Ottoman pattern travelled the road of imperialism which was so detrimental to Turkish culture and life.[15]

When the culture of the Ottomans was condemned and refuted, and folk culture was praised in such a romantic manner, it was logical for Gök Alp to engage in folklore research. He was indeed the forerunner of folklore studies and collecting in Turkey. He translated the word "folklore" into Turkish as "halkiyat," lore of the people, and used it until 1922. That year, however, he replaced it with the international term "folklore."

As early as 1912 he not only collected folktales but used them as the source of inspiration and versified them for children in order to spread nationalistic feeling among them.[16] This activity also involved versifying some episodes of the Book of Dede Korkut to create a national epic.[17] Later in 1922, perhaps after having realized his lack of talent in writing poetry, he started to publish tales in prose, altering their language slightly, as well as their style and the names of the tale characters, to suit his nationalistic cause.[18] Gök Alp found in Turkish folklore a great educational tool for implementing his ideology. In the works he published in verse or in prose, the geographical setting of the tale became the neglected Asian fatherland of Turks. The names of the heroes were replaced with the real or legendary heroes of Turkish history. At the end of one of his tales, for example, he says, "The heroine of the tale, Moon-Lady (Ay Hanım) is Turkey, the Star (Yıldız) is Islam, and the Stepmother (Üvey Ana) is England."[19]

Writing to Fuat Köprülü in 1922, Gök Alp states: "I am collecting here (in Diyarbakır) folktales. I hope to publish them in my *Küçük Mecmua* [The Little Journal]. I will also collect folk beliefs. We have been collecting the ancient folk songs in Diyarbakır. I am also doing ethnographic research among Arabs, Kurdish, and Turkish tribes, and hope to establish a small museum of ethnography here."[20] An article published by Gök Alp in 1922 describes his method of collecting tales. He says that "tales should not be collected from every teller. Only the best traditional teller should be selected. Folktales are the most valuable treasure of the nation. The ancient character and ideals of our nation are preserved in tales. . . . When all the tales are collected, those which are instructive for children and useful for national spirit should be selected, and the remainder must be thrown away."[21] Gök Alp's approach to the folktale resembles that of the romantic folklorists of Europe for whom folklore was beautiful and useful as long as it reflected forgotten national virtues and helped promote national unity.[22]

The Turkish War of Independence (1920-22) liberated the core of the Ottoman Empire, Anatolia and Thrace, populated only by Turks, from foreign occupation. The non-Turkish and non-Muslim population of the Empire remained outside the boundaries of modern Turkey. The concept of Turkish national culture which in the past was in conflict with the language, religion, and ethnic identities of other *millets* under the Ottoman system, was not an intellectual dream any more; it became a state policy whose implementation was facilitated by the ethnic and religious homogeneity of Turkey. The nationalist leaders of the new era, under the strong leadership of Mustafa Kemal Atatürk, introduced a sweeping reform program during 1923-30 to break the hold of Islam over the state, to alter the political structure of the Empire, and to modernize education and the legal system as well as customs and minds. The sultanate and caliphate were abolished, and a new republic was proclaimed. All religious schools were closed and teaching religion in public schools was stopped, the Islamic legal system was replaced with European law, and the Roman alphabet was adopted and the usage of the Arabic alphabet became a crime punishable by law.

These drastic changes, the new leaders felt, would not be successful or complete unless a sense of national pride stemming from a glorious past was introduced into the society to unify Turks in "joy and sorrow"; a new national culture was created by means of a common language which would be understood by everybody, intellectual and peasant alike. The Turkish Language Society, whose duty it was to purge the language of foreign vocabulary and to lead research and activities toward that goal, was established in 1932. The duty of unearthing the glorious role of the Turks in Asia and in the Middle East, especially in the pre-Islamic period, and discovering the contribution of the Turks to the civilization of the world, was given to the Turkish Historical Society, which was established in the same year.[23] Both organizations were suggested and supported by Atatürk and are still continuing their activities through a fund set up in his will.

In this age of state nationalism, folk literature was accepted as a major source of national pride. After all, there were the Turkish minstrels who created and transmitted folk poetry and who resisted the influence of Arabic and Persian and preserved the national language in their works. The majority of the population read, enjoyed, and understood their poetry. The language of this poetry had served as a viable means of communication for centuries among uneducated peasants, a means which the new intellectuals had been searching for to bridge the gap between the rulers and the ruled. Furthermore, a major part of this folk poetry, especially the poetry of Alevi and Bektaşi minstrels (members of a heterodox religious order) who had liberal attitudes toward religion, endowed the secular policy of the Republic with strong ideological support. Minstrels who had been ignored by the Ottoman intellectuals became culture heroes and days of commemoration to celebrate their memory were considered great cultural events in the new capital, Ankara. "Toward the folk" was the motto of the intellectuals and, in fact, was included as one arrow in the flag among five others which represented the main principles of the People's Republican Party, the party which was established by Atatürk and governed Turkey until 1950.

As early as 1920 the Ministry of Education established a Department of Culture to collect folklore, and included folklore research among the Ministry's publications during the first decade of the Republic. Foreign experts and scholars were invited to prepare reports to develop folklore studies, to organize folklore collection trips, and to establish folk museums.[24] İstanbul Conservatory for example, following the recommendation and advice of Béla Bartók, collected 2000 folksongs, and published many of them during 1925-35.[25]

Scholarly activities in the folklore field started in 1924 with the establishment of the Institute of Turcology at İstanbul University under the chairmanship of Professor Köprülü.[26] During the first two decades of the Turkish Republic, Fuat Köprülü contributed more than any other scholar to the study of folklore. Although he was an historian, he published books on Turkish folklore, and such articles as, "The Origin and Development of Turkish Minstrel Tradition," "Meddah, the Storyteller," "The Early Turkish Mystics," "Studies and Texts on Turkish Ashik Poetry," and "Kayıkcı Kul Mustafa and the Story of Genj Osman."[27] These were studies which were unprecedented and were published at a time when very few scholars knew what folklore meant. The following generation of folklorists, Boratav among them, received their folklore and literature training from Köprülü. As a pupil and friend of Ziya Gök Alp, Köprülü followed his master's nationalistic principles and applied them to the study of history, folklore, and literature. Besides the scholarly merit of Köprülü's work the reader will easily identify an ideological tone. He tried to prove that "the national spirit and the national preferences in arts and aesthetics of the Turkish people can be studied and found in folklore and folk literature."[28]

The first organization devoted exclusively to folklore studies, the Folklore Association (Halk Bilgisi Derneği), was instituted in 1927.[29] Supported by Mustafa Necati, Minister of Education who served as honorary chairman, the Association, although a private organization, enjoyed extensive official assistance. The official stationery of the Association was printed without charge at the printing office of the Grand National Assembly. And the entire stock of the Association's first publication was purchased by the Ministry of Education to be subsequently distributed free to all members and to the schools.[30]

The Folklore Association engaged in a nation-wide membership campaign, urged publication, and instructed its amateur members in folklore theory and fieldwork techniques. The first publication of the Association, a handbook for local collectors, indicated the guidelines for determining what should be considered folklore.[31] Such a guide was essential in Turkey where the word "folklore" was unknown until the 1920s.

The Association's conception of folklore and its approach to the subject did not differ from the emotional, romantic view of Gök Alp. In the first issue of the folklore journal *Halk Bilgisi Mecmuası*, published by the Association in 1928, the editors declared that they would include studies and collect materials to both educate the people and promote the cause of national unity.[32] In one article, the Secretary General of the Association went one step further by proposing a map of folk tradition which would feature the epics, tales, oral poetry, beliefs, language, traditions, and material culture of all Anatolia. By examining such a map, the folklorist could discover any deviation from the national culture and national language; he would then use appropriate means to assimilate the cultural anomaly for the benefit of national unity.[33] Thus, folklore would become a potent weapon in the struggle for a homogeneous nation with one language. Of course, the Secretary General, Ziyaeddin Fahri (Fındıkoğlu), was expressing his own opinion in the article; nevertheless, his views were characteristic of the nationalist extremism in Turkish folklore. As will be seen below, this extremism is responsible for terminating the teaching of folklore at Ankara University in the late 1940s. Although not in such a chauvinistic manner, romantic nationalism predominated in Turkish folklore studies until 1940. From this perspective, each folklore genre had a special value for the nation: proverbs reflected the high morals and philosophy of the Turkish ancestors, epics exemplified Turkish heroism, riddles demonstrated the cleverness and finesse of the Turkish mind, folk poetry revealed the natural sentiments of the people; in sum, folklore as a whole expressed the national spirit which had been undermined for centuries.

The Folklore Association died out in 1932. Its role was assumed at least partially by People's Houses, the government-supported social activity centers.[34] The first of these centers began operation in 1932, and in ten years they had spread to all Turkish cities. By 1945 they numbered 465. Among their activities folklore collection and publication were regarded as important subjects. Most of them published monthly or bimonthly periodicals which included topics on local folklore.[35] Besides the modest publications of each major People's House, the Central Office published a series in which several folklore studies appeared.[36] After 1945, the Central Office of People's Houses attempted to establish a Turkish Folklore Archive.[37] The only folklore journal published in Turkey during 1932-42 was the "Folklore News" (*Halk Bilgisi Haberleri*) from the İstanbul People's houses, a major source today for folklore collections.[38] Mehmet Halit Bayrı, a self-trained folklorist, must be given credit as the editor of the long lasting publication of "Folklore News".

In 1938, folklore, though limited to oral tradition, was added to the program of the Institute of Turcology in a newly established Faculty of Language, History, and Geography at the University of Ankara. In 1947 this program, including all folklore genres, became an independent chair under Professor Pertev Boratav. During these years, Boratav, with the help of graduates from the department and young assistants, established a Turkish folklore archive containing 15,000 pages of materials.[39] The department became the nerve center of folklore activities by keeping in touch with former students who were teaching in cities and towns throughout Turkey.

It was Boratav who introduced folklore to Turkey as an independent, scientific discipline. He enlarged the scope of folklore teaching and research to include verbal and nonverbal tradition. Boratav received his training in Europe, and was inspired partly by Arnold van Gennep and partly by the Finnish Historical School. It was this scholarly and objective approach to folklore that clashed with the conception that folklore should further the policy of extreme nationalism which controlled the ruling party after the Second World War. With the establishment of the opposition Democratic Party in 1945, and with the contribution of changing internal and external conditions, the dominant reformist People's Republican Party in Turkey reversed its position toward the radical reforms that had been achieved by the same party. The Village Institutes, a daring, radical approach to peasant education, lost their original character; the Land Reform Law was amended and was no longer effective in the distribution of large estates to landless peasants; teaching of religion was reintroduced into public schools; the state-controlled economic policies of the 1930s were discouraged; and the translation of Western literary masterpieces was stopped.

These changes were made possible through an alliance of the right wing of the ruling party and the newly established Democratic Party which went to the extreme right in cultural affairs. This new alliance, which controlled the Ministry of Education, had a powerful voice in the National Assembly. It launched an organized attack against three "leftist university professors" in order to create a favorable climate for the coming general election. Professor Boratav and the teaching of folklore at Ankara University were included in their target. It was argued that the national themes of folklore were not being emphasized; instead, international themes of folk narratives were taught to the students. The national character of folklore was neglected by Boratav as a matter of ideology. Heroes of Turkish epics, such as Köroğlu, were said to be depicted as social bandits who took from the rich and distributed to the poor. All this was interpreted as nothing but the initiation of class struggle within a classless Turkish society. The heroes should have been analyzed as representing the heroic features of the nation. The folk poetry studied in the university classroom was purposely chosen from among the examples which reflected the poverty and miserable life of the peasants; besides, these examples contained obscene expressions which were detrimental to the high moral principles of the Turkish youth.

These were general accusations, but nevertheless Professor Boratav was sent to trial after the official complaint forwarded by the Ministry of Education that "he criticized, in his teaching, Namık Kemal and Ziya Gök Alp," the two leading figures of Turkish nationalism. He was acquitted and returned to his teaching; however, the Minister of Education, Ş. Sirer, managed to pass a law in the National Assembly to cut the budget of the folklore program, and the teaching of folklore at Ankara University was discontinued in 1947. The outcry for academic freedom by a few university professors who had remained unintimidated by the anti-intellectual frenzy did not affect the decision. It is the result of that political move that today the Turkish universities do not offer a folklore program; Turkish folklore as an independent discipline is taught abroad, in Paris and at Indiana University in Bloomington.

Another blow to folklore collection and studies occurred when the Democratic Party came to power in 1950 with a sweeping majority victory. One year later the new government closed the People's Houses, the community centers where folklore studies found a friendly atmosphere and support. Consequently, folklore publications and collection lost the support of the University and the State, and local folklore periodicals were all discontinued.

After losing the support of these two institutions, folklore studies continued in Turkey on an individual basis after 1950. Although an independent folklore program does not exist in any Turkish university today, some university professors in ethnology, literature, religion, art, theatre, and even English are interested in folklore and do research and collecting in this field.

Since individual treatment of folklorists is neither possible nor reasonable in this short article, I would like just to note the main trends in folklore scholarship in Turkey. Boratav, who continues his research and publications at the Sorbonne, in Paris,[40] approaches folklore basically through the method of the literary folklorist without denying the value of cross-cultural emphasis and social background analysis. He employs one of these approaches, depending on the nature of the topic, and in this respect he does not follow one folklore school, but represents only himself with an eclectic methodology.

The romantic-nationalist trend established by Gök Alp and Köprülü is still dominant among their students though there is no well-known figure among them. They see the folk culture of Anatolia as the direct survival of Central Asiatic Turkish culture, especially of shamanism. Foreign influences represented by ancient Anatolia, the Middle East, and Balkan cultures are minimal and should be ignored. This opinion is heavily represented in various universities and has the support of the Ministry of Education.

A third tendency, which may be called the "humanist school" has developed since 1945. It considers Turks in Anatolia the survivors of ancient Anatolian and classical culture. Cevat Şakir, an artist and novelist who is known as the Fisherman of Halikarnassus, explains the opinion of the school in this way:

> The people who created the ancient civilization of Anatolia are the ancestors of the people living here today, i.e. Turks. The population of Anatolia, according to the first census taken at the time of the Roman Emperor Augustus, was 21 million, which is more or less the current population of Anatolia. Turks who came from Central Asia number not more than two million, a fact suggesting that they did not increase and change the character of the inhabitants, but mixed with them. That is why we are in fact the successors of classical civilization. Classical culture was born in Anatolia and was transmitted to Greece from there.[41]

The origin of this movement is connected with the establishment of the Faculty of Language, History, and Geography which included the Department of Classical Languages, Hittite and Mesopotamian Studies and does research on the ancient Anatolian culture as a possible source of Turkish nationalism. Atatürk encouraged and suggested its establishment. Between 1938 and 1945 the Ministry of Education supported this humanistic approach by establishing Latin programs in some selected high schools and translating the masterpieces of Western culture, including Greek and Latin classics, into Turkish. Metin And's studies in folk theatre, rituals, and folk beliefs brought new evidence to support the survival of ancient Anatolia in Turkish folklore.[42]

Several attempts were made after 1945 to bring folklorists together into a folklore organization. None of them was successful. An independent folklore organization or association which represents the folklore scholars is still nonexistent. The Ministry of Education which was responsible for stopping folklore teaching at Ankara University established a Folklore Institute within the Ministry in 1966. When I visited the Institute in 1970, it was a small bureaucratic organization with no contact with the folklorists of the country; the director, who is not a folklorist, was trying to bring an American expert to expand the activities of the Institute. Unless this pattern is broken and the Institute cooperates with the folklorists or is controlled by scholars, it seems that the new Institute will not contribute much to the folklore studies in Turkey and may just follow an extremist nationalistic approach again.

Although several scholarly journals today publish folklore research and encourage folklore collection, it is *Turkish Folklore Research*[43] which is exclusively devoted to folklore, and has survived for more than twenty years thanks to the individual efforts of the editors, Ihsan and Bora Hinçer, father and son. It follows the tradition of *Folklore News* by publishing the collections of amateurs as well as the articles of folklore scholars. In 1967 a second journal, *Folklore,*[44] appeared representing the Turkish Folklore Association, a private folklore entertainment organization which is interested in folk dance and folksong shows in Turkey and abroad.

Until the first decade of this century, interest in folklore, which began more than a century ago, had the limited aim of purifying the Ottoman language. This limited aim turned into a full cultural movement to discover the forgotten culture of the Turkish nation when the nationalistic movement rejected the main cultural traits of the Ottoman Empire in language, in literature, in art, and in politics. The Turkish nationalists found a fresh, unspoiled, and national source in Turkish folklore to fill the cultural vacuum created by the collapse of the Empire. The new source, they believed, would provide a strong power to unify the citizens of the new Turkish republic and would facilitate the modernization and the Westernization of the nation. As long as folklore research did not depart from this official view of nationalism, the state gave all possible support to folklore scholars. However, when nationalism was carried to extremes, it clashed even with the neutrality and objectivity of folklore studies.

Interrelations between folklore and the state, whether friendly or conflicting, became less intense when a new fever of economic development caught the country after 1950. The international jargon of that new era, such as "per capita income," "industrialization," "land reform," and "economic development," pushed into oblivion the importance and discussions of all cultural problems including folklore. Since then folklore studies have been conducted without state help by private individuals and individual organizations. The recent establishment of a National Folklore Institute has not altered this trend.

Indiana University
Bloomington, Indiana

NOTES

[1] Agah Sırrı Levent, *Türk Dilinde Gelişme ve Sadeleşme Safhaları* [Progress in Simplification of Turkish Language] (Ankara, 1949), p. 141.

[2] Ahmet Hamdi Tanpınar, *On Dokuzuncu Asır Türk Edebiyatı Tarihi* [The History of Nineteenth-Century Turkish Literature] (Istanbul, 1956), pp. 147-148.

[3] İbrahim Şinasi, *Durubu Emsal-i Osmaniye* [Ottoman Proverbs] (Istanbul, 1863), 2nd ed., 1870, 3rd ed., 1885 by Ebuzziya.

[4] Levent, p. 139.

[5] Pertev Boratav, "Hüseyin Rahminin Romancılığı" [Hüseyin Rahmi as Novelist], in *Folklore ve Edebiyat* [Folklore and Literature], vol. 2 (Ankara, 1945), p. 161.

[6] Ahmed Midhat Efendi, *Durubu Emsal-i Osmaniye-i Şinasi Hikemiyatını Tasvir* [The Description of the Morals of the Ottoman Proverbs Collected by Şinasi] (Istanbul, 1288 [1871]).

[7] Abdulhak Hamid, *Sabr ü Sebat* [Patience and Determination], Tanpınar, p. 435.

[8] Kenan Akyüz, "La litérature moderne de Turquie," in *Philologiae Turcicae Fundamenta,* (Weisbaden, 1965), p. 548.

[9] Pertev Boratav, *Folklor ve Edebiyat* [Folklore and Literature], vol. 1 (Istanbul, 1939), p. 49.

[10] Ibid.

[11] Pertev Boratav, *Halk Edebiyatı Dersleri* [Lectures on Folk Literature] (Ankara, 1943), p. 8.

[12] Fuat Köprülü, "Aşık Tarzının Menşe ve Tekamülü" [The Origin and the Development of the Ashık Poetry], in *Edebiyat Araştırmaları* [Researches on Turkish Literature] (Ankara, 1966).
[13] Niyazi Berkes, *The Development of Secularism in Turkey* (Montreal, 1964), p. 313.
[14] Ziya Gök Alp. *The Principles of Turkism,* trans. R. Devereux (Leiden, 1968), p. 23.
[15] Ibid., p. 28.
[16] Ergenekon 1912, Alageyik 1912, Küçük Şehzade 1913, Ülker ile Aydın 1913, Kızıl Elma 1913, Yaratılış 1917, Küçük Hemşire 1922, Kolsuz Hanım 1922. These tales are the products of that literary activity. Fevziye Abdullah Tansel, *Ziya Gök Alp Külliyatı* [Collected Works of Ziya Gök Alp], vol. 1 (Ankara, 1952).
[17] Gök Alp versified three episodes from the Book of Dede Korkut epic. These are: Deli Dumrul, in 1917; Aslan Basat, in 1917; and Tepegöz, in 1917. For more information see Tansel, *Ziya Gök Alp.*
[18] These tales are Keloglan, Tenbel Ahmet, Kuğular, Nar Tanesi, Keşiş Ne Gördün, Pekmezci Anne, Yılan Bey ile Peltan Bey, all written in 1922.
[19] Tansel, *Ziya Gök Alp.* p. 207.
[20] Fevziye Abdullah Tansel, *Limni ve Malta Mektupları* [Letters from Limni and Malta]; *Ziya Gök Alp Külliyatı* [Collected Works of Ziya Gök Alp], vol. 2 (Ankara, 1965), p. xxvi.
[21] Ziya Gök Alp, "Masalları Nasıl Toplamalı" [How Should the Folk Tale Be Collected?], *Halk Bilgisi Mecmuası* [The Folklore Journal] 1 (1928): 22.
[22] For the selected bibliography of the development of folklore in Europe see Linda Dégh, "Folklore and Related Disciplines in Eastern Europe," *Journal of the Folklore Institute* 2 (1965): 103-119; Richard M. Dorson, "The Question of Folklore in a New Nation," *Journal of the Folklore Institute* 3 (1966): 277-298.
[23] See Bernard Lewis, "History Writing and National Revival in Turkey," *Middle Eastern Affairs* 4 (1953): 218-227; Uriel Heyd, "Language Reform in Turkey," *Middle Eastern Affairs* 4 (1953): 402-409.
[24] Ignácz Kúnos, Béla Bartók, Gyula Mészáros, all Hungarians, were invited to and visited Turkey during 1925-35 to advise the organization of folklore studies or the establishment of museums and institutions.
[25] Pertev Boratav, "Les travaux de folklore Turc, 1908-51," *Anadolu* 1 (1952): 71.
[26] The following volumes which appeared among the publications of the Institute of Turcology should be mentioned as important contributions to folklore studies: Pertev Boratav, *Köröglu Destanı* [The Köröglu Epic] (Istanbul, 1931); A Baki (Gölpınarlı); *Melamilik ve Melamiler* [The Melami Order of Islam and the Melamis] (Istanbul, 1931); Fuat Köprülü, *XVI asır Sonlarına Kadar Türk Saz Şairleri* [Turkish Folk-Poets until the End of the Nineteenth Century] (Istanbul, 1930); Fuat Köprülü, *Kayikçi Kul Mustafa ve Gencosman Hikayesi* [The Story of Kul Mustafa, the Boatman and the Young Osman] (Istanbul, 1930); Muallim Rifat, *Maniler* (Istanbul, 1928).
[27] Other works in folklore by Fuat Köprülü are: "Turk Edebiyatinda Aşık Tarzinin Menşe ve Tekamülü Hakkında Bir Tecrübe" [An Essay on the Origin and Development

of the Ashik Poetry among the Turks], *Milli Tetebbular Mecmuası* [The Journal of National Researches] 1 (1915); "Türklerde Halk Hikayeciligine Ait Bazi Maddeler" [Studies on the Storytelling Tradition among Turks, Meddahs], *Turkiyat Mecmuasi* [Journal of Turcology] 1 (1925): 1-45; *Turk Edebiyatinda Ilk Mutasavvıflar* [The Early Mystics in Turkish Literature] (Istanbul, 1919), 2nd ed. (Ankara, 1966); *Türk Saz Şairleri* [Turkish Folk-Poets] (Istanbul, 1940), 2nd ed. (Ankara, 1962).

28 Köprülü, *Ilk Mutasavviflar*, pp. 1-2, 2nd ed.

29 Köprülü, *Halk Bilgisi Mecmuası* [The Folklore Journal] 1 (1928): 187. The executive committee members of the Association were: Ishak Refet (Işıtman), the deputy of Diyarbakır; Ali Riza, the superintendent of Teacher Training School, Ankara; Ismail Hikmet (Ertaylan), the superintendent of the lycée for girls, Ankara; Hasan Fehmi (Turgal), the general director of the libraries, Ministry of Education, Ankara; Hakki Baha, director of the Museum of Archeology, Ankara; Ziyaeddin Fahri (Fındıkoglu), the secretary general of the Association, the teacher of philosophy and sociology, lycée for girls, Ankara; Ihsan Mahfi, the teacher of language and literature, lycée for girls, Ankara.

30 Ibid. [The same page as the preceeding note.]

31 In the preparation of the first handbook [*Halk Bilgisi Rehberi* no. 1], *Folklore* by Arnold van Gennep was used as the main source. However, the chapters covering the collection of folksongs, language, folklore, and folk arts and crafts were written by Mahmut Ragip (Kösemihal), Hasan Fehmi (Turgal), and Ismail Hüsrev (Tökin). For the list of folklore publications of the Association see Mehmet Halit Bayri.

32 *Halk Bilgisi Mecmuasi* 1 (1928): 1-4.

33 Ziyaeddin Fahri, "Halk Bilgisi ve Milli Birlik" [Folklore and National Unity] *Halk Bilgisi Mecmuasi* 1 (1928): 141.

34 See İlhan Başgöz and Howard Wilson, *Educational Problems of Turkey 1920-1940*, Indiana University Uralic and Altaic Series no. 19 p. 149, for People's House.

35 For the list of the periodicals published by People's Houses see Avni Candar, *Bibliografya: Halkevleri Neşriyati* [Bibliography: The Halkevi Publications] (Ankara, 1940).

36 See Candar for the list of the publications.

37 This activity was initiated by Ahmet Kutsi Tecer in 1946.

38 *Halk Bilgisi Haberleri* [The Folklore News] 1 (1932)–117 (1942).

39 For the content of the Archive see Pertev Boratav, "Dil ve Tarih Cografya Fakültesinde Halk Edebiyati ve Folklor Arşivi" [The Folklore Archive at the Faculty of Language, History, and Geography], *Dil ve Tarih Cografya Fak, Dergisi* 1 (1942).

40 The following is a selected bibliography of Boratav's books:

Folklore ve Edebiyat [Folklore and Literature], vol. 1 (Istanbul, 1939); vol. 2 (Ankara, 1945).

Pir Sultan Abdal [A Nineteenth-Century Minstrel] (Ankara, 1947). Co-authored by Abdulbaki Gölpinarlı.

Halk Hikayeciligi ve Halk Hikayeleri [Folk Stories and Folk Story Tradition] (Ankara, 1947).

Typen Türkischer Volksmärchen (Wiesbaden, 1953). Co-authored by Wolfram Eberhard.
Conte Turcs (Paris, 1955).
Zaman Zaman Içinde [Once Upon a Time, Tales and Tekerlemes] (Istanbul, 1958).
Le Tekerleme, contribution a l'étude typologique et stylistique du conte populaire Turcs (Paris, 1963).
Er Toshtuk, epopée du cycle de Manas, translated from Kirgiz (Paris, 1965).

[41] Halikarnas Balikçisi, *Anadolu Tanrıları* [Anatolian Gods] (Istanbul, 1955), p. 7.

[42] Among others, the basic works of Metin And are: *Kırk Gün Kırk Gece* [Forty Days and Forty Nights] (Istanbul, 1959); *Türk Köylü Dansları* [Turkish Peasant Plays and Dances] (Istanbul, 1964); *Dionisos ve Anadolu Köylüsü* [Dionysus and the Anatolian Peasants] (Istanbul, 1962); and *A History of Theater and Popular Entertainment in Turkey* (Ankara, 1964).

[43] Ihsan and Bora Hinçer, eds., *Türk Folklor Araştırmaları* 1 (1950)–259 (1971).

[44] Ihsan and Bora Hinçer, eds., *Folklor* 1 (1969)–8-9 (1970).

FOLKLORE, NATIONALITY, AND THE TWENTIETH CENTURY IN SIBERIA AND THE SOVIET FAR EAST

Robert Austerlitz

First thesis: Folklore is less likely to survive in twentieth-century, urbanizing, industrializing societies than during previous centuries when these movements were less pronounced and less speedy.* I am aware of the opinion held by some folklorists that folklore will survive everywhere and forever, regardless of new socioeconomic factors. I share their view and would like to say that "folklore" here will be used to mean traditional inherited folklore (and not new, urban, metropolitan or industrial folklore—which exists). In this sense, therefore, I believe that the social revolution in the U.S.S.R., namely, the transfer of cultural allegiance from the tribe or from religious cohesion to the kolkhoz, to the factory, or to the work team entails a partial or substantial loss of ethnic identification and that this loss, in turn, entails a concomitant decrease in the vitality with which the *inherited* stock of folkloristic art is perpetuated. A hypothetical example: a Gilyak (see ethnic group 30 in table 1 on page 206) leaves his fishing and reindeer-breeding environment and clan to be trained as and eventually to become a teacher. He adopts a Russian (that is, Western) mode of life, meets over Soviet citizens (larger numbers of non-Gilyak than Gilyak), possibly marries a non-Gilyak, is perhaps inhibited because of his tribal background, and thus eventually disassociates himself—through his own effort or by default—from his native culture, including folklore (he will continue to have and perhaps even to create folklore, but it will not be Gilyak folklore). Such alienation is familiar to us from previous centuries and from all parts of the world, but is more pronounced, qualitatively and quantitively, in large, industrial, urbanizing

*The substance of this paper was first presented at the 1973 annual meeting ot the American Folklore Society (Nashville, Tennessee, November 14). A report on its substance was given before the Seminar on Soviet Nationality Problems of Columbia University on 11 December 1973.

countries such as the Soviet Union and in the twentieth century, known for its accelerating effect on history (planned economy, planned society, husbanding of resources in remote areas, mixing of non-urban populations in industrial centers, "russification," and the like).

Second thesis: There is a considerable difference, existentially and otherwise, between belonging to a small nationality (SN) and belonging to a large nationality (LN) in the Soviet Union. An LN [for example, the Tajik or the Yakut (8 in table 1) or the Buriat (16)] has a relatively strong historical consciousness and national awareness, often coupled with explicit reference to written or oral history. Assertion of this national awareness beyond a certain point may go counter to official Soviet ideology ("multi-national in fact, uniform in purpose"). This situation is well known in the case of some of the largest nationalities (Ukrainians, Armenians, Estonians) and less obvious or pronounced in the case of slightly smaller LNs, such as the Yakut and others. An interesting paradoxical situation emerges from this: LNs may be and are encouraged to nurture their folklore, music, and national dances as long as the assertion of nationalistic or separatist aspirations–past or present–is not overt or dangerous (as it might be in some epics). The paradox spills over into the world of the SNs. SNs are by nature in danger of extinction. Their economy is generally less essential to the U.S.S.R. as a whole. Whatever national awareness an SN may have, it will be overshadowed by the sheer numbers of the nearest LN and by that of the Russians (or Western groups of the U.S.S.R.). SNs are also encouraged to nurture their folklore and cultural heritage and since no danger or threat to the U.S.S.R. as a whole attaches to the assertion of this heritage, they are even freer in asserting it than LNs. Thus, we may overstate the situation somewhat by saying that SNs are pampered in respect to their culture whereas LNs must be circumspect in asserting it. Or, to exaggerate the situation even further, perhaps into the realm of the unrealistic, Gilyak shamanism is encouraged while the Ukrainian church is fettered.

Third thesis, or anchorage: Anchorage involves the fact that a given ethnic unit in the U.S.S.R. has or lacks affines beyond its borders (an affine here means another ethnic group related to the ethnic group under discussion. The most obvious index of affinity here is language). Thus, taking the Soviet Union as a whole, the Moldavians have anchorage outside the U.S.S.R. (in the form of the Romanians), as have the Estonians (Finns and others), and the various Turkic peoples of the U.S.S.R. (the Turks of Turkey), while the Latvians and Lithuanians have no anchorage outside the U.S.S.R. In table 1, the ethnic groups from 1 to 15 have anchorage beyond the U.S.S.R. (although it is not clear to me to what extent they are aware of it), the Buriat

(16) have very strong anchorage in the Mongols of the Mongolian People's Republic and other Mongol foci in the Far East, whereas groups 25 to 30 lack such anchorage. The Eskimo (31) have and are strongly aware of their ultra-U.S.S.R. anchorage, which is circumpolar (Alaska, Canada, Greenland, and potentially Denmark). Anchorage is a potential source of trouble and if not much has been made of it so far, it is only because the populations of Siberia hardly cause a threat to the weal of the U.S.S.R. But it ought to be reckoned with at least as an interesting theoretical construct. This notion of anchorage could be exploited also along religious and cultural lines: note its potential for discussing Lamaism, Islam, Roman Catholicism, Lutheranism (and the cultural superstructure these entail regardless of Soviet official atheism) as against the (anchorageless) Georgian and Armenian churches and Siberian shamanism.

Fourth thesis: There must be some significance in the fact that some SNs in Siberia have and others lack affines (as defined above) *within* Siberia. Thus, the Gilyak (30) are linguistically totally isolated and I know from my own field experience with a limited number of Gilyak (in Japan, 1954, 1956-58, 1962, and 1965) that they also consider themselves ethnically and culturally unique. The Orok (24), on the other hand, know that both their language and their culture are related to those of other, larger groups (fairly closely to groups 18-23 and more remotely to 17) and, I would venture to say, feel somewhat more secure for this reason. This thesis, therefore, involves anchorage within the U.S.S.R. and specifies that an SN with affines within Siberia or the Union feels less Ishmaelitic than one without affines, as is to be expected. The column marked "Branch" in column 4, table 1, provides examples of the potential for affinal cohesion. For example, the Vogul (2) are a smaller group than the Ostyak (1) and, I presume, derive some strength and satisfaction from having a big brother [Ostyak and Vogul, together, form the Ob-Ugric sub-branch of the Finno-Ugric branch (not shown on table 1 because it is located in part outside of Siberia) of the Uralic family (I). These are linguistic categories but should serve for this discussion].

Table one lists the thirty-two linguistic-and-ethnic groups which are relevant to this discussion. Column 2 gives the names by means of which these groups refer to themselves. The data in the two parallel columns under 3 are from *Itogi vsesojuznoj perepisi naselenija 1970 goda*, vol. 4 (Moscow: Statistika, 1973), pp. 9-11. They have been rounded out to the nearest hundred or (in the case of larger populations) thousand. The sub-column on the right under 4 gives the language family to which a given language belongs; there are seven such families, indicated by Roman numerals on the extreme right. "Altaic" is given in quotation marks because its status as a family is not

Table 1

	1	2	3		4		
	English name	Own name	USSR census		Linguistic-genetic		
			1970	1959	Branch	FAMILY	
1	Ostyak	xanti	21,000	20,000	Ob-Ugric	*Uralic*	I
2	Vogul	māńsi	7,700	6,400			
3	Yurak-S.	ńeńecʔ	29,000	23,000	Samoyed		
4	Tavgi-S.	ŋanasan	1,000	700			
5	Yenisei-S.	eńecʔ	?	300			
6	Ostyak-S.	sel'kup	4,200	3,700			
7	Kamassian	kaŋ-maže	- - -	1			
8	Yakut	saxa	296,000	233,000	Turkic	"Altaic"	II
9	Dolgan	dolgaan	4,800	4,000			
10	Khakas	(5 groups)	?	52,000			
11	Altai	oĭrot	?	35,000			
12	Shor	šor	16,000	15,000			
13	Tatar	(tribal)	?	70,000			
14	Tuva	?tuba	?	6,000			
15	Karagas	tuba, tofa	600	600			
16	Buriat	burĭaad	315,000	252,000	Mongol		
17	Tungus	ewenki	25,000	24,000	Tungus		
18	Lamut	ewen	12,000	9,000			
19	Negidal	elkem beye	500	400			
20	Goldi	nanai	10,000	8,000			
21	Olcha	nāni	2,400	2,000			
22	Udykhe	udexe	1,500	1,400			
23	Oroch	nāni	1,100	800			
24	Orok	wilta	?	400			
25	Yenisei-O.	ket	1,100	1,000	PS:1	Yeniseian	III
26	Yukagir	odul	600	400	PS:2	Yukagir	IV
27	Chukchi	luorawetian	13,600	12,000	PS:3	*Luorawetlan*	V
28	Koryak	čawču	7,500	6,300			
29	Kamchadal	itəlmen	1,300	1,100			
30	Gilyak	ńivx	3,700	4,400	PS:4	Gilyak	VI
31	Eskimo	ĭupik	1,300	1,100	- - -	*Eskaleut*	VII
32	Aleut	unaŋax	?	(300)			

as obvious or convincing as that of families I, V, or VII. Some languages do not belong to any family; they are called isolates and form rudimentary families in their own right: III, IV, and VI. Nevertheless, the languages listed under 25, 26, 27-28-29, and 30 are traditionally lumped under the collective term Paleosiberian (abbreviated PS in the table). Question marks have been used in instances where census data are not available or unclear. The bulk of some of these populations lies outside Siberia: the Tatar (13) are one example. Aleut (32) is spoken in the United States; it is mentioned only to show its affinity with Eskimo.

General remarks: (1) Christian missionary activity in Imperial Russia left less durable marks than similar activity in the New World, in parts of Africa, in India, and in Southeast Asia. This fact contributes mildly toward the preservation of their cultural heritage by some of the SNs of Siberia. (2) The railroad played a tremendous part in the opening of North America to nineteenth-century technology and concomitant economic and social developments. The role of the railroad was less dramatic in Siberia. (3) The economic opening of Siberia, especially since the 1917 revolution entailed the influx of higher-echelon technicians from the Western ("European") U.S.S.R. and presumably the recruitment of lower-echelon technicians from among some of the local populations. Compare this with the hypothetical example cited under my first thesis, above. (4) We may want to reckon with a vague notion such as "national awareness" which would issue from the points discussed under theses 2, 3, and 4 (large vs. small nationalities, anchorage, and affines within the area). The notion is necessarily vague but its ingredients, as spelled out above, are perhaps a little more concrete than the term itself implies. (5) Obviously, the economy and the role which each nationality plays within it, on a national or local scale, is the most important factor to be reckoned with. (6) Other factors which can be mentioned here, but which will not be considered, are: mobility within a certain area, political system or degree of administrative autonomy, contiguity with other groups.

From what has been said so far it should issue that the more a given ethnic group is exposed to industrialization, urbanization, and modernization the less likely it is that its native and traditional folklore will survive. Such a process of deculturation is all the more likely if the ethnic group is weak; that is, is small, lacks anchorage, and has no affines. All that is not unexpected and is, in fact, somewhat banal but it is hoped that the notions used in this discussion will make it possible to treat the problem more tractably than has been done traditionally.

Table two is an attempt to plot awareness (as discussed in general remark 4, above) against anchorage. The four cells which result from the

Table 2

		Awareness	
		strong	weak
Ultra-U.S.S.R. anchorage	present	Yakut (8) Eskimo (31) Buriat (16) 1	?Tungus (17-24) 2
	absent	3 Chukchi (27)	4 Kamchadal (29) Ket (25) Orok (24) Goldi (20) Yukagir (26) Gilyak (30)

matrix are not watertight or mutually exclusive. Rather, it is the polarity which obtains between cell 1 and cell 4 which deserves our attention. The message of table 2 is that weak awareness and lack of anchorage (cell 4) implies a threatened folkloristic future, as against strong awareness and presence of anchorage (cell 1). That may be so, but it is not a complete statement of the problem.

Table three attempts to remedy the weakness of table two by introducing economy. It is my feeling that as soon as a group is involved in the economy, its heritage is endangered. Obviously, large groups will suffer less or more slowly than small groups. If the group is not involved in the economy or only minimally involved in it, its heritage, conversely, is not endangered. At this point, the question of affines enters. If the group has affines, it will (a) tend to perpetuate its culture because of the affine's model or because of its very existence, but it will, at the same time (b), present ever so slight a threat to the republic's common weal, precisely because of these affines. The group without affines therefore has the advantage. This is why I think that the officialty will (to use the somewhat far-fetched example introduced under thesis 2) promote Gilyak shamanism; it presents no threat and can be used as a museum piece. The U.S.S.R.'s or the R.S.F.S.R.'s attitude toward the perpetuation of Gilyak culture could therefore be considered paternalistic as against, say, Chukchi (27) culture, which may

Table 3

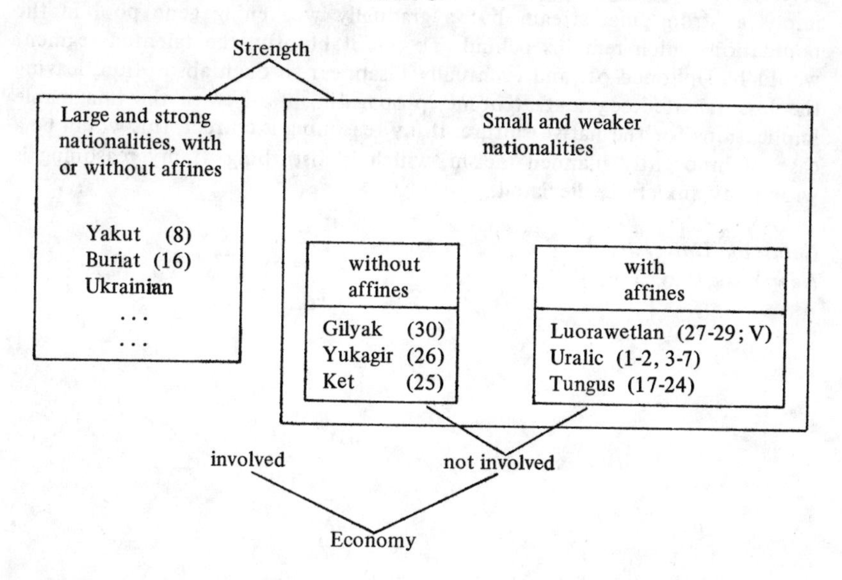

require a more vigilant stance (in reality, the Chukchi pose no threat, but still they are coastal, they have affines, and they are somewhat more numerous).

We therefore emerge with a final dilemma: in general twentieth-century terms, all national cultures, the small ones included, are theoretically doomed to eventual extinction. However, in specific terms, the smaller and the more insignificant (culturally, economically) a group, the more likely it is to be pampered and its culture kept alive. That seems to me to be the circular dilemma of folklore, nationality, and the twentieth century in Siberia and Soviet Far East.

If there is a moral to be drawn from this, it is that cultural questions of this kind should be posed by folklorists in the demographic-economic framework in which they belong.

There is one more thought, a disturbing one, which deserves mention in this connection. It seems to me that the gradual Westernization of the great native preserve that is Siberia has implications for the gene pool of the area. If the capable members of an ethnic group (where capable means ability to integrate, survive successfully, and reproduce in the new Westernized surroundings) are siphoned off into the mainstream of Soviet industrial society, the less capable ones, one may assume, remain behind. This would imply a strong mainstream but a gradually weakening gene pool in the population which remains behind. To put it bluntly, the talented segment would be siphoned off and eventually disappear through absorption, leaving the less talented segment at home, propagating itself, with the imaginable implications for the native culture. If my reasoning is correct, this would be a case of innocently planned racism, which is disturbing. If my reasoning is wrong, my anxiety is alleviated.

Columbia University
New York, New York

NATIONAL CHARACTERISTICS OF JAPANESE FOLKTALES

Richard M. Dorson

Anyone speaking of national characteristics depicted in folktales treads shaky ground, but Japan offers as strong a case as may be found anywhere.* Her geographical insularity coupled with three hundred years of self-imposed isolation have shaped a distinctive body of folk narratives. We will discuss three characteristics of this tale corpus: the predominance of the legend (*densetsu*) as a narrative genre; the dependence of legends upon religious folk beliefs (*minkan shinko*); and the intimate association of folktale telling with forms of traditional theater, themselves grounded in *minkan shinko*.

In the lexicon of folklorists the term "folktale" is often used synonymously with "magical tale" or Märchen, and is considered a fiction as opposed to the believed story or legend. This is not the sense employed by Stith Thompson in his study of *The Folktale*, which comprehended all forms of oral traditional prose narrative. At any rate the community of folktale scholars, including Thompson, has long given primary attention to the Märchen and disregarded the legend as artistically inferior. The Grimm brothers published collections both of Märchen and Sagen, but only the Märchen have enjoyed countless translations and editions and inspired subsequent collectors in every European country and on other continents to search for the prized "fairy tales." In Japan the same emphasis appears, with the *mukashibanashi* being elevated at the expense of the *densetsu*.

The first collection of Japanese oral narratives, the *Tono Monogatari* published in 1910 by Kunio Yanagita, consisted almost entirely of *densetsu* stored in the mind of a country youth. This volume, now happily for the first

*This paper was presented in Japanese translation to the Japan Folklore Society in Tokyo, July 28, 1975 in the symposium honoring the centenary of the birth of Kunio Yanagita.

time translated into English by Ronald Morse, should rank in importance with the Grimms' original 1812 collection of *Kinder– und Hausmärchen* as a landmark contribution to folktale studies. In both cases the work stirred a national audience with its revelation to intellectuals of the mental possessions of peasant folk, and in each case it ignited the energies of the collector-authors to establish a discipline of folklore studies within their countries.

In the genre of folk narrative alone Yangita-*sensei* has performed every conceivable task: collector, organizer, editor, classifier, theorist. Following his own fieldwork, he stimulated his countrymen to record folktales through his handbooks *Mukashibanashi no Saishū Techō* and *Mukashibanashi Saishū no Shiori*; he edited a series of volumes from different districts, *Zenkoku Mukashibanashi Kiroku* (1942-44); he systematically codified the collected tales in two indexes, *Nihon Mukashibanashi Meii and Nihon Densetsu Meii;* he founded a Japanese Folklore Institute and encouraged disciples, such as Keigo Seki, who further extended the classification; and he wrote theoretical studies relating folk narratives to animistic beliefs and to older literary sources. Yanagita-*sensei* wryly recalls his excessive zeal in seeking to stimulate collecting by amateurs through the *Techō*, a booklet containing synopses of a hundred folktale plots, with blank pages for the reader-collector to fill in the full stories. Of a thousand copies that he distributed, in hopes of getting them back completed, not one was ever returned to him! "My method was too businesslike, too American," he concluded.[1]

It might also have been that he was pressing too hard for *mukashibanashi*, that had he sought replicas of the farmer Kizen Sasaki's repertoire from Tōno, legends would have come flooding in. But Kunio Yanagita felt some disappointment in the Tōno stories, which seemed to him artless and providing only "two genuine folk tales of the kind folklorists in England and Europe were studying." [2] In the revised edition of the *Japanese Folk Tales* the translator, Fanny Hagin Mayer, has regrettably perpetuated the stereotype that magical fictions are more authentic and desirable than legendary traditions, and displaced forty-five "legends or popular fiction" with what she calls "forty-three genuine folk tales."[3] The master himself deplored the process whereby old folktales "were later dressed up to seem as though they actually happened."[4] Yet this is the folk process, particularly in Japan. Since only three of all of Yanagita-*sensei*'s hundred books have hitherto been translated into English, it is doubly unfortunate that one should be the *Japanese Folk Tales* (the other is the substantial social history he edited, *Japanese Manners and Customs in the Meiji Era*, and *About Our Ancestors*, his well known study of folk religious beliefs). Adapted for children, illustrated with the romanticized pictures customary in children's books, and weighted toward fairy tales, it is an attempt to render a Japanese version of Grimm. But Stith Thompson also contributed to this erroneous conception of Japanese folktales in his direction of Hiroko Ikeda's doctoral dissertation at Indiana University, subsequently published as *A Type and Motif Index of Japanese Folk Literature*.[5] He wished to see Dr. Ikeda fit the Japanese tale types into the categories of European animal tales, Märchen, and novelle on which the Aarne-Thompson tale-type index was based (Seki's index follows indigenous patterns). But the Japanese folk narratives with their bias toward legend belong to a different world.

Ikeda's informative and well-constructed index itself offers the best proof of this allegation. Of 439 tale types in the index, seventy-four, by Ikeda's own judgment, are classifiable as legends (one of the most frequent comments in the plot summaries is the phrase "often told as a local legend"), sixteen as true stories (only four of which overlap with legends), and five as myths (only one of which is also counted as a legend). The legend concept covers true stories, which are potential legends, and myths, which are older legends. But this count could be considerably enlarged if all the tale types dealing with historical figures, supernatural beings, and magical beliefs were included. Furthermore, it is clear that the index does not reflect the totality of such themes. For example, *kappa* surfaces in only three tale types, but these only suggest the hundreds of personal experiences and local traditions attached to this ubiquitous water imp.[6] Other demonic creatures are well represented: the fox (kitsune), with its mischievous powers of transformation, in forty-three story types; the badger (tanuki), another trickster-magician, in nineteen; tengu, the long-nosed mountain goblin, in eight; the snake, better characterized as a serpent-deity, in twenty; yamauba, the mountain ogress, in six; spider, usually depicted as monstrous, in eight; crab, often evil, in eleven. Rarer appearances are made by such demons as Ama-no-jaku, a she-devil credited in two tale-plots with shooting six suns while sitting on a pine stump, and with killing or transforming a princess born from a melon; nushi, twice mentioned as a guardian water spirit; and yamajiji, a mountain monster mentioned once. In addition the frequent roles in the tales of the cat (19), dog (14), and monkey (27) on occasion associate the animal with a god, a spirit, or supernatural powers. For example, type 300, "The Monkey-God Slayer," deals both with a punitive monkey deity demanding an annual human sacrifice and a dog who overcomes the deity and is then enshrined as a god. The folk belief that very old cats acquire supernatural potency is illustrated in types 215 B and C, in which a cat from a mountain temple vanishes each night, taking along the priest's ceremonial robe, to serve as priest for other cats; she obtains a new temple for the priest by causing a coffin to rise and descend and giving him credit for the miracle. Some animals and demons possess interchangeable characteristics; kappa, snake, dragon, nushi, watergod, and mudsnail melt one into another. Stories with such creatures are considered fictional animal tales in Europe, but in Japan they take the form of local legends about minor deities of mountains, lakes, and pools; they are fragments of a demonic mythology.

The most prominent human character in the narratives is the Buddhist priest, who takes part in fifty-eight tales, of which twenty-three fall into the so-called Priest and Acolyte cycle. While this cycle consists of comical anecdotes in which the acolyte seeks to emulate his master, the priest himself is a serious figure, a religious magician who continually combats fox enchantresses, mountain ogres, swamp serpents, deceitful badgers, and vexatious ghosts. Yamabushi, the priests of the particular sect of Buddhism associated with Shugendō, the ascetic mountain religion, are seen in five additional tale types, often blowing a conch shell to frighten a fox. More powerful than the Buddhist priest is Kannon, the Buddha of Mercy, assigned to four types–a small representation for the many local traditions about Buddhist statues who assume the injuries dealt their worshipers and who rebuke the impious. A special deity, Bimbo-gami, the god of poverty, emerges in two tale plots (types 735 B and 946), foiling poor people, unless they work hard or overcome fear, but otherwise the legion of kamis who preside over homes, grounds, and fields are unnoted. Indeed Ikeda's subject index lacks an entry for kami or for spirits, and reports only six appearances of ghosts–two of treasure guardians, four of unhappy revenants–a drop in the bucket of Japanese memorates about the vengeful dead. Unlike the Western ghosts, the Japanese ghosts may possess magic powers, as do other Japanese supernaturals, to transform and reward mortals.

Perhaps the most striking aspect of the legend-making process in Japan concerns the attachment of folkloric themes to historical personalities (see appended list). More than a score are named in the Ikeda subject index: Buddhist priests, samurai, scholars, judges, emperors, courtiers, a prime minister. Chronologically they range from the fourth to the eighteenth century, and are evenly distributed in nearly every intervening century. The earliest is Agatamori, renowned for his strength and temper, who in 379 A.D. hurled three gourds into the Kahashima River and commanded a poison-belching water snake to sink them or be destroyed–an episode found in the widely reported tale of *Hebi Muko* (type 312B "Snake Husband Killed"). The most recent is the celebrated judge Ōka Echizen-no-kami (1677-1753), to whom is attributed a cycle of clever judicial decisions lodged in traditional anecdotes. Sometimes international story forms become attached to well-known individuals. The account of "The Deceptive Land Purchase" (type 2400), related as an actual occurrence by Herodotus in ancient Greece and by North American Indians today, is told on the priest Jōye, son of the prime minister Fujiwara Kamatari and alleged founder of Tōunji Temple in Miyagi-ken. While traveling, early in the eighth century, he beheld a fair land with ninety-nine mountain ranges and valleys, and sought to acquire it for a temple. But a pair of supernatural beings living there would not relinquish the land. Thereupon Jōye planted his staff in the ground and asked simply for the loan of the ground covered by its shadow. They agreed, but the shadow blanketed the entire hill. Where in American Indian versions the white man treacherously tricks the red man out of his land through such stratagems, the Japanese cognates honor the trickster as the priest-hero. An older Japanese variant set in prehistoric times matches two deities against each other for the coveted land.

The force of the legend-making process can be documented in various instances in which a place-name encapsulates the tradition or a testimonial object gives it veracity. Crab Village and Crab Hill in Yamanashi-ken bear witness to the episode in type 326E ("The Mythical Crab") that pitted a traveling Buddhist monk against a weird being in a ruined mountain temple. Asked its identity, the creature replied with a riddle, which the monk solved as "A crab" and smacked the thing with a bamboo flute. The next morning he found a big crab dead under the temple floor. Villagers say the lines on the crab's carapace are the marks of the flute, and that the carapace in question is preserved in the temple. The riddle in the legend belongs to the so-called Odin type applying to a creature with an unusual number of appendages. Similarly several Buddhist temples treasure the tea kettle into which a grateful badger transformed itself so that the sale would profit its benefactor (type 325). Kibitsu Shrine in Okayama preserves the famed iron bow of the hero Yuriwaka who defeated an island of ogres in a blinking contest; Yuriwaka's footprint and his horse's hoofmark are visible on certain rocks (type 974).[7] Burnt rice grains are said still to be found on the site where defenders of a besieged castle, whose water supply was cut off, poured a stream of white rice over a horse in view of the enemy, to give the illusion of bathing the animal in water; the discouraged besiegers were about to depart when the ruse was discovered, so instead they laid waste the castle (type 993).[8]

We can only surmise the extent of as yet uncollected legendary themes in Japan's oral traditions. Occupational, urban, and industrial legends are still an unknown quantity. Unique in Ikeda's index is the tradition attached to gold mines throughout the country (type 960C "A Unique Survivor"), which tells of miners discovering a vein of gold ore shaped like an ox. After a feast of celebration they try, on New Year's Day, to pull it out of the mine with a rope when a cave-in buries all, save one survivor, a cook called from the scene by a mysterious voice. Although not included among Ikeda's types, legends of Japanese metalworkers abound. Writing on this subject, Nobuhiro Matsumoto alludes to the degenerated deity of the ironworking industry, the one-eyed, one-legged monster Hitotsu-me-tatara; to the legend behind the custom of setting up a corpse in the fireplace; and to the legend of Kogorō, the charcoal-maker, who through the intervention of a Buddhist or Shinto deity finds gold scattered around his charcoal kiln. Matsumoto speculates that "each occupational group perhaps had its own ancestral god to whom a separate belief system and a distinctive set of legends were attached."[9]

Densetsu evolve both from indigenous cultural matter in Japan and through the adaptation of European popular fictions to the cultural matrix. But to say that Japanese folk narratives gravitate to legend forms is an incomplete statement, for these legends exhibit special characteristics. In great part they embody elements of Japanese folk religion. As evident in Ichiro Hori's skilful analysis, that folk religion, or, more properly, that tissue of folk-religious beliefs, derives from the old animistic concept of mountains, trees, and animals as possessing souls, from the Shintoistic idea of protective deities, and from the Buddhist theology stressing the powers of priests and Buddhas.[10] The folk mind seizes on the dramatic supernatural and magical aspects of the religious systems and applies them to personal experiences or migratory tales. In this seedbed germinate the memorates and fabulates which, as folklorists are now demonstrating, grow into legend. Yanagita's *Legends of Tōno* comprises just this formation of first- and second-hand accounts of brushes with the demon and spirit world enveloping his village.

A newly published volume of American folklore can illustrate the process under discussion. The United States with its rationalistic Enlightenment intellectual roots is much leaner in supernatural legendry than is Japan, but pockets of fundamentalist Christianity fan the folk credence in a visible Devil, portents of death, and ghosts that rise from the grave. In *Ghosts Along the Cumberland*, subtitled "Deathlore in the Kentucky Foothills," William Lynwood Montell has presented familiar materials in an unfamiliar but logical way, by juxtaposing beliefs in the coming of death and the return from the dead with narrative testimonies involving those beliefs.[11] Some narratives are memorates pure and simple, while others are international tale types, such as "The Youth Who Wanted to Learn What Fear Is" (type 326), which also occurs in Japan in nine subtypes (Ikeda 326A-326J). Customarily the folklorist artificially separates the belief statement from the personal experience, and slights the personal experience in favor of the more polished legend.

The densetsu that teem in Japan unquestionably develop from a worldview in the minds of village folk, and townspeople too, that could be expressed in a series of folk belief testimonies. This worldview stresses mountainous areas as the locus of divinities and the abode of the dead, a point documented by a number of scholars, notably Kunio Yanagita, who appended a detailed essay on "Yamadachi and Yamabushi" to the collaborative *Studies in Mountain Village Life* that he directed. In discussing "Mountains and Their Importance for the Idea of the Other World" Hori indicates his debt to Yanagita's analysis of mountain beliefs.[12] Central to those beliefs is the folk conception of the deity or spirit of the mountain, Yama-no-kami, and secondary figures, such as the tengū and yama-uba, who share his awesome attributes. Yama-no-kami ruled over the animals on the mountain, took their shapes, possessed the land, and dwelt in certain trees. He held the power of birth and rebirth over humans and animals, and worshipers prayed to him for the healing of disease, the blessing of offspring and marriage partners, and easy childbirth. Apparently after the eighth century with the development of agriculture Yama-no-kami moved from the mountains to the rice fields for half the year and became Ta-no-kami. The custom of bringing down trees and branches from the mountainsides to the fields to celebrate the New Year fostered this evolution.

Mountain religion bred its own rituals and forms and places of worship, in the shrines on top of and at the foot of mountains, in pilgrimages to sacred mountains, in the use of a special language by hunters and woodcutters in the mountains, and in burials on mountain sites. Shugendō developed as a special sect of ascetic mountain worship served by the Yamabushi, the austerity-practising priests. The Bon festival linked souls of the dead with mountain fastnesses.[13]

The intimate alliance of this cluster of beliefs with the formation of densetsu can readily be seen. Reference to mountains is made in tale after tale in Ikeda's index. The Buddhist priest regularly visits or resides at a mountain temple; the yamabushi are dedicated to the worship of Yama-no-kami; foxes, badgers, ogresses, tengu, and other mysterious beings inhabit the mountains.

Following Yanagita's typology, Hori defined three classes of hunters' densetsu based on mountain beliefs, the Kōya and Nikkō types, named for mountains, and the Shiiba type, named for a village.

The Mount Kōya legend complex describes how Kūkai or Kōbo Daishi (744-835), founder of the Shingon sect of Buddhism, and the magnet of an extensive cycle of saints' legends, located his shrine on the mountain in honor of the mountain goddess and her son, and with their consent.[14] In this legend formation, the mountain deity guides visitors and grants them leave to erect temples on her preserves.

In the Nikkō type, the mountain goddess gives favors of special hunting rights to hunters who have served her well. Thus did the goddess of Mount Nikkō reward the hunter Banzaburō who befriended her by shooting an arrow through the eye of a great centipede, the deity of Mount Akagi and her sworn enemy (rivalry between mountain deities is a recurrent legend theme). Banzaburō himself became the guardian deity of hunters. Mountain ascetics of the Tendai sect of Buddhism adopted this legend.

In the Shiiba form, the mountain goddess tests the sympathy of two hunter brothers. While hunting on the mountain, they meet a young woman who has just delivered a child and asks them for food; Ōma, fearing the taboo attached to birthing, refuses, but the younger brother Koma shares his lunch with her, and she bestows prosperity upon him. A variant told by the Tōno legend-teller Kizen Sasaki mingles the second and third types. Banji (or Banzaburō) has no luck at the hunt, while his brother Manji shoots many deer, until they meet a beautiful woman in the mountains in labor. Manji refuses her aid, which Banji proffers. The woman bore twelve babies, and promised Banji that if he called out his name "Banji" he would enjoy good hunting. In thanks he celebrated a holiday on the twelfth of each month (later limited by hunters to the twelfth of December). If a hunter wishes to bring bad luck to a rival he shouts "Manji."[15] The twelve children of the mountain goddess, who is sometimes called Mrs. Twelve (Jūni-sama), represent the twelve months. To ensure easy delivery, a woman in labor may hang a scroll portraying Jūni-sama at her bedside, or her husband may lead a horse toward the mountain to invite the goddess.[16] Kizen Sasaki also tells a legend of the strongest wrestler in Japan, Yokoguruma Daihachi, who encountered the deity Sankichi in the guise of a small boy, and was led by him to his mother, the goddess of Mount Taihei. After he prayed at her shrine for seven cold nights, she appeared as a young woman with a baby, which she gave him to hold, and then left. The weight of the baby increased until (like the pangs of childbirth) it became almost unbearable; at the breaking point the woman returned, revealed herself as the mountain spirit, and conferred unconquerable strength upon Daihachi.[17]

The deep basis of the Buddhist element in such folk-religious legends can be appreciated from the similar examples recorded in the late eighth century by the monk Kyōkai in *Nihon ryoiki.* The author-collector, a monk of Yakushi temple in Nara, states, in words dear to a modern folklorist, "I dare to write down oral traditions," and set down three sheaves of thirty-five, forty-two, and thirty-nine stories dealing with the karmic retribution of good and evil.[18] These are all narrative testimonies to the miraculous events befalling those who believed, or scorned, Buddhist teachings and monks and Kannon. Often the mountain is the scene of the miracle, and some stories are very like densetsu collected in the twentieth century. These deal with the emperor who married a fox-wife and named her Kitsune ("come and sleep") (I:2); the remarkably strong boy born to a farmer as a gift of the thunder, who became an acolyte at Gangō temple and slew a huge fiend there that proved to be the ghost of a wicked slave, whose hair is still preserved in the temple (I:3); the bronze Buddha which cried "Ouch! ouch!" when a thief stole it from the temple of Jin'e and hammered at its limbs, and so caused the thief's detection II:22; variant II:23; the monkey-kami of Taga Shrine on the mountain Mikamu-no-take, who revealed to a monk that he had been reborn as a monkey since, in his previous incarnation, as a king in India, he had attempted to limit the followers of monks (III:24). In the collection of Kyōkai the most popular Buddha is Kannon, who appears in seventeen stories, and endures in four of Ikeda's tale types. An occasional pre-Buddhist miracle may have crept into Kyokai's net. He relates the tale of a twenty-year-old woman who in the year 782 became pregnant without sexual intercourse and after three years gave birth to two stones, five inches in diameter. A great kami named Inaba revealed through a diviner that he had fathered the stones, which were then enshrined in the woman's abode (III:31). This seems to be a Shinto tradition. Kyōkai comments: "We never heard a story like this from ancient times until today."[19]

A major current trend in folklore scholarship, particularly of the folktale, emphasizes the performance aspect of the transmission process. We speak now of the tale-teller and balladsinger as performers, and collect not simply texts but the contexts of storytelling events that set forth the mimetic, histrionic, and intonational qualities of the narrator and the responses and reactions of the audiences on a given occasion. Surely nowhere in the literature of folklore can a better case be made for the thesis of folktale-telling as performance than in Japan, for a common stock of story themes unites the classic traditional forms of Japanese theater with the repertoires of professional and village storytellers. Turning again to Ikeda's index, we see that sixteen tale types have been dramatized as Kabuki, seven as Noh, thirty-two as Kyōgen, and six as Jōruri. On the side of the urban and court professional storytellers, Ikeda identifies thirty-one tale types as rakugo and six as kōdan. These figures still do not do justice to the correlations, since over half the Noh repertoire of 223 plays deal with the possession of a mortal by a spirit or a god, the continual theme of folk legends.[20] And a correlation is lacking for the incidence of legend kernels in Bunraku.

A few examples may illustrate this point. The story of "Stone Pillow Murder" (type 327B) in which an innkeeper murders guests who sleep on a stone pillow, and mistakenly kills her own daughter who has changed places with a traveler she falls in love with, becomes localized in Japan as an actual occurrence. Noh, Bunraku, and Kabuki, as well as various chants mentioned by Ikeda, all present this tale of tragic retribution. "Death Tricked" (type 322), relating how a jester outwits death on earth and in the lower world, is told as a rakugo, written and performed by San-yūtei Enchō (1839-1900), and dramatized as a Kabuki that Ikeda recalls seeing in Tokyo. The writer himself saw a Kabuki in Tokyo in 1957 of Obasute-yama (type 981), grimly depicting, in the style of Jack Kirkland's long-running Broadway play *Tobacco Road,* a poverty-stricken family devouring every grain of rice in their bowls or spilled on the ground. This powerful legend of the impoverished mountain village that abandoned its aged at sixty also appeared in Noh, rakugo, poems, songs, and rhymes.[21] Obasute-yama further commands interest as a Japanese localizing of a European Märchen type that emphasizes the wise elder's solving enigmatic tasks (the story circulates in the United States as a "sick joke": a colleague at a history convention told me of the son and grandson carrying the aged patriarch in a basket to the place of abandonment; the son was about to leave the spot when the grandson asked him to bring away the basket; "Why?"; "I need it for you, Dad"). Legends of heroes lend themselves well to theatrical treatment. The adventures of Kōga Saburō (type 301A), who rescued a princess from an underground cavern, and later became the watergod of Lake Suwa, were performed in 1808 in the Kabuki play "Account of Kōga Saburō in the Cave," as well as in other plays and in Jōruri chants.[22] A Noh play, "Benkei on the Bridge," probably from the first half of the fifteenth century, presents the celebrated episode in which Benkei, the eight foot warrior-priest with the strength of a hundred men who fought in the civil wars of the twelfth century, met his match at Gōjo Bridge at the hands of a stripling.[23] The chanted epic plays known as Kōwaka-mai, popular at the Imperial court in Kyoto in the mid-sixteenth century, and still enacted by a troupe in Kyushu, contained in their repertoire a number titled *Yuriwaka*, concerning the Ulysses-like exploits of the champion who would sleep and stay awake for seventeen days and nights alternately, and who always fought with iron bows and arrows (type 974).[24]

From the performances of professional actors to the performances of professional storytellers, who relate kōdan of heroic warriors and rakugo of motely characters before urban audiences, is a short step. Both sets of performers employ variations on the same traditional legend plots. We can perceive the overlap in the selection from the *Hō-Dan-Zō*, the Treasure-Tale-Storehouse accumulated from the public storytellers in the early part of the present century by Post Wheeler (1896-1958), an American consular official in Tokyo. Here are a batch of anecdotes testifying to the shrewd, if harsh, decisions of Judge Ōka; an account of a grateful fox who rewarded a poor woodcutter by having him sell her in the guise of a beautiful maiden to a brothel-keeper; a legend of Straw Hat Temple and Straw Hat Village, named for the placing of a straw hat upon a Kannon in a ruined temple by a poor young girl to shield it from the rain, an act that won her the hand of the lord's son; a chronicle of a horse that suddenly began speaking the most derogatory comments about his master, who had unwittingly entombed a thief in a deserted shrine, whereupon the thief cursed the man and sent his spirit to possess the steed. Delivered in a high-flown, archaic prose, filled with delicious innuendoes and turns of phrase, these stories from the *hanashika* are far from the folk style, but they dip into the same stream of legendry and anecdote.[25]

Continuity in performance style as well as in story content exists between stage actors and professional storytellers. The master narrators of rakugo indeed belong to the theater; they present their tales on stage kneeling before the audience, and recreate characters and scenes through adroit miming, gesticulation, intonation and use of ideophones, and handling of props such as chopsticks or fans. In an essay illustrated with photographs of Katsura Bunraku in characteristic storytelling poses, Vena Hrdličkova has conveyed a sense of the artistry and training that distinguishes the professional teller of rakugo.[26] She observes how he can adapt his vocal range to simulate the gruff man, the shrill wife, the fearful apprentice, the arrogant clerk, and how realistically he sips noodles with an inhaling sound, gulps wine *kabu*, *kabu*, and weeps while eating. As a youth Bunraku frequented the theater, and his career combines histrionic and narrative gifts.

What then of the folk storyteller? If narrators of folktales in all parts of the world are considered performers—Harold Scheub, for instance, invariably refers to the Xhosa tellers of ntsomi whom he recorded in the Republic of South Africa as performers[27]—then surely in Japan, with its rich heritage of traditional theatrical arts, the village spinners of legends must shine as performing artists. The study of Robert Adams on Mrs. Tsune Watanabe indicates the possibilities for in-depth portraits of folktale raconteurs.[28] On a folklore observation trip to Okinawa in August 1975, sponsored by the Japan Folklore Society and the Committee to Celebrate the Centenary of the Birth of Kunio Yanagita, I observed Taro Kinjō, ninety-one, demonstrate his storytelling art. His continuous flow of expressive hand and arm gestures gave the narration a truly dramatic quality.

The traditional theater as well as the stock of oral legends is indebted to religious folk belief and observance. In shamanistic trance, hunters' ceremonies, and agricultural rituals some scholars see the origins of Japanese theater and dance-drama. Before their adaptation to the commercial urban stage, Noh and kyogen took the forms of religious rites and services in the countryside. Village folk regarded puppets as a magical means of calling down deities and spirits, and puppets are still employed in religious ceremonies. The dance-dramas known as geinō, with their special forms such as kagura, the temple dances, and dengaku, rice-planting dances, are associated with seasonal and ritual worship of gods.[29]

In a suggestive essay on "The Birth of the Japanese Theater," Thomas Immoos relates Noh and kagura and other dramatic forms to rites of magic propitiating gods of the animal and vegetable kingdoms. He describes a kyogen he witnessed in Miyazaki prefecture as derived from a ritual celebration of an annual boar hunt. In the play a mountain dragon-god entwines and swallows Tarō, the big-headed fool, but is shot by Yazō, the little bright boy, and forced to release Tarō, amid smoke, noise, excitement and the relish of youthful spectators. In such hunting and agricultural rites Immoos sees the seedbed of Noh dramas.[30]

Folk religion, folk theater, and folk legend all converge in the realm of Japanese storytelling.

Indiana University
Bloomington, Indiana

APPENDIX

Historical characters listed in Ikeda's subject index

NAMES	TALE TYPES	IDENTIFICATIONS	DATES
Abe no Seimei	413D 671	court diviner of Heian Period	9th-12th
Chiisakobe no Sugaru	465	famous courtier of Emperor Yūryaku	462 A.D.
Ōka Echizen-no-kami	653 (780) 920A (1645C) 1861	famous judge	1677-1753
Jikaku Daishi	956A	Buddhist priest who studied in China	838-847
Jōye	2400	ditto; son of prime minister, founder of temple	630?-714
Jōzō	930A	famous Buddhist priest in Kyoto	892-964
Kibi no Makibi	1645A	studied in China 20 years	694-775
*Kōbō Daishi (Kūkai)	751A	founder of Shingon sect of Buddhism	774-835
Minamoto no Yoritomo (Kajiware Kagemochi, a warrior, 554)	554 967	first Shogun to establish military government in Kamakura	1147-1199
Ōkuni-nushi	313 554	descendant of Susanowo and ruler of Izumo	mythical
Ōoka Echizen-no-kami Tadasuke	653 920A 1861	clever judge of Edo	1677-1751

Saigyō	921Z	Buddhist priest famed as poet	1118-1190
Sōgi	921Z	Buddhist priest famed as poet in *renga* style	1421-1502
Tawara Tōda Hidesato (=Fujiwara Hidesato)	738	strong hero who killed giant centipede	early 10th
Toyotomi, Hideyoshi	1540	farmer who became prime minister, fought Korea	1536-1598
Watanabe no Tsuna	971	one of four samurai serving General Minamoto no Raikō	953-1024
Yuryaku	465	21st emperor, ordered courtier to fetch thunder	456-479

Mentioned in notes but not in subject index

Ryōben	768C	famous monk	689-773
Agatamori	312B	man of great strength	379
Abe no Yasuna	671	father of Abe no Seimei	Heian period
Shuten Dōji	780A	legendary ogre-thief of Tamba Hills near Kyoto	10th
Ikkyū	612 1262*	talented patriarch of Daitokuji Temple, Kyoto (anecdotes) printed in *Ikkū Kantō Banoshi*, 3 vols. 1672)	1394-1481
Kitchomu	1262*	local character on Kyūshū	mythical
Taira no Suetake	768A	famous warrior, holds baby in Konjaku	11th
Kōga Saburū	301A	deity of Suwa	mythical
Yuriwaka	974	strong warrior, Imperial minister	mythical

NOTES

[1] Kunio Yanagita, "Introduction to the Japanese Edition," in *Japanese Folk Tales*, tr. Fanny Hagin Mayer (Tokyo: Tokyo News Service, 1960), p. 177. Works of Yanagita especially deserving of translation are: *Momotaro-no-Tanjo* (The Birth of Momotaro), a detailed discussion of folktales dealing with a hero's miraculous birth; *Kosho-bungei-shi Ko* (A Study of Oral Literature), considering the development of the folktale and its relationship to other forms of oral and literary tradition; and *Mukashi-banashi Oboegaki* (Memoranda on the Folktale), short monographs on nine well-known tales with extensive introductory and concluding remarks about the general structure and meaning of Japanese folktales.

[2] Translator's Introduction by Fanny Hagin Mayer to Kunio Yanagita, *Japanese Folk Tales, A Revised Selection* (Tokyo: Tokyo New Service, 1966), p. x.

[3] *Ibid.*, p. 9.

[4] Kunio Yanagita, "Introduction to the Revised Edition," in *Japanese Folk Tales*, tr. Fanny Hagin Mayer (Tokyo: Tokyo News Service, 1954), p. 293.

[5] FF Communications No. 209 (Helsinki: Suoamalainen Tiedeakatemia Academia Scientiarum Fennica, 1971). See also the classification of Keigo Seki identifying 470 tale types based on indigenous themes: "Types of Japanese Folktales," *Asian Folklore Studies* 27 (1966): 1-220.

[6] Thus see Eiichiro Ishida, "The Kappa Legend," *Folklore Studies* 9 (Peking, 1950): i-vi, 1-152; Richard M. Dorson, *Folk Legends of Japan* (Rutland, Vt., and Tokyo: Charles E. Tuttle Co., 1962), pp. 59-68.

[7] See also "The Tale of Yurikawa" in Dorson, *Folk Legends of Japan*, pp. 154-156.

[8] A text is given in Dorson, *Folk Legends of Japan*, pp. 231-232, "Oka Castle."

[9] Nobuhiro Matsumoto, "Japanese Metalworkers: A Possible Source for their Legends," in *Studies in Japanese Folklore*, ed. Richard M. Dorson (Bloomington: Indiana University Press, 1963; reprinted Port Washington, N. Y.: Kennikat Press, 1973), pp. 147-164.

[10] Ichiro Hori, *Folk Religion in Japan, Continuity and Change* (Chicago and London: University of Chicago Press, 1968).

[11] Published by University of Tennessee Press, 1975.

[12] Hori, *Folk Religion in Japan*, pp. 167-169.

[13] See Hori, ch. 4, "Mountains and Their Importance for the Idea of the Other World," Nelly Naumann, "*Yama no Kami*–die japanische Berggottheit," *Asian Folklore Studies* 22 (1963): 133-366 and 23: 2 (1964): 48-199; review by Matthias Eder of Gorai Shigeru, *Yama no Shūkyō* (Mountain Religion): *Shugendō*, Asian Folklore Studies 31: 1 (1972): 125-127; H. Byron Earhart, "The Celebration of Haru-Yama (Spring Mountain): An Example of Folk Religious Practices in Contemporary Japan," *Asian Folklore Studies* 27: 1 (1968): 1-24. The idea of Japanese folktales reflecting Japanese folk religion is discussed by Robert Smith, "On Certain Tales of the *Konjaku Monogatari* as Reflections of Japanese Folk Religion," *Asian Folklore Studies* 25 (1966): 221-233, which considers the selection made by Susan W. Jones, trans., in *Ages Ago: Thirty-Seven Tales from the* Konjaku Monogatari *Collection* (Cambridge, Mass.: Harvard University Press, 1959); Fanny Hagin Mayer, "Religious Elements in Japanese Folk Tales," in *Studies in Japanese Culture,* ed. Joseph Roggendorf (Tokyo, 1963), pp. 1-16; Matthias

Eder, "Reality in Japanese Folktales," *Asian Folklore Studies* 28: 1 (1969): 17-26. Eder is closest to my position, that Japanese folktales are primarily legends.

[14] For Kōbo Daishi see Dorson, *Folk Legends of Japan*, pp. 33-36, and references, p. 33.

[15] "Banji and Manji" in Dorson, *Folk Legends of Japan*, pp. 167-169.

[16] Hori, p. 167 and note 52.

[17] Dorson, *Folk Legends of Japan*, pp. 171-174, "The Strongest Wrestler in Japan."

[18] Kyōkai, *Miraculous Stories from the Japanese Buddhist Tradition*, translated and annotated with an introduction by Kyoko Motomochi Nakamura (Cambridge, Mass.: Harvard University Press, 1973), p. 158.

[19] *Ibid.*, p. 266.

[20] Thomas Inmoos, "The Birth of the Japanese Theater," *Monumenta Nipponica* 24 (1969): 412.

[21] Dorson, *Folk Legends of Japan*, p. 223, quoting Sanaro in *Asahi Evening News*, Tokyo, July 12, 1957, "A Memo on the 'Oak-Mount Song' "; Donald Keene, *The Old Woman, the Wife and the Archer* (New York: Columbia University Press, 1961), pp. xi-xiii.

[22] The legend of "Kōga Saburō" is in Dorson, *Folk Legends*, pp. 158-160.

[23] "Benkei on the Bridge" has been translated by Arthur Waley, *The Nō Plays of Japan* (New York: Grove Press, 1957), pp. 115-120. Two legends of Benkei are in Dorson, *Folk Legends*, pp. 163-164.

[24] Discussed by Ikeda, p. 218.

[25] Post Wheeler, *Tales from the Japanese Storytellers*, ed. Harold G. Henderson (Rutland, Vt.: Charles E. Tuttle, Co., 1964).

[26] Vena Hrdlickova, "Gramophone Recordings of the Representative Tales of Katsura Bunraku, a Professional Japanese Storyteller," *Journal of the Folklore Institute* 9: 2/3 (1972): 194-208.

[27] See for example Harold Scheub, "The Art of Nongenile Mazithathu Zenani, a Gcaleka Ntsomi Performer," in *African Folklore*, ed. R. M. Dorson (Garden City, New York: Doubleday Anchor Books, 1972), pp. 115-142.

[28] Robert J. Adams, "The Social Identity of a Japanese Storyteller" (Indiana University doctoral dissertation, 1972).

[29] Matthias Eder, "Japanese Folklore Science Today," *Asian Folklore Studies* 18 (1959): 310-314, reviewing volume 9 of the *Nihon minzokugaku daikei* (*Encyclopaedia of Japanese Folklore Science*) devoted to "Geinō to goroku ("Dramatic Performances and Amusements").

[30] *Monumenta Nipponica* 24 (1969): 403-414.

FOLKLORE AND NATIONALISM IN MODERN CHINA

Sandra Eminov

During some two thousand years of fairly constant Confucian orientation, educated Chinese emphasized the elitist traditions of the literati, while ignoring the folk and their lore. Confucianism and its trappings served an aristocratic class of bureaucrats who were supremely self-confident of their own cultural and class supremacy. This lofty, if somewhat virulent, ethnocentrism was shattered by the Opium War (1839-1842) and subsequent events in the nineteenth and early twentieth centuries. The political and military disasters of this period plunged China into decades of internal chaos and national self-examination: a once serene, advanced nation was transformed into weak and humiliated spheres of influence. Chinese intellectuals began to re-evaluate their heritage in the light of these unprecedented events. They came to realize that the old way of life was no longer viable. The traditional political system was disposed of through the successful Revolution of 1911: the despised Manchu (Ch'ing) dynasty fell, and the subsequent establishment of the Republic of China (1912-1949) marked the beginning of a new order with its own ideology. Chinese intellectuals repudiated Confucianism and monarchism as relics unsuitable for the modern world. Instead, they turned to new ideas, and to innovations in politics and culture.

Political disasters of the late nineteenth and early twentieth centuries served as a catalyst for great intellectual ferment in early Republican China. This ferment, nurtured for years among small circles of intellectuals, burst upon the public consciousness in September of 1915 with the first issue of *New Youth* (*Hsin Ch'ing Nien*), an influential (and quickly much-imitated) magazine. In the initiatory number of *New Youth* its editor, Ch'en Tu-hsiu (later, one of the founders of the Chinese Communist Party), published his essay "Call to Youth." In this electrifying polemic, Ch'en encouraged young people to discard the shackles of Confucianism and the traditional culture, and to cultivate an attitude opposite to that of Confucianism: independent, scientific, aggressive, and progressive. "This article had the effect of a bombshell whose impact shook the very heart of the Chinese intellectual world."[1] Ch'en's article initiated perhaps the most important period in modern Chinese intellectual history, known as the New Culture Movement.

In addition to continued attacks on Confucianism, *New Youth* published translations of western writers. At first, these translations were published in the literary ("classical") style, which was considered the only acceptable form of written communication even in the early twentieth century. Soon, though, the magazine signaled another major change in the course of modern Chinese history with its publication of Hu Shih's "Some Tentative Suggestions for the Reform of Chinese Literature" (January, 1917). This article, which ushered in the "literary revolution" aspect of the New Culture Movement, proposed the use of the modern spoken language in place of the ancient, effete literary style. Such a proposal was radical, if not downright horrifying, for literature and the Confucian literary style had been the mainstay of China's intellectuals for centuries. As the literary historian Wu-chi Liu has written, "until Hu appeared on the scene with his novel ideas, even the manifestos of reformers and revolutionaries had kept to the classical style of writing as if there could be no other."[2] A positive call to arms in favor of utilizing the despised *pai-hua*, or "common language," was unprecedented. In unequivocal language, Hu Shih wrote, "I advocate the adoption of colloquial expressions and words in writing poetry and prose. It would be much better to use the living words of the twentieth century than the dead words of three thousand years ago . . ."[3]

Hu's literary plea was an immediate success. The literary revolution was launched, and numerous magazines copying the style of *New Youth* quickly appeared. *New Youth, New Tide* (*Hsin Ch'ao*), and other magazines gave space to unfamiliar ideas for students and intellectuals who had become alienated from traditional Chinese culture. They had rejected Confucianism, but no alternative was immediately apparent. Many, particularly the thousands of Chinese who had gone abroad for extended periods of foreign study, had become partially westernized; they disdained the ways of old China and longed for the strength and superiority they imagined they saw in the example of the modern West.

Progressive magazines printed numerous articles about the new philosophies which returning students brought from the West and via Japan. For a time, myriad Western philosophies vied for acceptance among China's modern thinkers. Western-style liberal democracy was the panacea most often promoted by writers, although simplified (and sometimes garbled) versions of idealism, materialism, anarchism, and other "isms," appeared in the pages of modern Chinese magazines.

Many scholars, however, rejected the idea of total Westernization. While agreeing that Confucianism was unsuitable for a modernized China, they wished to retain positive aspects of Chinese culture in order that their cultural identity not be lost. One extreme interpretation of "positive traits" foreshadows later developments. This is the Soviet Union-influenced stance of Ch'en Tu-hsiu. In an ideologically oriented essay in the second issue of *New Youth*, Ch'en Tu-hsiu declared himself "willing to risk the enmity of all the pedantic scholars of the country to raise the banner of 'The Revolutionary Army in Literature. . . .' " On this banner would be written three principles:

(1) To overthrow the decorative and flattering literature of the aristocracy and to create a plain, simple, and expressive literature of the people.
(2) To overthrow the stale and over-flowery literature of classicism and to create a fresh and sincere literature of realism.
(3) To overthrow the unintelligible and obscurantist literature of the hermits and to create an understandable and popular literature of society.[4]

Thus, the New Culture Movement almost immediately spotlighted two recognizable trends in the thinking of modernized intellectuals. One was the literary reform position of scholars like Hu Shih; the other was the politically inspired, activist approach of scholarly politicians like Ch'en Tu-hsiu.

One result of the political-literary New Culture Movement was an unprecedented interest in the folk, their colloquial oral literature, and their non-Confucian contributions to the nation. The repudiation of Confucianism produced a profound void in the lives of educated Chinese. With the old society and traditions in decay, the old symbols had fallen into disrepute. New, untarnished symbols were needed, and China's modern intellectuals now turned to the folk to provide these symbols.

Following the urging of Hu Shih to "use the living words of the twentieth century," folklore researchers at first concentrated on oral literature, particularly folksong. The first organized effort in this direction began in February, 1918 when the Department of Folksong Collection was begun at National Peking University. Professors Liu Pan-nung, Ch'en Chun-tien, and Chou Tso-jen guided this Department and also edited a short-lived journal, the *Bulletin for Nationwide Contemporary Folksong Collection*. Students were directed to collect "folksongs concerning the customs and habits, the history and society of the respective places. . .songs of far-off soldiers, rustics, longing girls and sorrowful women, in so far as they have natural beauty and are not obscene . . . "[5] Eventually over 3000 folksongs were collected from various provinces, but publication was unsystematic and plagued by political and financial adversity.

After the first collecting efforts of students at National Peking University, folklore studies developed rapidly. Events in the political arena furthered interest in the folk, especially after the May Fourth Movement was ignited by the infamous "Shantung decision" at the Paris Peace Conference in 1919. Shantung Peninsula in northeastern China had been leased to Germany as part of an "unequal treaty" (1898). China expected to recover all rights to the Peninsula as part of the settlement of World War I. However, in April of 1919 the Allies, representatives of Western enlightenment and liberal democracy, agreed to "transfer" to Japan privileges which Germany had enjoyed for two decades. This decision caused Chinese nationalism to reach new heights with the May Fourth Movement: "The news from Versailles immediately provoked an outburst of indignation and intense patriotism among the Chinese students, who spontaneously organized a great patriotic mass parade on May the fourth in protest against the unlawful Versailles decision concerning the fate of Shantung."[6]

After the Shantung decision and the resulting May Fourth Movement, even most of those who had promoted "total Westernization" were repelled by a civilization which, they felt, had proved to be morally bankrupt. China's disillusioned intellectual leaders discarded Western models for the remaking of their culture and pride. One result was heightened interest in the Chinese folk and their culture as a third alternative to Confucianism and Westernization.

In 1920 the Department of Folksong Collection gave way to the Peking University Folksong Research Society (*Ko-yao yen-chiu hui*). Ku Chieh-kang, Chou Tso-jen, and Yu Ch'en-chien were founding members. In December of 1922 the Society began its journal, *Folksong Weekly* (*Ko-yao chou-k'an*), under the direction of Chou Tso-jen and Ch'ang Hui. *Folksong Weekly* was to be the first major continuing folklore publication in China. During the two and a half years of its active life, *Folksong Weekly* received a total of more than 13,000 folksong contributions from every province of China, more than 2,000 of which were published in the pages of the *Weekly*.

For all their collection activity, however, the folklorists of the Folksong Research Society were not unbiased scholars. The Editor's Introductory Note to the first issue of *Folksong Weekly* reveals that, in addition to true folkloric aims, literary criticism and nationalism-through-poetry were integral parts in their concept of folklore research: "The aims of collecting folksongs are two; technical and literary . . . . Now we collect and print them to prepare the way for technical study. This is our first aim. From these sources we may select some good songs in the light of literary criticism. . . . Therefore, the work is not only to make manifest the hidden light of the people, but also to promote the development of the national poetry."[7] These poetic "hidden lights of the people," then, were to furnish models for reinvigorating the literary language. The literary folklorists of the early 1920s promoted folklore research for the sake of literary reform: from its beginning, folklore study was utilized for nonfolkloric aims.

Folklore study was blossoming. However, the same intellectuals who led the Chinese Folklore Movement were victims of the transition from Confucianism to modern nationalism. For many, "haunted by the ethics of the old tradition," pursuing folklore studies meant sacrificing their reputations. However, intellectuals were no longer allowed—at least in theory—to consider themselves superior to the masses. Some folklore researchers rationalized the dilemma by fervently throwing themselves into studying folklore for "social reform," or for "bringing new ideas to modern Chinese literature." One such enthusiast was Ch'ang Hui, a member of the Peking Folksong Research Society. In an article written in 1922, Ch'ang noted that "in order to study folksongs, not only is [an appreciation of] literature important, but also important is the understanding of the people's psychology. In order to investigate the people's psychology it is extremely necessary to pay attention to books concerning folk customs (*min-su*) . . . We should from now on study *min-su-hsüeh* (Folklore) enthusiastically!"[8] The circular reasoning found in Ch'ang Hui's argument is typical of many folkloric pronouncements which relied on bombast rather than logic.

Studying folklore "enthusiastically" became more important as the folklore movement became more politicized. A trend toward a social-political orientation was evident as early as 1923, with the founding of the Custom Survey Society of National Peking University. Members of the Society and interested outsiders were asked to collect specific information through the use of a lengthy questionnaire. Additionally, the Society planned to collect written sources and to create a folklore museum. The emphasis, however, was on the questionnaire devised by Professor Chang Ching-sheng. This document dealt with the "environment," "thought," and "customs" of the people through fifty-four specific questions, most of which concentrated on customs that were considered part of the old Confucian way of life. These customs, regarded as reactionary elements to be swept away by the New Culture Movement, included "idolatrous processions and performances along the procession," "concubines and slave-girls," "brothel frequenting," and "abandoned children."[9] With such an emphasis, it is perhaps not surprising that, of the three thousand questionnaires distributed, only forty-one completed copies were returned to the Society. By the middle of 1924, the Custom Survey Society was disbanded. This event did not signal an end to interest in social reform through folklore investigation. Only two years later, Y.C. James Yen established the Chinese Mass Education Movement in Ting Hsien,[10] and from 1926 on, many folklore researchers stressed social reform (mainly the abolition of backward customs and beliefs) through education.

Social reform and education of the masses was one goal of folklorist-intellectuals of the 1920s. Another, equally important goal was to revise and refurbish the image of the intellectual in modern Chinese society. The modern period was proving to be highly antipathetic to China's intellectuals. The literati were commonly depicted as parasites of the old order, bureaucrats who served the interests of the aristocracy at the expense of the lower classes. The modern Chinese intellectual felt a pressing need to disassociate himself from this old image, and to find a new identity for himself as a positive force in the new China. Folklorists were especially concerned with the problems of intellectuals and their relation to the folk. In his 1925 Preface to *Mount Miao Feng* (*Miao-feng Shan*), a study of customs associated with the annual offering to the spirit of a temple on that mountain, Ku Chieh-kang outlined the problems of intellectuals who had not yet freed themselves of the old identity. In former times, he admitted, the literati felt themselves superior to the peasantry; they did not comprehend the lives of the people, but considered them lowly creatures. Such class distinctions were dispensed with, in theory, at the founding of the Republic, for the Constitution clearly stated: "All people are equal under the law." This fine sentiment remained little more than that, however, for many intellectuals still harbored class prejudices, and a serious lack of mutual understanding was apparent. Ku called for more understanding of the masses and increased social harmony through a study of the folk and their ways, for "if one only *listens* to the slogan 'to the people,' we'll be unable to attain the *reality* of 'to the people.' " In this article Ku presented folklore studies as a means through which one might discover the reality of 'to the people,' and thus bring about increased social progress and harmony.[11] In short, then, the goals of scholars like Ku Chieh-kang were two: to bring forth the folk and their culture as a viable third alternative to the rejected ways of Confucianism and Westernization, and to find within this alternative tradition a new, acceptable identity for the Chinese intellectual. Ku and his followers believed that both goals were attainable, and they pursued these ends through the gathering and interpretation of folk materials.

The work of the famous critic and scholar Hu Shih and his students "was directly or indirectly devoted, in effect, to redefining the idea of 'Chinese,' through a process of reordering the relationship of past and present."[12] Simply stated, scholars led by Hu Shih and his student Ku Chieh-kang sought a new definition of "Chinese" through an investigation of the Little Tradition, particularly in the area of oral literature. Using an historical approach, folklore researchers brought to bear upon the records of the past new, non-Confucian methods of interpretation. The new interpretations, in turn, were to help destroy old traditions and to authorize new ones. In this way Hu and his group hoped to find validation for a revised, nonaristocratic interpretation of Chinese history and tradition.

Hu Shih pioneered this approach, carrying out extensive research into the historical relationships between aristocratic and folk literature. He concluded that

> every new form, every innovation in literature, had come never from the imitative classical writers of the upper classes, but always from the unlettered class of the countryside, the village inn, and the market-place. I found that it was always these new forms and patterns of the common people that, from time to time, furnished the new blood and fresh vigor to the literature of the literati, and rescued it from the perpetual danger of fossilization.[13]

The work of Hu and other researchers was imbued with a kind of Sinicized romanticism much like the romanticism of Johann Herder's *Volksgeist*. The notion that the folk possessed a special, long ignored oral literature that preserved uniquely Chinese virtues and traditions, was an idea which captured the imagination of the new intellectuals. The classical literature of the past was now interpreted as a stale, class bound phenomenon, while the oral poetry of the masses was seen as a truly Chinese creative production of a national, collective nature. This nationalistic interpretation of folk literature became extremely popular during the Republican period. A typical stance was that taken by another prolific folklore researcher, Lou Tze-k'uang. Lou, writing on the "national character" of folklore, remarked that folklore is not created by individuals, but rather is a product of groups of people. The nature, conduct, emotions, and even the background of their lives appear in the oral literature of such folk groups. Indeed, said Lou, if folklore were lacking in national character, it would lose its unique place in the lives of the people.[14]

While folklore researchers were becoming more reform oriented, events outside the academic world prompted unexpected changes in the Folklore Movement. Charismatic nationalist leader Sun Yat-sen died March 12, 1925. China was left divided between the power of military warlords in the north and Kuomintang (Nationalist Party) rule in the south. In May, 1925, the

Kuomintang officially severed all connections with the north of China and turned its efforts towards cooperation with the Soviet Union. The internal political and military struggles prompted many scholars to leave Peking for the south of China, a move which caused the Folksong Research Society to be disbanded. The diaspora of National Peking University faculty (1925) occurred at a time when membership in the Folksong Research Society was large and its activities numerous. Ninety-seven issues of *Folksong Weekly* had appeared by this time, several monographs had been published, and Society-sponsored collections of folksongs and folk expressions had been made in all regions of the country. With the demise of the Folksong Research Society, the Folklore Movement regrouped in the south.

In the south, the Chinese Folklore Movement was popular and prolific. Lou Tze-k'uang has noted that, with many transplanted scholars forsaking active life for the library, "a high tide of research occurred, much of which concerned folklore."[15] During the 1920s and early 1930s, numerous volumes of collected lore were published. These included "several tens of thousands of folksongs, more than three thousand folktales, many thousands of proverbs and riddles, hundreds of folk plays, and . . . a great treasure of folk customs, festivals, superstitions, and medicinal beliefs."[16]

The "high tide of research" in the south brought about a better understanding of folklore concepts and techniques. Folklore collection had begun with vaguely defined programs which contained more of idealism than sound methodology. However, folklore enthusiasts were aware of the folklore movements of other countries, and Western scholars sometimes lectured on folklore at Chinese universities. In the first issue of *Folksong Weekly*, the Editor's Introductory Note had quoted Baron Guido Vitale, an early collector of Chinese songs and tales.[17] Perhaps the first major contribution towards comprehending "folklore" as it was defined in the West came with Ts'ai Yüan-p'ei's 1926 article "Talking about Folklore" (Shuo min-tsu-hsüeh). Ts'ai, who had been chancellor of National Peking University during the tumultuous New Culture Movement, was in the south at Nanking when he wrote, "*Min-tsu-hsüeh* [folklore]is a branch of learning which examines the cultures of peoples so as to further the descriptive or comparative studies [of the cultures]. . . . But in German the singular form for *Völkerkunde* is *Volkskunde* which comes from the English word Folklore. This English term was created by W.J. Thoms in 1846 to replace the term Popular Antiquities . . . ."[18] Ts'ai's article marks the first time that "folklore" was seriously understood as a disciplined social science in China. Some folklore scholars thereafter attempted to utilize the methodologies and tools of Western folklore research.

The southern phase of the Chinese Folklore Movement got off to a quick start at Sun Yat-sen University in Canton. There, the Institute of History and Philology was founded in August, 1927. Under the direction of Fu Ssu-nien, a former student leader in the May Fourth Movement, the Institute developed a folklore project which came to include a Folklore Society (Min-su Hsüeh-hui, 1927), a Show Room of Folklore Objects (Feng-su wu-p'ien ch'en-lieh-shih, 1928), and an extensive program of folklore courses (1928). The first publication of the Folklore Society was the journal *People's Literature and Art* (*Min-chien wen-i*), which appeared in November, 1927. The lead article for the first issue was by Tung Tso-pin, an archaeologist who wrote extensively in *People's Literature and Art*. Expounding on the popular slogan of "two cultures," Tung complained that the aristocracy had totally dominated Chinese culture for more than a thousand years, and that "all literature was the instrument of their play and pleasure. The obligations of morality and the laws of government were used as screens to hide their wrongs and as weapons to slaughter the common people."[19] Tung's remedy for this dire situation was a familiar one. He urged the readers of the journal to overthrow the outmoded, corrupt literature of the aristocracy, to become informed and appreciative of the literature and art of the people, and to unite to promote a fresh and living art and literature. Articles such as this one are forceful reminders that, while some intellectuals were attempting to develop folklore as a scholarly field, many continued to publish material which was mainly political in nature.

After twelve issues, the Folklore Society enlarged the scope of its journal and changed its name to *Folklore* (*Min-su*). In addition to literature and art, the journal now included articles on customs and folk beliefs. A weekly which ran continuously from March, 1928 to April, 1930, *Folklore* became the most versatile journal of the early Folklore Movement. Additionally, Sun Yat-sen University published numerous folklore monographs in several series.

By the late 1920s, folklore research in China appeared to be moving in two distinct directions. One direction was towards a more scholarly, informed treatment of folklore materials. Professors at Sun Yat-sen University's folklore department introduced their students to new concepts and methodologies in courses such as "Method of Studying Legends" (taught by Ku Chieh-kang), "Psychology and Folklore" (Wang Ching-hsi), and "Introduction to Folksongs" (Chung Ching-wen).[20] Inspired by the *List of Types of Indo-European Folk-tales*, translated from Charlotte Burne's 1914 *Handbook of Folklore* by Chung Ching-wen and Yang Ch'eng-chih, some students began comparative folktale studies. Also, the Finnish historical-geographical method, first explained to Chinese students by R.D. Jameson, became popular among folklore researchers. Jameson, the Westerner who first brought word of Kaarle Krohn's *Die folkloristische Arbeitsmethode* to China, expounded on the Finnish method in an article entitled "Comparative Folklore Methodological Notes."[21] In general, folklore activity among nonactivist scholars now moved to a stage "characterized by an effort to combine fieldwork materials and experiences with speculative treatment."[22]

The other main trend in folklore research of the late 1920s was a strengthening of efforts to utilize folklore for social and political ends. Nationalistic postures of varying extremity were assumed by proponents of the "education" and "political" schools of folklore study. "The political school," wrote Ku Chieh-kang, "wishes to glorify the national spirit; the education school wishes to transform customs. . . ."[23]

Sociologically and politically oriented folklore workers gained momentum in the 1930s. After the development of rural reconstruction plans, folklore journals came to be filled with the idea of using folklore studies in order to modernize society. The most extreme expression of this school of thought appeared throughout the 1930s in the journal *Mass Education* (*Min-chung chiao-yü chi-k'an*). In this journal, the literary approach to folklore was entirely abandoned. Writers espoused a "functional" method, which "aimed only to discover the sociological role of a custom or art form in order that reformers might better know how to implement their programs."[24] The education school of the Chinese Folklore Movement proved extremely antagonistic to scholars of less activist persuasions. When the Ting Hsien experimental village project published its first report in 1933, the idea of "study for study's sake" was denounced vigorously. Understanding the realities of the people's lives was considered only the beginning of their work: social reform was the goal.

During the 1930s, many researchers were more reform oriented, and the Communist approach to folklore already was felt in some areas (particularly in "liberated" Kiangsi, where a peasant drama troupe, the Central Blue-Shirt Ensemble, presented a series of dramatic performances with socialist themes). However, a significant number of serious scholars remained loyal to the less activist "literary" school. During the mid-1930s, these scholars—even as government displeasure caused folklore studies to become less popular—produced works of significance. Interest in the Folksong Research Society was sufficient to revive that organization in 1935, and fifty-one issues of *Folksong Weekly* were published between April 1936 and April 1937. The reincarnated Society emphasized the use of folk literature for the invigoration of the national literature, and 825 songs from twenty provinces were published. The Society was once again terminated—

this time permanently—when Japanese troops invaded China in 1937.[25]

Also important for Chinese folklore scholarship was the publication of several major works during the mid-1930s. These included Ch'en Ju-heng's *Brief History of Storytelling* (*Shuo-shu hsiao-shih*), which appeared in 1936. Ch'en traced the recorded history of storytelling in China back to Buddhist monks' religious tales of the T'ang dynasty (AD 618-906). Later records reveal secularized tales. Although Ch'en's book could not illuminate the non-Buddhist oral tradition which undoubtedly existed simultaneously, the *Brief History* uncovered a previously unknown aspect in the development of tale literature in China.

In 1938 appeared a seminal work in Chinese folkloristics, Cheng Chen-to's *History of Chinese Folklore* (*Chung-kuo su-wen hsüeh-shih*). Showing the tendency of Chinese folklorists to define "folklore" as "oral literature," Ch'en traced the rise and development of folksongs, ballads, folk drama, and other narrative genres.

Ku Chieh-kang, Cheng Chen-to, and other folklorists led a movement which, for a few years, tried to assist China in its difficult metamorphosis from Confucianism to a radically different way of life. If the Folklore Movement had arisen under other circumstances, it might have flourished and grown. However, the Chinese Folklore Movement blossomed in a highly charged atmosphere; the demands of developing nationalism and political expediency took precedence over unbiased scholarship. According to Wolfram Eberhard, "folklore studies, even at their inception in China, were a tool for other movements, and not an independent scholarly field."[26] Scholars turned to the folk primarily because the pressures of a disintegrating elitist oriented culture forced them to seek alternatives. Promoters of literary reform and agents of social change all directed their energies towards the beleaguered rural masses, but they did so as nationalists, not as uninvolved scholars. They moved with the desire to save China through a reinterpretation of her history and culture, much as Hu Shih had reinterpreted the history of Chinese literature.

At first, folklore researchers believed that this lore, and folk culture in general, could help to shape a new identity for the Chinese. The people and their oral tradition were to serve as acceptable, nonaristocratic symbols of the new China. All too soon, though, the political tide—which largely had been responsible for the birth of the Chinese Folklore Movement—turned against the study of folklore. By the late 1920s, it was obvious that the Revolution of 1911 had been a success in certain ways: China no longer was a crippled, semi-colonial nation; the Chinese people no longer were burdened with recent, unwelcome feelings of inferiority towards the West. Throughout the countryside there raged a political and military struggle between the forces of Chiang Kai-shek and those of Mao Tse-tung. However, *all* the people were nationalists; all felt the pride and strength of independent Chinese nationhood. With renewed confidence on the ascent, interest in the remedial powers of folklore and folk culture waned.

Even worse, folklore came to be regarded as a hazardous, reactionary field of study during the Chiang Kai-shek regime. The Nationalist Government launched an "anti-superstition" campaign which soon was directed at scholars who were studying the customs and beliefs of the rural folk. Folklorists "were accused of keeping alive the superstitious beliefs and attitudes of an era which. . .should be allowed to die." Unhappily for the Folklore Movement, folklorists also "tended to emphasize local differences, even to isolate local subcultures."[27] Fortunately, serious folklore scholars continued to conduct research and to publish numerous collections, essays, and historical investigations. Folklore societies and publications continued to exist despite the displeasure of the Nationalist Government during the 1930s. In 1937, however, with the beginning of the Sino-Japanese War, the Republican phase of the Chinese Folklore Movement was effectively at an end.

As in so many other countries, nationalism and the Chinese Folklore Movement very nearly coincided; the rise of nationalism encouraged interest in folklore and "the people" in general. Folklore was never, however, a field of purely scholarly interest, as it was closely tied to the political and intellectual struggles of early twentieth-century China. When the tremendous insecurities and uncertainties of the period were overcome, the study of folklore no longer appeared to be vitally important. On the contrary, to investigate folk beliefs or local traditions seemed suspect in a period when the modernity and unity of the entire nation were being stressed. Nationalism and Chinese folkloristics had risen together, but while nationalism flourished and still remains a potent force in China, the non-Communist phase of the Chinese Folklore Movement was a short-lived phenomenon.

The Chinese Communist Party (CCP) developed a sophisticated, purely political attitude toward folklore quite early. Folklore was utilized for political, ideological reasons in 1930, in the "liberated" area of Kiangsi in Northwest China. "Revolutionary" tales and songs were circulated among the soldiers, while peasants from the area comprised the Central Blue-shirt Ensemble (Chung-yan lan-shan-t'uan), a drama troupe that presented a series of dramatic performances with themes such as "down with the local big-shots," "redistribution of lands," and "seeing lovers off for the Army."[28] In the liberated area of Shensi, a local dance-and-story form, *yangko* (which formerly was used to express simple boy-meets-girl tales), was modified to present similarly politicized stories.[29] Such ideological experiments in applied folklore served as field data for decisions promulgated at the crucial Yenan Forum on Art and Literature.

At the 1942 Yenan Forum on Art and Literature, Mao Tse-tung presented his ideas about Chinese art and literature, including folk literature. In Mao's celebrated "Talks at the Yenan Forum on Art and Literature," he stated the dramatic objective of the Yenan Forum: ". . . to make art and literature a component part of the whole revolutionary machine. . . ."[30] To attain this objective, Mao elaborated the Marxist based theory that guides folklore on the Mainland to the present day.

According to Mao Tse-tung, the source of all art and literature is man's social life. Since in a socialist society the intended audience for any art form is a combination of the workers, peasants, and soldiers, art and literature must reflect truthfully the lives of such people. Furthermore, art and literature are primarily *ideological* expressions. They must adopt the standpoint of the masses and present, in language intelligible to the common people, the ideology of the proletariat—as guided by the Chinese Communist Party. Only this approach, Mao reasons, will be acceptable to the masses. Art and literature taking this ideological stand, presenting the lives of the common people, will be "popular," or "diffused throughout the masses." The task of art and literature is not merely to be popular at a certain level—it also must be ideologically elevating. In order to elevate the masses, then, art and literature must present the life of the masses "on a higher level and of a greater intensity than real life, in sharper focus and more typical, nearer the ideal, and therefore more universal."[31]

Implicit in the theory that art and literature are primarily ideological expressions is the idea that politics takes precedence over artistic considerations. Therefore, while artistic perfection is to be strived for, the artist's or writer's main concern must be that of strict obedience to and preservation of the Chinese Communist Party line. Enemies of the party are to be exposed and vilified; party allies are to be united with, helping them to discard what is backward (including feudalism, superstition, blind worship of tradition, and so forth) and promote what is revolutionary. In order to accomplish these goals, artists, writers, folklore workers, and all workers in the broadly interpreted area of art and literature must identify with the common people, study their language, get to know and understand them thoroughly. In order thus to identify, to fuse their ideas and feelings with those of the masses, workers must go among the people, work and live with them, and study the precepts of Marxism-Leninism with them.

Mao's realization that folklore could be utilized for political propaganda and modernization was put into nationwide practice soon after the establishment of the People's Republic of China (1949). At first, communist-style folklore research was conducted by the Research Institute of Literature in the Chinese Academy of Science. The Research Institute was soon relegated to a special role in folklore studies, primarily dealing with the oral literature and linguistics of China's minority peoples. Other folklore research and propaganda work was delegated to the Research Society of Chinese Folk Literature and Arts (Chung-kuo min-chien wen-i yen-chiu-hui), established for this purpose in February, 1950. Well-known folklore researchers of the early communist period included folklorists of long standing (Ku Chieh-kang, Chung Ching-wen, Ch'ang Hui) as well as workers whose qualifications were mainly political (Kuo Mo-jo, Chou Yang, Chia Chih). Chairman of the board of directors of the Research Society was Kuo Mo-jo, a well known leftist literary theoretician; Chung Ching-wen served as vice-chairman.

In an article published in 1951, Chung Ching-wen applied the socialist viewpoint specifically to the area of folklore. The article, "Some Basic Understandings About Folk Literature and Arts" (Tui-yü min-chien wen-i ti i-hsieh chi-pen jen-shih),[32] reaffirmed that folk art and literature arise from the social life and struggles of the masses. Quoting Gorkij, Chung found socialist support for the idea that the oral tradition of the people must be known in order to understand the true history of the laboring classes. This article foreshadowed the extreme emphasis that the Chinese Communist Party was to give to folklore and its use for political purposes.

Policies concerning folklore in the Peoples' Republic of China have occurred in a series of "waves" of reform. In the course of these waves may be seen the tendency of the CCP to promote an idea in an excessive, sometimes overwhelming, manner. The demands of the party, executed with fanatical, insensitive zeal by party cadres, are often followed by mass confusion and resistance, resulting in retreat and temporary compromise by the party. After a cooling off period, the compromise is negated by subsequent demands which are more extreme than those which originally resulted in chaos.[33]

Chinese Communist folklore policies and the results of those policies may be seen most clearly in the case of folk drama. Folklorists had ignored folk drama during the Republican period. Since 1949, however, the greatest activity of communist folklore workers has been in this area.

Mao Tse-tung revealed a political interest in folk theater as early as 1944. After seeing a revolutionary play presented by the Yenan Peking Opera Theatre, he wrote a letter which commented on the traditional theater:

"history is made by the people, yet the old opera (and all the old literature and art, which are divorced from the people) presents the people as though they were dirt, and the stage is dominated by lords and ladies and their pampered sons and daughters."[34] Such "feudal" content was, with "superstition," the first aspect of folk theater to be attacked on a nationwide level after the declaration of the People's Republic of China.

The National Conference on Opera Reform was held in November of 1950. Following the party line, the Conference reaffirmed the policy of using traditional Chinese drama for political propaganda. In addition, steps were taken to halt the excesses of some cadres who implemented local drama policy. *All* traditional theater had been banned in some areas by cadres who called its very existence feudal and superstitious in nature. The Conference therfore recommended that the final decision on banning any play should be reserved to the Ministry of Cultural Affairs.[35]

Other measures were taken to centralize control over traditional drama. In 1951, the Chinese Opera Research Institute was established to systematize opera reform. New operas and revised traditional operas were produced for current use. The "correctness" of these dramas was insured by government-appointed editors. In October, 1952, another opera reform conference was held in Peking. This gathering promulgated a new policy of "thematic reform." Just two months later, on December 26, 1952, a new set of regulations required that theatrical troupes register with the government and submit performance schedules for approval by the authorities. State-controlled troupes also were required to spend at least two or three months each year as mobile units, giving performances in factories, villages, and army units.

These measures caused unexpected results. New plays were held up for months while being checked through the intricacies of administrative red tape, while the acceptable repertoire of traditional plays was cut and cut again. Skilled actors stopped performing because local cadres considered their old roles undesirable. Many professional dramatists were afraid to write until the party position was made clear.

Party retreat and compromise came with a limited "thaw" in 1956. At a National Conference of Drama Workers, the Ministry of Culture proposed reconsideration of traditional plays to enrich the available repertoire. Most traditional drama had been prohibited for containing superstitious elements, particularly ghosts and other supernatural beings. In order to break the stalemate in the Chinese theater, the party compromised its ban on superstition to allow the portrayal of ghosts with "rebellious and folk qualities"[36] on the stage.

A second wave of drama reform was attempted during the Great Leap Forward campaign of 1958. From revising old plays, the party escalated its policy to promoting new plays with modern, revolutionary themes. *The White-haired Girl* is perhaps the most famous example of this type of play, which utilized a disastrous combination of traditional music and singing with modern costumes, make-up, and stage settings. The new direction of drama reform proved so unacceptable to the public that the party compromised again in 1959. The slogan "Walking on Two Legs" reaffirmed the party's desire to popularize plays with revolutionary proletarian themes. Still, Chou Yang (then Deputy Minister of Propaganda and party spokesman for folk literature policy) declared, "We should not expect too much."

In 1963 all ghost plays were banned. In 1964, a vigorous propaganda campaign included festivals of modern opera (still using traditional Peking opera techniques) and frequent comments in various organs of the party press. Editorials attacking the bourgeois ivory tower attitude of theater workers appeared. Traditional plays depicting the Confucian ideals of family loyalty and filial piety remained banned, as well as those containing superstitious and feudal elements. Some traditional plays, particularly those pointing out evil social customs, corrupt landlords, heroic peasants, and other socialist themes, were promoted in the official repertoire. Old plays, though, were susceptible only to marginal revision. The traditional operas could not be reworked sufficiently to promote specific party policies of ideology without causing a worse disaster than *The White-haired Girl*.

The Great Proletarian Cultural Revolution of 1966 brought new, extreme developments to folk drama. Chou Yang, who formerly had participated in drafting party folklore policies, was accused of conspiring to impede the reform of Peking opera, and ousted as a "counter-revolutionary revisionist."[37] Contemporary revolutionary dramas were encouraged and publications like the English language journal *Chinese Literature* began to teem with articles about new plays with titles like *Esteemed and Beloved Chairman Mao*, *You Are the Red Sun in Our Hearts*, and *I Love Best to Read Chairman Mao's Works*. At the same time, drama workers were criticized, and the need for them to remold their ideology was emphasized. The party stressed the evil influence of the old operas on actors and audiences.

A pattern and goal may be discerned from this frenzied activity in the area of folk drama. Surely, party directives have not been entirely successful in their attempts to transform traditional theater into revolutionary theater. Also, the worldview of the Chinese peasant has not been completely changed by the new plays. However, some significant changes may have been effected by the CCS's use of folk drama.

Quantitatively, the party has been extremely successful, increasing the number of professional dramatic groups from 1,000 in 1949 to 3,513 in 1959, while amateur drama troupes grew from 1,000 to 5,000 in 1951 to 240,000 rural drama troupes and 40,000 workers' troupes in 1959.[38] In the years subsequent to the most recent of these statistics, the number of people involved in the Chinese drama most surely has increased.

Most importantly, the internal content and structure of Chinese traditional drama has been transformed to promote social change. Traditional opera was what James Peacock[39] has termed "cyclical"; that is, the final action takes place in the same milieu as the opening action. Though the hero may better his personal circumstances or overthrow a dynasty, the milieu remains the same. Society is not changed; a new dynasty replaces the old one. Recent revolutionary drama in China is of the "innovative" variety. The first scene, depicting the oppression of the past, backward tendencies, or an unjust situation, is always traded by the last scene for something totally *new*. The creation of a new social order, a more progressive comrade, or the obliteration of feudalistic institutions are commonplace on the Chinese Communist stage. This innovative structure is combined with a linear, continuous movement which builds to a climax and is resolved in the successful achievement of a socialist goal. Peacock maintains that "there is some cause to think that [this] type of form encourages emotional dispositions which facilitate the modernization process."[40]

The movement in revolutionary proletarian plays is towards some social or political goal. The action usually unfolds with the help of basic Chinese Communist strategies: the exposure and solution of the problem follows the mass line, with direct involvement and participation of the common people. For example, in Lao Sheh's *Dragon Beard Ditch*,[41] the filthy, disease spreading ditch is brought to the attention of the party by the people, who then participate in its renovation.

In a conscious attempt to psychologically influence the masses, the party portrays social action and heroes with which both the audience and the actors can empathize and identify. The audience is encouraged to identify with actors who use socialist means to move towards their goals. Thus, as James L. Peacock claims, the audience is able to "vicariously exercise heroic means ordinarily kept packed away. . . in this way the participants develop a proclivity to favor certain roles, situations, goals, or means on occasions when daily life offers a chance to choose which role one will play . . . ."[42]

In China, drama is a major source of emotional and moral education. According to James L. Peacock, modern revolutionary plays attempt to instill in an audience the "mental drive. . .to engage in and complete *any* action. . .that is 'modern' . . . ."[43] That the instillation of this mental drive has not been completely successful in China may be due to the fact that, as Alan Liu has noted, "Peking has severed the media from the people. Instead of helping the peasants to adopt modern practices, Peking has alienated them."[44] It still remains to be seen whether the Chinese Communist Party's persuasive propaganda techniques, as manifested in the modern theater as well as in other genres, are powerful and subtle enough to eradicate a tradition so central to the lives of the people, and to replace it with the products of modern socialist realism.

The CCP has followed similar policies in other areas of folklore. While some traditional tales and songs of the "old tradition" were published during the first few years of the Communist regime, the party has always tended to modify and modernize folklore materials. Recently, the emphasis has been on the production, popularization, and collection of nontraditional "revolutionary" lore. In 1958, the Great Leap Forward Folksong Collecting Movement collected "endless versions" of songs about the people's "working spirit," "mobilization for the Great Leap Forward," "Great Leap in in steel foundry," and other songs designed to wipe away feudal tradition and arouse class consciousness. During the same year, the major party folklore journal, *Folk-Literature* (*Min-chien wen-hsüeh*), started to publish "bandit lore." Mao's rural-based People's Liberation Army (PLA) turned folklore workers to searching for lore about other examples of peasant rebellion and heroism. *Folk-Literature* published stories of the 1900 Boxer Rebellion, and revolutionary legends and songs about the T'aiping Rebellion of 1850-1864 and the Nien Rebellion of approximately the same period. The 1960 collection *Nien-chün ko-yao*, by Li Tung-shen, has been published in English as *Folksongs of the Nien Army*.

Folklore workers in current China are not unaware that folkloristics takes quite different forms in other countries. As longtime party spokesman Chia Chih has remarked, folklore has two "face values"; it is artistic work, and it is valuable material in respect to culture and science. Two face values implies two different methods of dealing with folklore. "As scientific research materials, there must be an emphasis on the faithfulness of recording. . .as literary work. . .for the purpose of providing the people with a comparatively refined work, it is our opinion that a proper arrangement and reworking (of the material) should be effected."[45] The CCP viewpoint is that "popularization" of revolutionary lore is first necessary in order to elevate the people's political and social consciousness (much as James Peacock described for the case of folk drama). "Scientific research" is envisioned in the vague, undefined future.

In the meantime, folklore items from the Mainland prominently feature traits unfamiliar to the lore of traditional China. Where pre-Communist texts stress overcoming impossible situations by appealing for supernatural assistance, Chinese Communist texts emphasize man's ability to control his environment and overcome all obstacles. In the words of a recent "new nursery rhyme,"

> Hey, ho,
> Rumtiddytum!
> Little red soldiers,
> Here we come.
> Chairman Mao's words
> Never forgotten,
> Out in the fields
> We pick the cotton . . . [46]

"Chairman Mao's words never forgotten," contemporary Chinese scholarship continues to place politics over other considerations, and folklore study continues to reflect the preoccupations of the current regime.

Indiana University
Bloomington, Indiana

NOTES

[1] Sung-k'ang Huang, *Lu Hsün and the New Culture Movement of Modern China* (Amsterdam: Djambatan Publishers, 1959), p. 9.

[2] Wm. Theodore de Bary, et al., editors, *Sources of Chinese Tradition* (New York: Columbia University Press, 1960), Vol. II, p. 157.

[3] Wu-chi Liu, *An Introduction to Chinese Literature* (Bloomington: Indiana University Press, 1966), p. 263.

[4] Huang, p. 13.

[5] Wei-pang Chao, "Modern Chinese Folklore Investigation, Part I," *Folklore Studies* I (1942): 59. This journal is now retitled *Asian Folklore Studies*.

[6] Huang, p. 18.

[7] Chao, p. 56.

[8] Hui Ch'ang, "T'an Pei-ching ti ko-yao," *Hu-shih wen-ts'un* 4: ii (1925): 350-351. Quoted in Yen, p. 39 (see footnote 18).

[9] Chao, pp. 65-67.

[10] See Sidney D. Gamble, *Ting Hsien: A North China Rural Community* (Stanford, California: Stanford University Press, 1968).

[11] Chieh-kang Ku, *Miao Feng Shan* (Canton: Chinese Folklore Society of Sun Yat-sen University, 1928), pp. 3-5.

[12] Laurence A. Schneider, *Ku Chieh-kang and China's New History: Nationalism and the Quest for Alternative Traditions* (Berkeley: University of California Press, 1971), p. 2.

[13] Shih Hu, *The Chinese Renaissance* (Chicago: The University of Chicago Press, 1934), p. 52.

[14] Tze-k'uang Lou, *Wu shih nien lai te Chung-kuo su wen hsüeh* (Taipei, Taiwan: Chi-ch'eng Publishing House, 1963), p. 4.

[15] *Ibid.*, p. 3.

[16] Wolfram Eberhard, ed., *Folktales of China* (Chicago: The University of Chicago Press, 1965), Paperback edition, 1968, p.xxxiv.

[17] see Baron G. A. Vitale's collections, *Pekingese Rhymes* (1896) and *Chinese Merry Tales* (1901).

[18] Chun-chiang Yen, "Folklore Research in Communist China," *Asian Folklore Studies* 26: 2 (1967): 2, translating from Ts'ai Yüan-p'ei, "Shuo min-tsu-hsüeh," Chung-kuo min-tsu-hsüeh hui, ed., *Ts'ai Yüan-p'ei min-tsu-hsüeh lun-chu* Taipei, Taiwan: Chung-hua shu-chu, 1962), p. 1.

[19] Schneider, pp. 138-139.

[20] Wei-pang Chao, "Modern Chinese Folklore Investigation, Part II," *Folklore Studies* 2 (1943): 82.

[21] R.D. Jameson, "Comparative Folklore Methodological Notes," *Ch'ing-hua chou-k'an* 31, #4645. Peking: Ch'ing-hua University, no date given.

[22] Yen, pp. 39-40.

[23] Chieh-kang Ku, "Kuan-yü mi shih," *Chung-shan ta-hsüeh min-su chou-k'an* 4, #23 (1928): 20.

[24] Schneider, p. 147. Much information on the Education School is contained in Schneider, pp. 143-148.

[25] Chao, 1942, pp. 71-73.

[26] Wolfram Eberhard, "The Use of Folklore in China," *Studies in Chinese Folklore and Related Essays.* Indiana University Folklore Institute Monograph Series, Vol. 23. Bloomington: Indiana University Press, 1970. p.15.

[27] Eberhard, 1965, p. xxxiv.

[28] Yen, pp. 9-11.

[29] Jack Chen, *The Chinese Theatre* (New York: Roy Publishers (no copyright date. Introduction dated 1948).

[30] Tse-tung Mao, *On Art and Literature* (Peking: Foreign Languages Press, 1960).

[31] *Ibid.*

[32] Ching-wen Chung, "Tui-yü min-chien wen-i ti i-hsieh chi-pen jen-shih," *Min-chien wen-i hsin-lun-chi.* (Peking: Pei-ching Shih-fan ta-hsüeh, 1951).

[33] Alan P. L. Liu, *The Use of Traditional Media for Modernization in Communist China* (Cambridge, Mass.: Center for International Studies, MIT, 1965).

[34] "Mao Tse-tung's Thought Victorious in the Theatre," *Chinese Literature* 3 (1967).

[35] Alan Liu, p. 21.

[36] *Ibid.*, p. 26.

[37] "Mao Tse-tung's Thought Victorious in the Theatre," *Chinese Literature* 3 (1967).
[38] Alan Liu, pp. 44-45.
[39] James L. Peacock, *Rites of Modernization: Symbolic and Social Aspects of Indonesian Proletarian Drama* (Chicago: University of Chicago Press, 1968).
[40] *Ibid.*, p. 10.
[41] Sheh Lao, *Dragon Beard Ditch* (Peking: Foreign Languages Press, 1956).
[42] Peacock, pp. 8-9.
[43] *Ibid.*, p. 248.
[44] Alan Liu, p. 90.
[45] Chih Chia, "Ts'ai-lun min-chien wen-hsüeh kung-tso ti liang-t'iao tao-lu," *Min-chien*
[46] "New Nursery Rhymes," *Chinese Literature* 10 (1972): 87.

INDEX

OTHER BOOKS FROM SLAVICA PUBLISHERS

Henrik Birnbaum: *Common Slavic Progress and Problems in Its Reconstruction,* xi + 436 p., 1975.

Malcolm H. Brown, ed.: *Papers of the Yugoslav-American Seminar on Music,* 208 p., 1970.

Catherine V. Chvany: *On the Syntax of Be-Sentences in Russian,* viii + 311 p., 1975.

Frederick Columbus: *Introductory Workbook in Historical Phonology,* 39 p., 1974.

Dina B. Crockett: *Agreement in Contemporary Standard Russian,* iv + 456 p., 1976.

Ralph Carter Elwood, ed.: *Reconsiderations on the Russian Revolution,* x + 278 p., 1976. (Papers from the Banff '74 Conference)

Folia Slavica, a journal in the fields of Slavic, Baltic, and Balkan linguistics and philology, first issue March 1977.

Richard Freeborn, R. R. Milner-Gulland, and Charles A. Ward, eds.: *Russian and Slavic Literature,* xii + 466 p., 1976. (Papers from the Banff '74 Conference)

Victor A. Friedman: *The Grammatical Categories of the Macedonian Indicative,* iii + 210 p., 1977.

Charles E. Gribble: *Medieval Slavic Texts, Vol. 1, Old and Middle Russian Texts,* 320 p., 1973.

Charles E. Gribble: *Russian Root List with a Sketch of Russian Word Formation,* 56 p., 1973.

Charles E. Gribble: Словарик русского языка 18-го века/ *A Short Dictionary of 18th-Century Russian,* 103 p., 1976.

Charles E. Gribble, ed.: *Studies Presented to Professor Roman Jakobson by His Students,* 333 p., 1968.

Raina Katzarova-Kukudova & Kiril Djenev: *Bulgarian Folk Dances,* 174 p., numerous illustrations, 2nd printing 1976 (1st printing, Sofia 1958).

Demetrius J. Koubourlis, ed.: *Topics in Slavic Phonology,* viii + 270 p., 1974.

Michael K. Launer: *Elementary Russian Syntax,* xi + 140 p., 1974.

Alexander Lipson, *A Russian Course.*

Thomas F. Magner, ed.: *Slavic Linguistics and Language Teaching,* x + 309 p., 1976. (Papers from the Banff '74 Conference).

Kenneth E. Naylor, ed.: *Balkanistica: Occasional Papers in Southeast European Studies, I(1974),* 189 p., 1975; *II (1975),* 153 p., 1976.

Vasa D. Mihailovich and Mateja Matejić: *Yugoslav Literature in English: A Bibliography of Translations and Criticism (1821-1975),* ix + 328 p., 1976.

Hongor Oulanoff: *The Prose Fiction of Veniamin A. Kaverin,* v + 203 p., 1976.

OTHER BOOKS FROM SLAVICA PUBLISHERS

Jan L. Perkowski, ed.: *Vampires of the Slavs* (a collection of readings), 294 p., 1976.

Lester A. Rice: *Hungarian Morphological Irregularities,* 80 p., 1970.

Midhat Ridjanović: *A Synchronic Study of Verbal Aspect in English and Serbo-Croatian,* ix + 147 p., 1976.

David F. Robinson: *Lithuanian Reverse Dictionary,* ix + 209 p., 1976.

Don K. Rowney and G. Edward Orchard, eds.: *Russian and Slavic History,* viii + 311 p., 1977. (Papers from the Banff '74 Conference).

Ernest A. Scatton: *Bulgarian Phonology,* xii + 224 p., 1976.

William R. Schmalstieg: *Introduction to Old Church Slavic,* 290 p., 1976.

Michael Shapiro: *Aspects of Russian Morphology, A Semiotic Investigation,* 62 p., 1969.

Charles E. Townsend: *Russian Word-Formation, corrected reprint,* xviii + 272 p., 1975.

D. N. Ushakov, ed.: Толковый словарь русского языка, original edition in 4 volumes, Moscow, 1934-1940; reprint (slightly reduced in page size, corrections indicated throughout, 4 volumes bound in 3), 1974.

Worth, Dean S.: *A Bibliography of Russian Word-Formation,* xliv + 317 p., 1977.

Maurice I. Levin: *Russian Declension and Conjugation: A Structural Description with Workbook,* x + 159 p., 1978.

Paul Debreczeny and Thomas Eekman, eds.: *Essays on Chekhov,* ca. 200 p., 1978.

Jules F. Levin: *Reading Contemporary Russian,* ca. 400 p., 1978.

Charles E. Townsend: *The Memoirs of Princess Natal'ja Borisovna Dolgorukaja: Original Text, Annotated, with Facing English Translation and Historical and Linguistic Commentary,* ca. 200 p., 1978.

Mateja Matejić and Dragan Milivojević: *An Anthology of Medieval Serbian Literature,* 1978.